CONTENTS

CONTENTS

JEANETTE RAYMOND

Implementing Pastoral Care in Schools

WITHDRAWN FROM STOCK

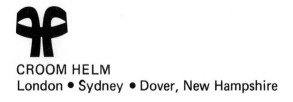

CROOM HELM
London • Sydney • Dover, New Hampshire

40704

© 1985 Jeanette Raymond
Croom Helm Ltd, Provident House, Burrell Row,
Beckenham, Kent BR3 1AT

Croom Helm Australia Pty Ltd, Suite 4, 6th Floor,
64-76 Kippax Street, Surry Hills, NSW 2010, Australia

British Library Cataloguing in Publication Data

Raymond, Jeanette
   Implementing pastoral care in schools.
   1. Personnel service in secondary education
   I. Title
   373.14   LB1620.5
   ISBN 0-7099-2273-6
   ISBN 0-7099-4211-7 Pbk

Croom Helm, 51 Washington Street, Dover,
New Hampshire 03820, USA

Library of Congress Cataloging in Publication Data

Raymond, Jeanette, 1952-   .
   Implementing pastoral care in schools.

   Bibliography: p.
   1. Personnel service in secondary education – Great
Britain. 2. Teacher-participation in personnel service
– Great Britain. 3. Teacher-student relationships –
Great Britain. 4. Students – Great Britain – Attitudes.
5. School discipline – Great Britain. I. Title.
LB1620.5.R39   1985   373.14'0941   85-14978
ISBN 0-7099-2273-6
ISBN 0-7099-4211-7 (pbk.)

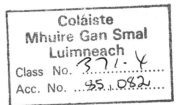
Printed and bound in Great Britain
by Billing & Sons Limited, Worcester.

ACKNOWLEDGEMENTS

I would like to thank all the pupils
and teachers with whom I worked and am currently
working for indicating the need for this book.
I would also like to thank Doug Jones for his support and encouragement in relation to this work.
To Gwyn Walters who read and re-read the work,
grateful thanks for your time and patience. For
the helpful and useful comments given by Clive
Francis and Avril Protheroe many thanks. Lastly,
thanks to Stella Davies and Malcolm Burnell for
their invaluable assistance with the art work.

PREFACE

There has been a growing demand for materials and
suggestions for techniques to use with secondary
school pupils during tutorial periods. While some
schools use these ideas as part of a planned programme of guidance and counselling, others appear
to require items to fill gaps on the timetable.
In this book, tutorials are seen very much as the
core of the pastoral system within a school, which
cannot be divorced from the ethos of the school,
teacher motivation and support systems, and the
carrying out of preventive work with pupils.
    As many form tutors and year tutors have not
been specifically trained to develop personal and
social skills in pupils, using systematic procedures, this book presents detailed guidelines
for the interested and or inexperienced teacher
to follow. The topics covered have been collected
from ideas contributed from a combination of pupils,
teachers and the author's daily work with the above
two groups. The skills of working with small groups
is outlined to help the tutor organise and facilitate pupils learning from each other.
    Several techniques for stimulating pupils,
and for aiding them to reflect on their lives and
how they manage their personal difficulties are
given, so that tutors will be able to choose methods
to suit their purpose, and compare pupil responses
with their colleagues.
    In this book I have stated that if pastoral
care is for the welfare of pupils, then their
opinions and perceptions have to be afforded greater
prominence. Teachers may not be used to doing
this as a matter of course, and so a chapter has
been written to help staff begin this task with
confidence. Many different methods of eliciting
pupil perceptions are presented, with actual

examples of pupil responses. The use made of pupil opinions can be far reaching on the way the school plans its operations. I have therefore given hints as to how this information can be utilised by staff for the mutual benefit of teachers and students.

Authors frequently comment that good schools make their pupils feel worthwhile, and encourage in them a sense of belonging. As yet few writers have given specific ways in which this can be done for all pupils, and I have described techniques for so doing. Making pupils partners in the process of schooling means finding out what they do not understand about the school, and what it is trying to do for them; and having done so, assisting them to comprehend and contribute to it. The items for this chapter evolved from my many discussions with classes of pupils, and include teacher style and expectations, the school hierarchy, school reports, and the banding and setting system.

Most of the problems that teachers have to cope with in their dealings with pupils involve interpersonal relationship difficulties, as experienced by students. A whole chapter has been given over to the use of social skills training, so that tutors can help children manage their problems better, in a practical and meaningful way. This chapter and others show an appreciation of the difficulties that tutors have in effectively counselling large numbers of pupils as individuals. As such, all the methods outlined in the book discuss techniques for use in the group setting.

Assisting pupils to cope with stress is probably one of the most important functions of a pastoral team. The recognition of symptoms of anxiety and different ways of controlling stress is presented in step by step format for tutors to make use of. These include the skills of relaxation, thought control, and predicting levels of distress in various situations as a first step in self control. Other life skills such as planning time, study skills, and handling interviews are also included in the pastoral programme. Developing self awareness, and self identity goes hand in hand with self management skills. Thus, the latter two items have been included as an integral part of the curriculum in pastoral work.

Many schools like to have a set of topics that the pastoral team use as a basis for their daily work with students. The development of a pastoral curriculum has a chapter devoted to it, with examples of content and the best time

to approach each topic. Tutors are referred to
the relevant chapters in the book for an in depth
explanation of how to set about each item, and
the relevant strategies to use, where they are
covered in detail.

The responsibilities of senior management
in supporting and helping tutors has not been overlooked. The book presents some details of what
type of problems tutors encounter in their pastoral
work, and evaluates the role of the school in contributing to their difficulties. Suggestions are
made for senior teachers to assist tutors by setting
up in-service training courses within the school,
and by giving practical help in the form of team
teaching and encouragement from colleagues. Teacher
motivation and pupil enthusiasm are inextricably
linked in this book, and pastoral care for both
groups is a theme which receives much emphasis.

I have tried in this book to give teachers
some useful tools to aid pupils in their daily
lives in school. In the hope that they will feel
that they are doing worthwhile jobs, tutors have
to see some purpose in their tasks. I have stressed
how tutors can help each other by preventing pupils
from experiencing an excess of distress and lack
of motivation. If pupils are that much more able
to manage their lives, then they will show a greater
contentment in school, and so present teachers
with fewer management problems. Staff should therefore become more willing to take on their difficult
jobs with a greater sense of keenness.

Several authors have expressed a note of cau-
tion about structured pastoral work producing a
population of conforming children who may not respond to situations appropriately. This has been
taken account of in the book. The emphasis throughout is for pupils to be presented with several
alternative ways of solving their difficulties,
so that they can choose the most apt one for their
particular circumstances. Tutors are given the
task of facilitating the adoption of relevant tac-
tics for each individual pupil, and to evaluate
its effectiveness.

Finally, in an attempt to avoid the use of
sexist language I have found it necessary to use
the 'his/her' format in certain parts of the book.
I hope that readers will not find this too cumber-
some.

CHAPTER ONE

APPROACHING THE TASK

Most schools would like to think that they are
concerned about all aspects of their pupils' lives
while they attend school, and to this end have
created pastoral care units such as forms and form
tutors, year groups and year tutors or houses.
Such pastoral units are expected to aid pupils
in their academic, social and emotional functioning.
These units are organised at different levels.
On one level are form tutors who are often expected
to carry out the "nitty gritty work" of pastoral
care. On another level are to be found year tutors
who have responsibilities for co-ordinating the
pastoral and guidance services provided for pupils
in a particular year group. On yet another level
come the senior members of staff, such as heads
of section or school, and deputy headteachers who
may well be instrumental in defining the objectives
of a pastoral system and advising on how they should
be implemented.

Prerequisites for an Efficient Pastoral System

The type of organisation described above has the
potential to offer a great deal to pupils and staff
provided certain prerequisites are attended to.
First, it is essential for schools to ensure that
the setting up of a pastoral structure of tutors
or houses is not in itself mistaken for the actual
function and process of pastoral care, (Best, et
al 1980). It has often been assumed that creating
a post of pastoral responsibility meant that 'pastoral care' would be taking place ipso facto.
Schools must state clearly what they expect from
their pastoral system if the tutors involved are
to be effective in their task, and are to be seen
to be so by the pupils. It is not uncommon to

1

find schools where tutors have no real idea as
to the nature of their task apart from the knowledge that they are supposed to carry out certain
administrative duties. Tutors therefore experience
a whole range of conflicts. They operate within
a system that has no explicit aims, but which nevertheless expect tutors to act as much more than
glorified clerks.

Form tutors are seen by many authors at the
heart of the pastoral system (Hamblin 1978; Blackburn 1975; Baldwin & Wells 1979-81) and rightly
so. However, for them to be able to do their jobs
effectively the school needs to consider its second
prerequisite condition. This involves support
and help for its staff, which will include form
tutors. No school should contemplate setting up
a pastoral care programme for its pupils until
it has adequately gauged the nature and amount
of assistance its staff need to solve their difficulties. At present the pastoral systems that
exist in schools actually work by solving TEACHER
problems as opposed to offering care and guidance
to its pupils. These problems tend to be those
of classroom control, non-school attendance, in-
fringement of school rules and anti-social activities such as fighting, and solvent abuse. Teachers
who are faced with these problems tend to use the
pastoral chain of command to send awkward pupils
to those with pastoral responsibility. Most teacher
energy and resource in pastoral care goes on solving
problems for teachers and not those as seen from
the pupil perspective.

Take the case of a boy who arrives late at
his lessons over a period of time. The teachers
who teach this pupil may report him to his form
tutor, who may give him a little warning and some
friendly advice. If this does not work the pupil
is sent to the year tutor, or to the head of section
for further warnings or punishment. If this too
proves ineffective, teachers may send the pupil
to a deputy head for action to be taken. Sometimes this may be done directly by bypassing all
other staff in the hierarchy, or only one member
of that system. For example a year tutor may refer
the child to the deputy head directly for admonish-
ment. This is not pastoral care. It is more like
a system where staff, who get little help in their
daily interactions with pupils, are encouraged
to give vent to their stresses by passing the buck.

The identification of those members of staff
who need help, especially in matters of classroom

control and in communicating with pupils should be part of any school's function if it is concerned to meet the needs of both staff and pupils. This can be done by monitoring the number of times teachers request help from their colleagues either directly, by asking for someone to come into their rooms to settle a rowdy class, or indirectly, by sending a procession of children out of class to be punished by senior staff. In addition, most schools will be aware of which teachers are referred to frequently in relation to poor communication and relationships with pupils. They will also realise by listening to pupils and parents which teachers do not explain their topics adequately, and as a result do not get their homework assignments carried out by the pupils. Rather than concentrate solely on berating pupils for homework not done, senior staff need to ensure that teachers are putting over their lessons in a comprehensible manner. The school has a duty to assist these members of staff by sharing good teaching techniques with them in helpful ways instead of not doing anything in the mistaken belief that they would be unprofessional by pointing out weaknesses.

If the needs of teachers are being met in this way, then there is a greater chance that staff can start to define and meet pupil needs. If teachers' needs go unrecognized and unmet, then the needs of pupils will also remain unfulfilled. This can give rise to a depressing cycle of events where both staff and pupils have negative experiences of school. See Figure 1.

The third prerequisite that a school should ensure before setting out on a pastoral programme is to define clearly what type of role its pastoral system is to have. Too often pastoral care systems are nominally for the care of pupils but in fact are really systems of discipline and control. While it may be totally unrealistic to separate these two functions, a school which does not have clear aims about the pastoral organisation will find that neither tasks are undertaken with any long term success. The pastoral system more than any other, reflects the ethos of the school, and can do a lot to help create the kind of atmosphere in which both staff and pupils are motivated. The pastoral system can deliberately set out to produce the conditions necessary for success in school by building into its programme adequate facilities for feedback from staff to pupils and vice versa. This will assist the school in discovering whether

3

FIGURE 1

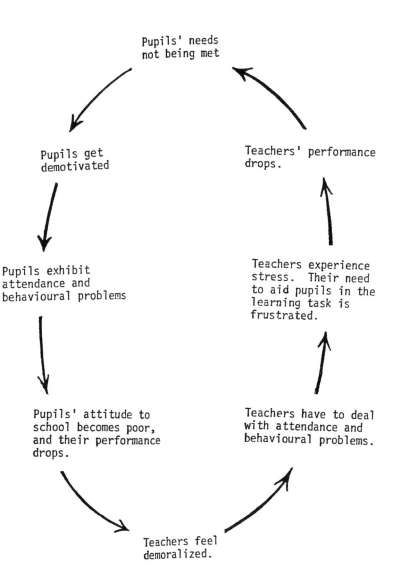

Pupils' needs
not being met

Pupils get
demotivated

Pupils exhibit
attendance and
behavioural problems

Pupils' attitude to
school becomes poor,
and their performance
drops.

Teachers feel
demoralized.

Teachers have to deal
with attendance and
behavioural problems.

Teachers experience
stress. Their need
to aid pupils in the
learning task is
frustrated.

Teachers' performance
drops.

the ethos of the school is having an effect on
pupil performance, motivation, attendance and
participation, as so many researchers have indicated
is possible (Reynolds et al 1976; Reynolds
& Sullivan 1981; Ousten et al 1980; Rutter et al
1979 and Gregory 1980). If a school wishes its
pastoral care system to radiate a genuinely caring
atmosphere, then that has important implications
for its pastoral programme, which must then become
preventive in its aims.

As well as having opportunities for feedback
from pupils to staff, and staff to other members
of staff, the school has a duty to make certain
that those tutors who are doing the 'caring' at
the coal face receive relevant training, support
and constructive advice. See Figure 2. Only in
this way can a pastoral system have a wider role
than simply responding to crises, otherwise known
as the 'fire engine' service.

The Pastoral Duty

The core of a pastoral programme for pupils should
be that of motivating pupils and fulfilling their
needs. This is a formidable task and one which
schools spend a lot of time trying to do with vary-
ing degrees of success. If schools are to have
any real chance of achieving this aim, then they
have to use as their foundation stone, the pupil
point of view. While a great deal has been written
about pupils' problems, these are usually taken
from the adult perspective, with pupils rarely
being asked themselves, (Marland 1974; David &
Cowley 1979; Holden 1971; Jones 1979 and Hamblin
1978). Pastoral staff should use their expertise
and experience in working with pupils to ask them
the right kinds of questions so that children can
express their needs and views. Teachers should
allow pupils the opportunity of providing staff
with feedback on how they perceive and receive
what is being offered to them. In this way the
pastoral system can evolve to meet the changing
needs of pupils in terms that pupils will see as
relevant. As Williamson (1980) states, the essential duty of the teacher involved in pastoral work
is to understand how a child interprets what the
school is offering. It is the meaning that children
place on the messages given to them that is of
signficance. If pupils do not construe what the
school is offering them in the manner in which
it was intended, then the school is failing to

FIGURE 2

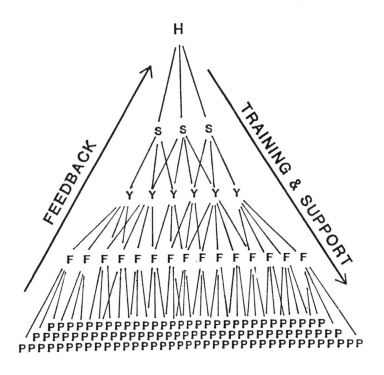

KEY   H=Head Teacher   S=Senior Teachers

Y=Year Tutors   F=Form Tutors   P=Pupils

communicate with its consumers, and pupils could well turn out to be casualties of the system.

Seeking the pupils' opinions and feelings about school life will inevitably lead to tutors having to cope with criticism levelled at their colleagues. They will also have to make some attempt at looking at the school and assessing its role in producing difficulties for its students. Teachers and pupils interact together inside a living institution, and there are bound to be times when both groups cause each other problems. This is natural and healthy. What is not healthy is when all problems are seen to be lodged with pupils. Taylor (1980) says that teachers in pastoral work must be able to 'inform, explain, advise, contradict, direct, and ENDORSE SOME CRITICISM of their colleagues'. If proper facilities exist for feedback from pupil to staff, and from staff to senior staff, then this can lead to positive changes being made via effective teacher support groups.

Allowing pupils to give their verdict on school and indicate areas in which more help is needed, gives them the impression that they are valued members of the school. This is likely to present them with incentives for taking a greater part in the life of the school. Their keenness will be translated into higher levels of motivation and greater gains in their work and social life. This in turn makes teachers feel that their job is worthwhile and raises their spirits. Thus a good pastoral system which wants to create a positive ethos, acts as a MEDIATING INFLUENCE between staff and pupils to establish high levels of morale on both sides. See Figure 3.

The Pastoral Programme

Having maintained that pastoral care has a bearing on the ethos of a school, and that taking account of pupil perceptions helps fashion an encouraging atmosphere for both staff and pupils, we can now ask ourselves what the pastoral programme itself needs to have as its basic tenets. Pastoral care needs to be PREVENTIVE in outlook. It also needs to be DEVELOPMENTAL in its approach, and SKILLS BUILDING in its techniques. These three principles go hand in hand, and should be seen as mutually reinforcing.

Specifying the tasks and objectives of pastoral care needs to be undertaken in some detail if schools are to be successful in their work.

FIGURE 3

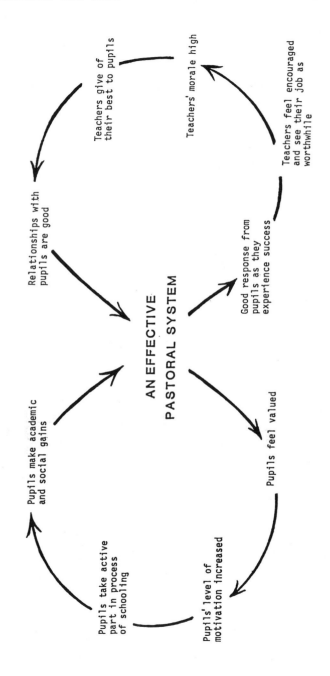

APPROACHING THE TASK

This is best conceptualized on three levels. The first level involves the general maxims of pastoral care, which are stated above. The second level concerns the areas in which the principles of pastoral care can be put into operation. These are:-

1. The teaching of life skills.
2. The teaching of social skills.
3. Developing the self identity, self image and self awareness of pupils.
4. Maintaining a partnership with pupils.

The third level spells out what particular topics each of the four broad areas should encompass. All three levels are depicted in Figure 4.

Life and Social Skills

Social skills are usually taken to refer to the skills of interaction and communication in a variety of contexts. They are really the building blocks of more complex tasks such as dealing with authority, coping with conflict, making relationships and generally being able to handle any social encounter in all types of settings.

Pupils report frequently that the things that cause them the most difficulties in school are interpersonal relationships, especially with teachers (Raymond 1982b). This indicates that they have difficulties in implementing the relevant social skills as necessary. Part of a pastoral programme should therefore address itself to this issue.

Tutors doing pastoral work are often involved in coming to the rescue of children who experience difficulties in their peer relationships. These problems include pupils who cannot make and maintain friendships, as well as those who find it difficult to cope with teasing, threats, and perceived rejection. These problems are faced by and dealt with by pupils everyday, but rarely with the skills needed for effective response. Teachers cannot protect the inadequate youngsters all through their school days. They can however train children to be more assertive, to be sociable and to conduct relationships with the minimum amount of stress. The teaching of social skills is thus a valuable part of the pastoral curriculum.

The school is a major socialising agent for young people outside the family (Hopson & Hough 1976). They therefore have a responsibility to

FIGURE 4

TASKS OF PASTORAL CARE

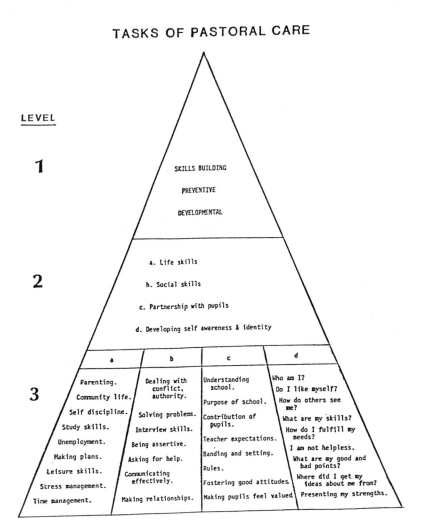

LEVEL

1

SKILLS BUILDING

PREVENTIVE

DEVELOPMENTAL

2

a. Life skills

b. Social skills

c. Partnership with pupils

d. Developing self awareness & identity

3

a	b	c	d
Parenting.	Dealing with conflict, authority.	Understanding school.	Who am I?
Community life.			Do I like myself?
Self discipline.	Solving problems.	Purpose of school.	How do others see me?
Study skills.	Interview skills.	Contribution of pupils.	What are my skills?
Unemployment.	Being assertive.	Teacher expectations.	How do I fulfill my needs?
Making plans.	Asking for help.	Banding and setting.	I am not helpless.
Leisure skills.	Communicating effectively.	Rules.	What are my good and bad points?
Stress management.		Fostering good attitudes.	Where did I get my ideas about me from?
Time management.	Making relationships.	Making pupils feel valued	Presenting my strengths.

execute this task in as conscientious a way as they do the teaching of academic subjects. Button (1980) says that the activities conducted during pastoral sessions need to be based on skills that can be used inside and outside the school setting. This is a common sense statement but one which is often overlooked. Schools are fitting pupils for life, and lifeskills should play a large part in any pastoral programme. While some subjects on the school timetable attempt to fulfil this role, e.g. domestic science, woodwork, gardening, etc. the pastoral programme needs to concentrate on personal qualities and coping skills so that it can complement the crafts that are taught in other parts of the school schedule. Employers are increasingly looking for just these qualities, for instance, those of time and stress management, the ability to cope with conflicts and to make decisions. These are all life skills and they can be systematically taught (McGuire & Priestly 1981).

Sometimes schools blame the home background for inadequacies in pupils, such as poor personal and social skills. However, it is worth remembering that every school has in its hands the future generation of parents, who unless they receive proper life and social skills training in school may not be able to pass on to their children the requisite skills. While families have a role to play in teaching social and life skills, they tend to do it by example, allowing children to follow in their footsteps. In many instances this isn't sufficient, and schools do need to back it up with a more structured and planned approach to learning life skills. Schools have a golden opportunity to help shape the next set of parents by deliberately preparing them for coping with difficulties in life and solving personal problems. Pupils who leave school with very poor life skills are going to be disadvantaged when it comes to putting into use the academic knowledge they might have gained from the traditional curriculum. Through social and life skills teaching, pupils will be better equipped to make relevant decisions, handle unpredictable situations, and take care of their needs and those of others in the community by engaging in purposeful activities, as opposed to anti-social and self destructive behaviours such as self abuse with alcohol, or losing the zest for life when unemployed.

APPROACHING THE TASK

Developing self awareness and self identity

Turning out pupils who are mature and well adjusted
is also a valid task for the pastoral team of a
school. The development of the personality needs
to be undertaken in a much more systematic fashion
than at present. Adolescence is a time when youngsters find out about themselves. They begin to
discover their self identities and self image (Wall
1982). Self awareness becomes a crucial factor
in adolescent development. Learning about themselves in safe and structured ways will help adolescents turn out as well adjusted with the necessary levels of independence to get the most from
the communities they live in, as well as being
able to contribute to them.

The importance of a positive self concept
has been well documented in the performance of
academic and social tasks, and it rests with pastoral care teams to aid pupils to develop good
pictures of themselves. They have to learn how
they see themselves, as well as how they are perceived by other people. The wider the gap in this
field, the greater the personal problems a pupil
will face. Comparing the two, helps pupils to
develop a greater congruity between the way in
which they see themselves, and the manner in which
they are perceived by others.

Pupils need to find out what their attributes
and skills are, and not just in terms of
what lessons they excel at in school. They need
help not only in discovering their good and bad
points, but also in how to use their strengths
and weaknesses to their advantage. Personality
development in pastoral care should include the
scope for pupils to become fully aware of their
attributes, both by taking account of the views
of their peers, and by self questioning. Youngsters
also require assistance in finding out what their
personal needs are, and how to go about trying
to meet them. For instance if a pupil has a need
to be 'needed' by a group of peers, what methods
are used to satisfy that need? Are they advantageous, or do they work in counterproductive ways?
Learning about which parts of their lives they
can control directly, and which parts of their
lives they cannot control is essential for mental
health. Learning how not to be helpless and dependent is a vital part of personal growth. The pastoral programme of a school can play a very important role in allowing pupils the opportunity to

discover how to help themselves, and how to accept help for those parts of life which they are not able to directly manage or control.

Partnership with Pupils

Doing preventive, developmental and skills building work in pastoral care, means having a working partnership with pupils. If pupils are to respond to the pastoral programme as outlined so far, they need to feel that they have something to contribute to the school and its functioning. Pupils should be encouraged to work together with staff so that they become aware of mutual expectations and agree overtly, and jointly, on methods of fulfilling them.

In order to do this, they have to be given sufficient information and explanation of their school, both in terms of its structure and function. Pupils should have some discourse with teachers about the purpose of school, its aims and how it achieves them. This ensures that teachers and pupils work towards common goals and not against each other. In this way pupils can be made aware of their part in helping the school achieve its objectives. If there is a measure of agreement on what these aims are, then pupils are much more likely to want to play their part in the scheme of things.

Schools also need to help children to foster positive attitudes to school by making them feel valued. This can be done in many ways, including giving emphasis to the perceptions of the pupils, explaining the banding and setting system, and that of reporting on pupil progress. These issues cause a great deal of confusion to pupils who can never gain the most from their days in school if they never fully comprehend the methods used to allocate them to lessons, or the system of reporting, which can often be quite subjective, and revealing more about differential teacher standards than about pupil performance.

Some of the difficulties that arise in teacher pupil relationships derive from the many different sets of expectations teachers have of pupils, but which are rarely made explicit. These expectations range from aspects of behaviour inside and outside classrooms, to matters of work presentation etc. Sometimes pupils have to endure many months of trying to determine just what is acceptable in one set of circumstances, but which may not be acceptable in another because the teachers concerned have differing standards. Pupils therefore have to learn by trial and error, but suffer many frustrations while doing so. This can lead to alienation and de-motivation. Teachers too may feel frustrated in their main task, which they often regard as to 'teach' or impart knowledge, by spending a lot of time reminding pupils of their personal rules and expectations. Helping pupils cope with differential teacher style and expectation should form part of a pastoral curriculum, so that pupils may learn more quickly and efficiently how to cope with previously confusing and frustrating situations.

Working in Small Groups

Much of the tutorial work that teachers undertake during their pastoral sessions will involve working with small groups within a class. This requires much pre-planning and organisation of tasks, and materials. It will also involve teachers in conducting their sessions in different ways to those that may be customary in normal teaching routines. Often team teaching can be very useful in tutorial groups, and should be considered seriously by all schools embarking on a structured pastoral programme. Teachers can get around the groups with greater ease and frequency, and perhaps, just as importantly, they can help, support and complement each other.

Subsequent chapters in this book provide extensive guidelines on techniques for handling different topics, with several examples of materials for use by the busy teacher. Before using those materials it is as well to review some of the rules for working with groups within a class.

1. <u>Group size and composition</u>: the tutor should aim to have between four to six pupils in each group. If classes are very large then groups may have to be slightly larger, but as group size increases so certain members become inhibited, while others allow the keen ones to do all the work. Four pupils to a group is probably a minimum for a reasonable set of ideas to be aired and discussed. Smaller groups tend to get 'hung up' on a certain way of thinking and rarely cover in depth the topic under consideration.

It is recommended that groups have equal numbers of boys and girls, where possible. The only exception to this is when the topic calls

for boys and girls to consider separately an issue
from the point of view of their gender. Sometimes
teachers find that adolescents become embarrassed
when discussing sensitive issues such as relationships with the opposite sex etc. and it may be
necessary to have all girl and all boy groups for
these issues if it is felt to be needed.

Where classes are of mixed ability children,
the composition of the groups should reflect that
mixture. If all the less articulate children were
grouped together, it is unlikely that they would
be able to express their ideas without a more elo-
quent peer to bring forth their views.

2. <u>Forming a group and instructing it in
its task:</u> Groups should be formed as informally
as possible, bearing in mind that they should have
a mixture of ability levels, equal numbers of boys
and girls, and a maximum of six pupils. It is
imperative that children do not choose to be with
their friends for all group discussions, as this
will not serve the purpose of the group to come
up with new ideas and think about ways of coping
with specific issues. For cross-fertilization
of ideas to occur, the teacher should form a group
at random. One rule of thumb can be the four -
six pupils sitting near each other provided they
do not happen to be close friends.

Each group should have a spokesperson and
leader, who may or may not be the same person.
The function of the spokesperson is to inform the
other groups of the views of that group. The leader
should ensure that all the tasks given to the group
are carried out within the specified time, and
that all members of the group have made a contribution.

The instructions given to each group by the
tutor should be as non-directive as possible. Pupils
will be expecting their teachers to guide them
along a certain path as this may be their experience
during more formal academic lessons. The tutor
should have ready all the materials for each group
and simply give them a time within which they are
to complete their task. The tutor should inform
the groups that there are no right or wrong answers,
as again many pupils get stuck in their deliberations, searching for the 'right' answer. Pupils
should be encouraged to express their own feelings
and views as honestly as possible, while being
prepared to hear many other points of view.

Often a group task will require individual
children to make up their minds about a topic.

Some pupils will feel unable to do this, and will therefore opt out of group discussions. The tutor should, in these instances, encourage those pupils to listen to the arguments, making a list of pros and cons, so that at the end of the discussions they have sufficient information with which to come to some conclusion.

  3. Assisting groups in their tasks: once each group has been formed, the leaders and spokespersons elected, the job of the tutor should be to mingle with the groups and stimulate discussion. Younger pupils in particular will still claim that they don't know what to do, simply because they have been given a free hand to think and discuss as they like. Often the tutor will have to ask pertinent questions to facilitate a discussion that for some reason did not get going, or one that died before time, perhaps because the leader was unsure of the task in hand. Many pupils will need a few reminders and demonstrations of how to complete their handouts, and this too the tutor can do while visiting each group before the time limit for discussion is over. This is a highly taxing part of the tutors role, as each group will be making different demands, and will be looking for reassurance that they have done their job 'correctly'. The tutor must not fall into the trap of looking for and complementing a certain type of response from individual pupils. The tutor must also be careful not to spend too much time with any one group for fear of influencing their judgements too much, and not giving assistance to other groups who may need it.

  4. Facilitating discussion between groups: after all the groups have finished their talks, the tutor should select one group at random to present their conclusions to members of the other groups. If the spokesperson fails to present the views of the group in a coherent way, the tutor can assist by asking questions which would elicit the required responses. Questions such as 'what did your group feel about...?' may help the spokesperson. Additional questions to ask are:

> 'Did you come to any conclusions about..?'
> 'What did most of your group think was the way round for...?'
> 'What did you decide to do for the best in this case?'
> 'Did you feel that the ideas given to you will work for...?'

When each group has presented its ideas, all the information should be available for the class to see at a glance. The tutor should, where possible, make a summary of each group's views on the blackboard, or a large sheet of paper, in view of the whole class. This is essential for guiding class discussion. Pupils should be encouraged to develop their ideas using evidence either from their own experience, their knowledge gained from media sources, or the strength of a logical argument. The teacher needs to act as 'devils advocate', presenting the opposing arguments or points of view, but never making a judgement about the rights or wrongs of an issue. The job of the tutor is to allow the children to come to conclusions, form views, and begin to think along new lines via discussion and debate.

The tackling of sensitive or emotional issues can sometimes pose problems for both tutors and students. The role of the tutor should be to channel feelings and views to a reasonable conclusion. Occasionally this may involve tutors in using some of their own experiences to help pupils in their understanding of certain points. This is a very useful strategy to employ, and one which gives credibility to the teacher in the eyes of the pupil. Some teachers feel that letting down their guards in this way may encourage pupils to take advantage of them in their formal lessons. This is an understandable fear, but one which rarely occurs. Pupils find it quite easy to separate tutorial sessions from academic lessons, and are quite at ease in relating to the same member of staff in two different ways.

What ever techniques are eventually used by tutors, their final aim should be to present the class with all points of view that emerged from the discussion, and guide them in considering the consequences of following one particular point of view. The class should leave the tutorial session with some definite views that they can justify to themselves. They should on no account be left more confused or worried than before the tutorial began. Tutors also need to bear in mind that it is perfectly reasonable for pupils to leave the session with quite different points of view, so long as it fits in with that pupil's circumstances. It will be on rare occasions that the tutor will aim for a concencus of opinion from the whole class. At times pupils will be asked to consider themselves as individuals and perhaps consult their peers about their perceptions of the individual concerned. In these cases, the tutor must encourage the individual point of view to have full expression.

5. <u>Changing the composition of groups</u>: some topics may require several units of discussion. In order that class members do not get stuck with the same group members for each of the group tasks, it is a good idea to alter the composition of the groups. This can be done either by changing just half the members of one group with half the members from another group, assuming there is an equal number of groups within the class, or pupils could rotate from group to group, with one member always staying constant. It is also an opportune time to change the spokesperson and group leader, so that all pupils will have the chance to play all roles within a group.

Working in pairs within groups can be a useful way of ensuring that no pupil is ever left out of discussions. When tasks call for individual pupils having to seek out information from their peers, then working in pairs within a group is possibly the best way of achieving this aim. The leader must then collate all the information so that the spokesperson can communicate it to the rest of the class. If children do work in pairs for some tasks, then the pairing of pupils also needs to be changed constantly.

6. <u>Giving the groups some purpose</u>: All groups function best if they have a specific purpose in mind. For the tutor, there are groups within a group (the class) and each has a purpose. The aim of the large group, which is the class, may be to think about a topic and come up with some ideas for the future. However, within the class, each small group must also have a special task to perform, and the tutor must make it quite plain what that is. Each group must be asked to present a case for an argument, ways of handling a problem situation, advice for peers on a difficult issue or simply ideas on how they, as a team, would go about a task. If pupils are not given a definite aim, they will have no incentive to perform that task.

Similarly, when each small group has performed its task, the tutor must bring the individuals together by giving them a joint target to aim for. This could take the form of a project that pupils do during their free time, or something that they conduct within the school such as a survey etc.

Alternatively if they have been thinking about helping peers with difficulties in homework, peer relationships etc. then they should all have some observation tasks to carry out and report on at future sessions. Sometimes it will be necessary to get pupils to try out a new skill, or practice others that they know of, but use infrequently. This could serve as the basis for later meetings. Where pupils have undertaken a task about their own experiences in school, it may be of benefit to get them to make up a little booklet where they write advice for the next set of pupils who may have similar experiences. This type of task will help to round off topics neatly, and give pupils the feeling that something has been accomplished from their work. Too often tutors report that their pupils resent tutorials and show no interest in discussions. This is possibly because they have not been encouraged to see some end result in it. With the help of some of the above ideas, this problem should not occur.

Further details about working with groups can be found in Stanford (1977) and Hopson & Scally (1981).

Problems Faced by Tutors and How to Support them:

Most tutors who undertake pastoral duties may well be somewhat alarmed at their role as outlined so far. This may be for several reasons. One of the major reasons revolves around the type of training form tutors and year tutors receive. In a study on how form tutors perceived their role, 89% of respondents felt that they had not been adequately trained for their role as tutors (Raymond 1982 a). Those who felt that they had been adequately trained, did so because they saw their role very much as the carrying out of administrative functions. The aspects of pastoral care that tutors found most difficult were those involving preventive work, developing social and life skills in pupils, helping pupils cope with their everyday problems, and encouraging a self awareness in youngsters. Tutors indicated that these tasks presented them with difficulties both personally and professionally.

A further reason why tutors find these tasks difficult relates to the bureaucratic nature of the pastoral structure in schools. While form tutors are seen at the heart of an active pastoral care service, they often work in double bind situations. They have responsibilities for the welfare and personal growth of pupils on the one hand, but on the other hand are encouraged to pass on their 'problem children' to year tutors or senior staff. This gives form tutors little incentive to take their duties seriously, and it is not uncommon for form tutors to retreat into administrative duties as a result. Of course, senior staff may take on the job of dealing with 'problem children' simply because form tutors are not equipped to handle them. This then becomes a vicious circle where tutors are given a task to do but are not trained to do it, and where the real tasks are taken away from them, thus never making it necessary for them to receive the requisite training.

The form tutors who feel that they must abdicate responsibilities for dealing with issues are going to feel less in command of situations than is necessary. They are also likely to become demotivated if they cannot accomplish what others expect of them officially, but DO for them unofficially. Pupils will not, in these circumstances, perceive form tutors as pastoral staff with status and will not respond to them accordingly during pastoral sessions.

Another reason why tutors find pastoral tasks somewhat difficult to implement is the lack of support and advice they receive from their colleagues. In most schools there is an unwritten law, that teachers are responsible for their own discipline and for conducting their classrooms. What goes on within their own four walls is their own business, and it is not proper to intervene unless absolutely essential. Unfortunately, this attitude permeates into pastoral work as well, making it very difficult for staff to admit that they need ideas or advice on how to tackle new topics and maintain an interest in the pupils. It is perhaps of even greater concern, that where teachers admit to having little or no training in pastoral work, that their colleagues do not deliberately set out to encourage and support them in a systematic way.

A third reason perhaps, as to why form tutors resist their wider pastoral roles rests on issues of credibility within the staff group of a school. While many teachers in senior and middle management levels of a school may actively welcome pastoral work as outlined previously in this chapter, they may not have actually conducted such sessions themselves, and have little empathy with those who

are elected to carry it out. There is thus a credibility gap, and one which will take a long time
to fill. It is not until form tutors who are now
engaging in preventive, and skills building work
with pupils become the senior management of
tomorrow, that that gap will be filled.

The organisation of a pastoral system, the
lack of relevant training and the credibility issues
all engender many conflicts and difficulties for
form tutors. As a result many have tried to resist
the introduction of new tasks being laid at their
doorsteps. They have done this by stating clearly
in a number of studies that they see their role
primarily in terms of administration, carrying
out activities such as marking the register, giving
out notices, and collecting in things from pupils
required by school (Silcox 1981; Raymond 1982a).
These findings are borne out by surveys of actual
practice where tutors were found to spend more
time on administration than on welfare, and that
as a result pupils were unlikely to seek them out
with problems (Figg & Ross 1981).

Taking all these problems into account it
appears that there can be a mismatch between what
form tutors believe their role and function to
be, and what is prescribed for them by others.
In addition form tutors may be doing things that
bear little resemblance to the way in which tutors
themselves see their task. All these mismatches
serve to create further conflicts in tutors (Doherty
1981) and need to be resolved if schools are to
implement successfully a pastoral programme.

Supporting Pastoral Teams

If and when a school has defined the aims of its
pastoral programme, it should then give that programme, its best chance of being adopted enthusi-
astically, by setting up two levels of support
groups. The first level centres around year tutors.
This group should get together on a regular basis
and discuss the content of pastoral programmes
for the coming term. They need to discuss what
problems pupils are facing in all areas of their
school life and communicate this information to
each other. In this way no single teacher is ever
made to feel inadequate, as the difficulties are
seen from the pupil view point, and a better understanding can be gained of pupil behaviour as a
result. Year tutors need also to discuss the techniques that could be used to help pupils handle

their immediate problems.

The next level of support group involves form tutors meeting, and comparing notes on content of pastoral sessions, useful techniques, things that were not successful and any novel approach that may have been tried with good results. Tutors can learn a lot from each other, and discover a great deal about the response of pupils to different ways of tackling a topic. In addition they need to appreciate that all classes will not respond to a topic even if the techniques used were apparently identical. The factors that the individual teacher brings to the session, together with the mood of the students can alter the outcome of such sessions.

Tutors need to bring to a forum of their peers the topics that pupils bring up as worthy of exploration, especially when they relate to issues of school organisation, teacher style or simply a lack of understanding of certain aspects of school life. This will give tutors some perspective on whether their students are unique in their views or whether there is some common element in their expressions which need a new or different approach by staff.

While it would be most beneficial for form tutors within a particular year group to meet regularly, it may also be worthwhile for form tutors from different year groups to get together from time to time, as often similar topics are covered and/or reinforced at different times of a pupil's career in school. Tutors can get some feedback about how children whom they tutored previously, are responding, and whether they have gained anything from sessions conducted in the past. For those form tutors who are simply starting for the first time, it would be very useful to hear about the problems of doing preventive and skills building pastoral care. This can be reassuring, and help inexperienced tutors to seek help at the earliest opportunity.

In addition to year tutors and form tutors meeting on their own, attempts should also be made for year tutors of a particular year group to meet with the form tutors of the same year group to exchange ideas. This could take the form of a mini pastoral session for the form tutors, in which they are encouraged to express their worries and fears about doing a particular topic, or using a technique that they may not be comfortable with. The year tutor should ask other form tutors who

are at ease with that technique, to give helpful
hints to those experiencing difficulties using
it. The year tutor needs to act as a facilitator,
so that tutors come away feeling well equipped
to handle their pastoral sessions in the future.
It is important that year tutors attempt to maintain
this delicate balance, in order that form tutors
continue to want to participate in such meetings.
Where possible, tutors should be paired up, so
that they learn skills from one another in the
classroom setting. The year tutor should promote
team teaching, by taking one of the tutorial groups
concerned, while two form tutors participated in
a session with another group.

Another function of joint meetings between
year tutors and form tutors, is to get together
as a team and work out what they expect of pupils
in all facets of school life. To achieve this,
teachers have to find out from their colleagues,
what they require, so that they can stress the
unwritten rules of school. This enables staff
to communicate effectively about individual pupils,
groups of pupils, and the procedures staff ought
to adopt in order to meet their needs. A lack
of communication between staff often gives rise
to potentially tragic circumstances. For instance,
a fourth form boy who was known to be very sensitive
was spoken to in a rather off hand manner by the
games master when he asked to be excused a games
lesson. This boy got very upset and broke down.
He remained distressed for a very long time after-
wards. He was unusually sensitive at this time
because his parents were getting divorced. His
year tutor was aware of this, as was the teacher
of his favourite subject. However, these members
of staff had failed to communicate the information
to anyone else, hence the games master's remark,
which hurt the boy more than it need have done,
had the teacher been made aware of the lad's circumstances.

When staff are clear as to the expectations
of their colleagues, and the requirements of pupil
groups, they should be able to give consistent
messages to students. Teachers will also be able
to reinforce each other, and ensure that staff
demands, and pupil needs are matched as closely
as possible, and that both have a chance of being
met.

Staff discussions and agreements on what they
expect of pupils should be reviewed periodically.
Teachers, like other people, differ in their levels

of tollerance, and they may inadvertently give pupils the impression, that on certain issues they differ in their level of flexibility. These signs can differ from day to day, hour to hour, depending on the moods of the staff and pupils they are involved with. As a result, it cannot be taken for granted that any plan will work without hitches, unless meetings are held regularly to discover whether their joint intentions are being implemented in practice. In this way pastoral care can truly take on a preventive role, and staff can gain support from each other in disciplinary tasks. If pupils are not conforming to staff expectations, then the pastoral team has a duty to find out whether in fact the messages they thought they were giving pupils, were properly received. The pastoral teams must also discover what if any difficulties the pupils have in putting into effect teacher expectations. The problems encountered by children in carrying out many of the tasks set by their teachers, can highlight the social and life skills that the pastoral team need to tackle. Skills building and preventive work can co-exist and complement each other therefore, as neither is taken on board in a vacuum, but from the standpoint of the pupils. Staff themselves, can use these forums as sounding boards to check out the expectations of their colleagues, and try where possible to be consistent with pupils across the board.

When tutors are aware of each other's expectations and experiences of tutorial work, they are much more likely to give each other help in informal ways. This should then obviate the need for the pastoral system as a whole to act only in times of crisis, or simply to solve teacher problems. Furthermore, teachers can be of greatest help to pupils when they are being helped themselves. They will be able to help pupils become aware of, and try to sort out their problems long before they reach breaking point.

Finally, form tutors and year tutors must together plan and discuss the pastoral programme that they hope to use. This will increase the chances of tutors being motivated in their work, as they have been personally involved, and are not merely carrying out the wishes of senior staff, or the headteachers. Some seminars or training sessions where particular techniques are discussed would be of immense value. If the year tutor with one form tutor were to conduct role-play sessions with the rest of the group it would probably be the best way of teaching a new skill. Video tapes of tutorial sessions could also generate much constructive discussion among tutors, guided by the year tutor.

Schools must, of course, allocate sufficient time for staff to support each other, and conduct the kind of meetings outlined in this chapter. The pastoral sessions too, must be given the status they deserve if tutors are to be expected to perform their duties therein as well as they do their other lessons.

This leads us back to the prerequisites that were mentioned at the beginning of this chapter. If schools want a caring and effective pastoral system, then they must attempt to provide the time needed for it to occur, and the relevant supports to their staff groups. Future chapters in the book should make their task much easier with practical guidelines for the handling of a number of pertinent issues in pastoral care.

CHAPTER TWO

ELICITING AND DISCUSSING PROBLEMS WITH PUPILS

Those organisations which offer a service to the
public are well aware of the importance of consumer
attitudes and beliefs about their products. The
Education system should be no less cognizant of
the views of pupils for whom they provide a service.
Pupils' perceptions of schools and teachers has
been shown to be significant in explaining the
behaviour of children in certain situations, and
the manner in which teachers themselves rate pupils.
(Davidson & Lang 1960; Phillips & Callely 1981;
Thompson 1975; and Woods 1976). Teachers are more
likely to have difficulties with pupils who have
negative perceptions of school. Raymond (1985)
found pupil motivation to be low in a class of
pupils whom teachers rated as disruptive, primarily
because pupils perceived the style of teacher-
pupil interaction to be discouraging. A pastoral
care system would need to be aware of such pupil
perceptions if it is to make school a more positive
experience for all pupils, and in the process,
prevent unmanageable situations from arising.

Valuing pupil perceptions is one of the hall-
marks of a good pastoral care system. By doing
so pupils are made to feel that their views are
of worth, and are taken into account. They can
also be made to feel that they are integral members
of the school and have their contributions to make
to the creation and maintenance of its ethos. Rutter
et al (1979) have indicated that the most successful
schools in their study were those that had
a pleasant and encouraging atmosphere, irrespective
of catchment area or size of school. The consultation of pupils, and giving them some part to
play in its day to day running usually created
a positive ethos.

Schools are places where many sets of people

communicate with each other. One of the most frequent and important sets of interactions occurs
between teachers and pupils. Teachers have the
task of informing children about the school, what
is on offer, and what is expected of pupils. Often
this is done implicitly and it is not easy
to measure its impact on pupils. Therefore finding
out from pupils how they perceive the communications
of the school via teachers is an essential part
of a pastoral system. Only then can some sort
of dialogue take place about common experience
for teachers and pupils. Without it, relationships
are bound to be strained and morale low amongst
both teachers and their pupils.

Advantages in Seeking the View of Pupils

For Teachers

There are many advantages for teachers in seeking
the view of pupils about school life, and about
the personal experiences of pupils which may pose
them difficulties.

    1. It allows the staff to check that their
communications with pupils are clear and unambigu-
ous.
    2. It permits the school to take corrective
action if there are gaps in pupils' awareness about
pertinent issues in school e.g. rules of dress,
homework, modes of talking to teachers, expected
behaviour in different situations etc.
    3. It shows up which areas need greater
elaboration and reinforcement before pupils indicate
their confusion by a deterioration in their general
demeanour and behaviour.
    4. It indicates which messages need to be
made more explicit especially in terms of teacher
expectations. Most pupils learn from their peers,
siblings and past pupils what teachers expect of
them. If they learn from teachers, it usually
takes place after they have contravened a rule.
It is often too late by then, and learning occurs
through punishment and fear instead of by having
definite goals to aim for. For instance, many
pupils need to be given very explicit messages
about how to ask for help, communicate their
anxieties, report on their views without being
'cheeky' etc.
    5. It defines a problem area for groups
of pupils and for individual pupils in concrete

terms, so allowing the teachers to be of maximum assistance.

6. Teachers can gain a better understanding of the difficulties encountered by pupils by looking at life from their point of view. It therefore permits staff to provide help that can be easily assimilated and used by pupils.

7. By listening to pupils discuss their perceptions of school and things connected with school that are of concern to pupils, solutions are often forthcoming immediately. Methods for solving problems offered to pupils can then be preventive rather than curative in nature.

8. It offers an insight into pupil motivation which is the province of all pastoral and academic staff. By discovering those things that encourage and discourage pupils from attending school, performing well in lessons, and taking a full part in school life, schools can adapt and evolve their system to meet the needs of its pupils.

9. It encourages communication between teachers about their discussions with pupils in a way that does not make any teacher feel threatened or inadequate.

10. By discovering why pupils think and behave in certain ways, teachers have in their power some means of changing situations for the better, which reduces teacher stress. (Dunham 1977; Hargreaves 1978; Galloway et al 1982).

For Pupils

Advantages are also gained by children when their perceptions are sought about school and their personal problems.

1. Pupils learn to express and communicate their feelings and difficulties in an articulate manner.

2. Pupils, by expressing their opinions may discover a solution in the process of describing their problems.

3. Pupils are made more aware of the trigger situations that lead them to experience situations in unpleasant ways.

4. Pupils can discover how and why situations ended in ways that had negative consequences for them.

5. By listening to their peers, pupils can be exposed to alternative methods of perceiving and coping with difficult experiences.

6. Pupils will feel encouraged to evaluate what is being offered to them in a constructive way instead of just opting out of things that they do not like.

7. By being given the opportunity to discuss their difficulties pupils are less likely to engage in antisocial behaviour as a means of expressing their dissatisfaction.

8. Pupils can develop new relationships with teachers, and see staff as agents who can offer help and advice before crisis points are reached.

Issues of Importance in Pupil Perception

On what kinds of topics should teachers seek the views of pupils? Basically there are two broad categories from which perceptions could be drawn; that is those related to SCHOOL FACTORS and those related to PERSONAL and SOCIAL FACTORS.

Most teachers who have a specific responsibility within the pastoral framework of a school are used to receiving complaints from other members of staff about individual pupils and their misdemeanours. In other words, they are usually privy to the views of their colleagues, and can therefore only deal with the problems as presented to them by other teachers. Pastoral staff then become problem solvers for teachers as opposed to pupils. Looking at difficulties from the point of view of a pupil will involve a change in the terminology that is used to describe problems. For instance a so called problem for staff called 'truancy' may have to change to 'what has school got to offer you?'. Persistent failure to bring books and equipment to school which could be labelled as a 'couldn't care less attitude, refusal to work' can be altered to 'why are your lessons so uninteresting to you, that you do not see the need to come prepared to take part?'

School factors and personal factors therefore have to be defined from the perspective of pupils before their opinions and perceptions can be sought. Often these factors overlap and need to be considered together.

PROBLEM AREAS FOR PUPILS

School Factors

Purpose of School

What has it got to offer?

Banding and setting system

Hierarchy within school

Rules

Teacher expectations

Teacher style

Tests and examinations

Attendance

Uniform

Privileges

Discipline system

Personal Factors

Planning and use of time

Homework

Conflicts with staff

Conflicts with peers

Coping with interviews

Being treated fairly

Awareness of own skills

Awareness of own needs

Handling responsibilities

Exerting own identity

Becoming independent

Coping with stress

ELICITING AND DISCUSSING PROBLEMS WITH PUPILS

Methods of Eliciting Pupil Perceptions

The way in which individuals perceive one another, and the situations in which these interactions take place is a very complex process (Warr & Knapper 1968). It involves a person's internal belief system, their expectations of events in a particular situation based on previous experience, and the direct immediate experience of an event. These things combine to produce a perception by an individual of another person or event. For instance, a pupil may have a belief that teachers provide children with information to increase their knowledge. The pupil may also have an expectation that teachers should demonstrate new skills and explain topics clearly and repeatedly until the pupil has understood. If a pupil then encounters a teacher who does not put over a topic clearly, and expects the pupil to find out for him/herself how to execute a new skill, it is likely that the pupil will perceive that situation as 'boring' and the teacher as a 'bad teacher'. Future inter-actions between the teacher and pupil will take on a more negative dimension as a result.

Pupils also have beliefs about themselves and their peers which influence their perceptions of situations where they interact. These percep-tions may cause relationship difficulties. The case of Mark in the fourth form illustrates the importance of person perceptions and the difficulties in eliciting them. Mark was a shy lad who had minimal contact with teaching staff outside lessons as he caused no trouble in school. He would panic in many of his lessons if he failed to keep up with his peers, and thus experienced a great deal of stress. He would come out in rashes, and stress related herpes, which meant his having to stay away from school for periods of time. This boy found it very difficult to express himself in words, and did not like teachers to single him out for attention in front of his class mates either for a telling off or even an innocuous interaction. Eventually it was revealed that the lad perceived his teachers to be uncaring and so never asked them for assistance. He assumed that when teachers called out his name, for any purpose whatsoever, his class mates would suspect that he had been up to something of a less than honourable nature. Not only would Mark refrain from communicating with staff about his feelings, but also he refused to allow his parents and outside agencies doing

so for him in case 'it made things worse for him'.
Mark had been through a very miserable and stressful
three years in school before his perceptions of
what was going on, and what he thought about
teachers and pupils was brought out, and acted
on, by aiding him to test out his views and modify
them accordingly.

The methods of evoking pupil perceptions are
many and various, each useful in a different way,
according to the situation in hand. Most of the
methods need to be sensitive and meaningful to
the pupil. Direct questioning of a pupil can sometimes lead to antagonism, as pupils are not used
to being spoken to about their personal feelings,
least of all when they relate to school matters.
Pupils are suspicious of teachers who suddenly
begin talking to them about their personal feelings,
when they are more accustomed to interacting with
them in a more distant and impersonal manner. As
a result, pupils may not always be as frank and
open with staff as would be required if anything
positive was to come from such episodes. Apart
from being sensitive and meaningful, methods of
eliciting pupil perceptions have to be indirect
and quite structured. Both pupils and teachers
need to feel safe and secure in disclosing things
about themselves without fear of repercussion.
Teachers should feel that they are able to collate
and handle emotions that may be threatening to
them or the school; as pupils are bound to describe
situations in school which have distressed them,
and they may reflect badly on some part of the
school organisation or a colleague. They also
need to accept that pupils reporting their perceptions of school life are genuine in their views,
however unrealistic these may seem to staff. It
is not uncommon for teachers to dismiss what pupils
tell them as untruths or exaggerations. This can
only damage the relationship between pupils and
teachers, and should be avoided as far as possible.
Pupils who are dismissed as liars or 'trying to
pull a fast one' become very reticent in their
conversations with teachers, and will be reluctant
to reveal anything of note in the future. In their
pastoral work, teachers need not act as judges
or arbiters of the truth. If they are to assist
pupils in their difficulties, then it can only
be done if pupils' views are accepted as authentic
and used as a starting point. Two pupils could
have had an identical experience in the same lesson
with the same group of people and the same teacher,

but each will have their own unique perception of it and each will be as valid as the other.

As perceptions are very complex the methods used to get at them need to be broad and diverse enough to encompass them. Basically there are five methods that are of value in the school setting. These are(a) Interviewing and questioning, (b) self report schedules, (c) rating scales, (d) card sorting techniques and (e) role play.

Interviewing and Questioning

Asking the right type of questions which give pupils scope to present their views in an articulate manner is a skilled business. Teachers often ask questions which involve factual recall as opposed to questions which stimulate thought and problem solving skills. They are used to encouraging responses from pupils which have either a right or a wrong answer (Gall; Hargie 1978).

In the context of pastoral care work, the teacher needs to develop a new set of techniques with regard to questioning, so that meaningful responses are forthcoming from pupils, Munro and Manthei (1979). 'Have you got any problems?' is the kind of question which is likely to stultify pupils in their self reflection and self disclosure. It is known as a closed question, which requires a simple choice of 'yes' or 'no'. It gives the teacher very little scope for developing the conversation. Many teachers have used that technique in their pastoral role and have reported back saying that they had nothing to work on with the pupils, as pupils did not come up with any problems. From the pupils' point of view that is a non question, as they are likely to say 'why are you asking me that type of question, as school itself is a problem'. More open questions can produce information of some significance and can lead to useful pastoral sessions where both teacher and pupil gain from the experience. Questions that may be of value in this context are:

'In what situations do you feel confused?'
'In what situations do you feel trapped?'
'How did you feel when you were not allowed in at break time?'
'What kinds of thing annoy you in school?'
'What kinds of things make you nervous?'
'When do you feel that no one understands you?'
'What sort of things do you feel are unfair?'

ELICITING AND DISCUSSING PROBLEMS WITH PUPILS

'What sort of things discourage you in school?'

Often a mixture of open and closed questions is necessary to enable pupils to channel their thoughts when appropriate, and think in a more diversified manner at other times. This is especially important when pupils are in classes of mixed ability groupings. To ensure that all pupils are aware of the topic under discussion, and that they are adequately cued in, a closed question to begin with helps focus all the pupils' minds on the theme. Later open questions encourage pupils to consider their own feelings, and implications for thinking and acting in certain ways. For instance a tutorial session on planning time to include homework may begin with a closed question such as:

'Is it necessary to plan out time so that we can fit in homework with everything else we want to do?'

This type of question will only allow pupils to answer in the affirmative or in the negative. However, it will have introduced the idea of Planning to those who may never have considered it seriously, and it will also have suggested that Planning is often a purposeful activity.

The next step would be to ask more open ended questions, which could stimulate pupils into thinking about their own plans if they have any, and about those they may have in the future e.g.:

'What would happen if we didn't have any plans in our free time?'
'Your parents must have many things to do during the day if you are to have all the things you want and need on your return from school. How do you think they plan their time to make sure these things happen?'

The use of open and closed questions together is known as a multiple question. It helps pupils concentrate on one specific point at a time while still permitting a wide range of view.

Alternating between closed and open questions is a useful device in class interviews, but it should also be peppered with the kind of question or remark which throws back at pupils what they have said, to check on their meaning, and if necessary expand on it. In this way pupils are certain of not having their views misrepresented.

The following extract taken from an interview with a group of third form low set of pupils indicates how their views about school were sought in order to discover what if any aspects of school life were problem areas for them. Pupils sat in a circle around the author (in the role of tutor) to maximise eye contact between the entire group.

TUTOR: What do you think about school?
What kinds of things do you like and
dislike?   OPEN
PUPIL A: Uniforms, we should be allowed
to wear what we like.
PUPIL B: I think teachers should wear
uniform. There is not enough strict-
ness in this school. There is not
much authority, because they haven't
got any school uniform on.
TUTOR: So you think that if the teachers
wore something that made them look the
same then you would have more respect
for them?   THROW-BACK
PUPIL B: Yes.
TUTOR: Let me ask another one of you why
do you think that some teachers don't
have enough control over you, since
that is what (pupil B) is suggesting?
Do you think its got anything to do
with the way they look?   MULTIPLE
PUPIL C: Not sure.
TUTOR: Have you got any idea why you
agree with (pupil B), why you think
the teachers don't have enough
discipline? Do you think its because
they don't want to discipline you, or
they couldn't care less?   CLOSED
PUPIL C: No idea.
TUTOR: You haven't any idea at all, but
you would like them to be more strict
with you, would you?   CLOSED
PUPIL C: (nods head in the affirmative).
TUTOR: In what way? What do you want
them to do that they are not doing
now?   OPEN
PUPIL D: It would be better to have
the cane rather than lines as with
lines you keep doing them all the time,
but if you have the cane its over with.
TUTOR: So you don't think its a very
good punishment to have lines.   THROW-BACK

What about what (Pupil B) was saying
that if teachers looked the same, if they
looked strict you would have more respect
for them. Do you agree with that?   CLOSED
CLASS: Yes.
TUTOR: What do you want them to wear to
look strict?   OPEN
PUPILS: Black gowns.
TUTOR: Why do you think black gowns make
people look strict and authoritative?   OPEN
PUPIL E: It makes them look pretty
terrifying.
TUTOR: Are there teachers you know of
who don't wear gowns, but you are still
terrified of?   CLOSED
CLASS: Yes.
TUTOR: Think of one now, tell me what it
is about them that makes you terrified
of them?   OPEN
PUPIL F: Its the way they come on to you,
its as if they are going to kill you.
TUTOR: Can you explain that a little
bit more. Is it the way they look at
you, or the way they talk?   MULTIPLE
PUPIL F: The way they look.
TUTOR: How do they look?   OPEN
PUPIL F: They stare at you.
TUTOR: They stare at you, anything else?   THROW-BACK/
                                                  OPEN

PUPIL G: They shout at you.
TUTOR: They shout at you. Why does that
terrify you?   THROW-BACK/
                                                  OPEN

PUPIL G: Its loud.
TUTOR: So loudness and staring terrify
you, anything else?   THROW-BACK/
                                                  OPEN

PUPIL E: Size of them.
TUTOR: The size, the bigger they are the
more terrified you are, is that right?   THROW-BACK/
                                                  CLOSED

PUPILS: Yes.
TUTOR: Aren't there any little teachers
whom you are terrified of?   CLOSED
PUPIL E: Yes, the science teacher, he is
small, but what I've heard off a couple
of people, he is supposed to be hard.
TUTOR: What do we mean by hard?   OPEN
PUPIL F: Tough.
TUTOR: What do we mean by tough?   OPEN
PUPIL H: They hit you.

36

TUTOR: They hit you. Can you tell me
the difference between a hard teacher
and a soft teacher?   OPEN
PUPIL I: A teacher who isn't strict
talks softly, they don't shout or
anything. They say they will but nothing
happens.
TUTOR: So they threaten you, but don't
carry out their threats.   THROW-BACK
What is a hard teacher like?   OPEN
PUPIL J: They shout.
PUPIL K: They push you about.
PUPIL L: They act bigger.
TUTOR: Yes, but how are they different
to soft teachers?   OPEN
PUPIL L: They say, 'if you keep on,
you'll go through the wall'.
TUTOR: So they threaten you.   THROW-BACK
PUPILS: Yes.
TUTOR: But we said that soft teachers
threaten you as well.   THROW-BACK
What is the difference?   OPEN
PUPILS: There is a difference. They do
it.
TUTOR: They carry out their threats.   THROW-BACK

This extract illustrates how to use different types
of question to stimulate pupils into explaining
complex issues such as discipline and control in
relation to its effect on them. None of the views
they had were immediately accessible by direct
questioning. They had to be led via the use of
open questions to consider specific issues and
pin point exactly what and why they felt as they
did. Where pupils found it difficult to respond,
the tutor used a number of closed forced choice
questions to provide a structure and platform for
pupils to explain themselves. The tutor made no
judgement about what pupils expressed and this
is a vital point to bear in mind. It allowed pupils
to continue to give freely of their opinions, and
it allowed the author to feedback information to
staff to aid them in their dealings with these
pupils.
       The teacher's role in using the interview
and questioning technique is to help pupils to
explain their feeling in a manner that is clear
and well thought out. In this way teachers can
get together in teams with year tutors and heads
of school to make informed and well planned decisions about the structure and content of the

pastoral system.   In the case of the interview
quoted above, it helped provide staff with possible
reasons for the behaviour of those pupils with
different teachers.   Pupils were indicating quite
forcefully the kind of style of discipline that
they responded to best, and why they failed to
take much notice of disciplinary styles in other
situations.   The pastoral team could have used
this information in two ways.   First, they could
have supported and assisted their colleagues in
improving their methods of control.   Second, they
could have worked out a pastoral programme whereby
pupils were given some skills in coping with differential teacher style.   Such strategies would ensure
that action was taken to prevent minor disciplinary
matters from escalating into major   management
issues.
         The teacher should also aim to offer pupils
a series of alternative view points so that pupils
indicate whether their perceptions were truly reflecting their feelings or not.   They can do this
by either, rejecting the alternatives suggested
or, using the other ideas, to elaborate on their
original views.   Presenting pupils with alternatives
also allows them the chance to change their perceptions from negative to a more positive dimension.
By looking at the same situation in another way
they may be less upset or confused about it. Putting
positive constructions on previously unpleasant
events gives pupils new ways of thinking of future
experiences which may cause them distress.   The
teacher also needs to act as a sort of sounding
board, echoing the views of pupils, and throwing
at them new ways of thinking about common and age
old problems.   This is not to argue that all unhappy
pupil experiences can be magically altered to happy
ones, but pupils are at least encouraged to develop
the skills of looking at issues from other peoples'
points of view, and to have a new perspective on
describing and coping with problems.

Self Report Schedules

It is often necessary to find out what individual
pupils think about themselves, and how it relates
to the way others perceive them, or how it relates
to the interaction between themselves, their
teachers, and the school as a whole.   Asking them
questions in front of their class mates may be
embarrassing, as they may not be ready or able
to handle any ridicule that could arise.   There

may also be occasions when pupils need to have their thoughts directed in a particular way, and in these instances self report schedules are of immense value to pupils and to the teachers.

Self report schedules enable pupils to indicate their thoughts, opinions, beliefs and feelings about a certain topic in a number of ways. Pupils may be involved in describing themselves, listing their skills, or comparing what they feel about a topic with the views of peers. Children may also comment on a system operating within the school and suggest ideas of improvement. Some schedules require pupils to complete sentences e.g. The Sort Of Person I Am (Hamblin 1978); while others allow pupils to list their own statements under general headings, e.g. Who Am I (Kuhn & Mcpartland 1954). In other schedules pupils rate themselves as 'Like Me' or 'Unlike Me', in relation to a set of statements pertaining to specific problems (Coopersmith 1967). Schedules for looking at group behaviour from the point of view of the pupil have been developed by Button (1974). Still other schedules ask pupils to respond by agreeing, disagreeing, or saying they are unsure to a list of statements.

Teachers are very busy people, and often do not have the time to make up schedules when the need arises. Some useful ones have therefore been devised for use by teachers who engage in pastoral work. They focus on the areas of pupil motivation, relationships, homework and revision, and school rules and community life.

Pupil Motivation

There are many aspects to the level of motivation which pupils may have in school to achieve their work, and to behave in ways that would maximise their opportunities for success. Waller & Gaa (1974) state that looking at the needs of a pupil and whether they are being met, can be a useful tool for the analysis of that pupil's behaviour. Many authors have suggested a list of basic needs that people have, the most well known of which is that provided by Maslow (1968;1970). Amongst the needs that he listed are those of safety, esteem and the desire to know and understand. Many of these needs are provided by teacher style and interaction with pupils. Bennett (1976) showed how the teacher can influence the attainments and behaviour of pupils via the teaching style adopted. Finlayson & Loughran (1976) revealed that pupils were more effected by the way the teacher communicates with the whole class, rather than with individual pupils, once again emphasising the manner of teacher interaction with pupils. Reynolds & Murgatroyd (1977), Hargreaves (1975), Ousten (1981) and Pik (1981) have all discussed the differences between schools, where pupils are made to feel important by having a structure that is immediate in its response to pupils as opposed to one that is delayed and bureaucratic in style, passing on the task from one level of management to another.

All these aspects of a school's operations will affect pupil motivation. Children who are being taught by staff who cannot control them without calling in other members of staff will not feel safe in their lessons, and their performance is likely to drop. Poor communication between staff and pupils, and an ineffective system of discipline can prevent pupils from fulfilling their needs to know, understand and build up self esteem.

It is helpful for pastoral staff in school to discover what effect these parts of the school organisation have on the motivation of the pupils. A self report schedule for this purpose can be an economical way of achieving this. Since such schedules may remain annonymous, pupils can respond truthfully without fear of being singled out for reprisals. It would also give the pastoral team information about which lessons and teachers need extra support, and which facets of school life need modification in order to raise levels of motivation amongst pupils. A set of three schedules which look at pupils' reasons for attending school, the things that encourage them, and the things that discourage them, is given below.

This type of self report schedule is of particular advantage when trying to deal with disenchanted pupils who may often absent themselves from school, rarely do any work in lessons, or with those who are disruptive. By comparing the responses of apparently well motivated pupils, and those who are not, it may be possible to set up schemes whereby the former group could exchange their views and skills. For instance if some pupils indicate that they rarely get praise for work well done or handed in on time, then those who do, can pass on some of their strategies for ensuring that they do get praise and are acknowledged for their efforts.

Opportunities are also evident for staff to shape the opinions of pupils on those aspects of

REASONS FOR ATTENDING SCHOOL

1.	It is the law.	YES	MAYBE	NO
2.	My parents force me.	YES	MAYBE	NO
3.	My parents bribe me to come to school.	YES	MAYBE	NO
4.	It's a place to be with my friends.	YES	MAYBE	NO
5.	I can learn something to do during the day.	YES	MAYBE	NO
6.	I need to have something to do during the day.	YES	MAYBE	NO
7.	I enjoy the sports facilities.	YES	MAYBE	NO
8.	I enjoy making teachers angry.	YES	MAYBE	NO
9.	I enjoy pleasing teachers.	YES	MAYBE	NO
10.	I might get a row off my parents if they find out I have not been to school.	YES	MAYBE	NO
11.	Some lessons are interesting.	YES	MAYBE	NO
12.	It is somewhere to be if the weather is bad.	YES	MAYBE	NO

ANY OTHER REASONS:

ELICITING AND DISCUSSING PROBLEMS WITH PUPILS

THINGS THAT ENCOURAGE ME IN SCHOOL

1. Praise for work well done.   YES   MAYBE   NO

2. Praise for work handed in
   on time.   YES   MAYBE   NO

3. Being given a reason for an
   order.   YES   MAYBE   NO

4. When I am given a chance
   to explain my side of
   things.   YES   MAYBE   NO

5. When I am spoken to in a
   pleasant tone of voice.   YES   MAYBE   NO

6. When I am spoken to without
   sarcasm or hurtful remarks.   YES   MAYBE   NO

7. Being allowed to ask
   questions in class without
   being made to feel guilty.   YES   MAYBE   NO

8. Being allowed to take a
   greater part in lessons
   instead of just writing/
   copying.   YES   MAYBE   NO

9. Teachers who can make pupils
   get down to their work and
   not let some pupils spoil
   lessons for everyone else.   YES   MAYBE   NO

10. Teachers who tell me exactly
    where I stand with them.   YES   MAYBE   NO

11. Teachers who can give their
    own punishments, instead
    of calling in other staff,
    or sending me to another
    member of staff.   YES   MAYBE   NO

12. Teachers who tell me exactly
    what I have done wrong
    before punishing me, instead
    of expecting me to work it
    out.   YES   MAYBE   NO

Any Other Comments

ELICITING AND DISCUSSING PROBLEMS WITH PUPILS

THINGS THAT DISCOURAGE ME IN SCHOOL

1. When different teachers tell me to do different things - making me confused.   YES   MAYBE   NO

2. When lessons take a long time to begin because the class cannot settle down, no matter what the teacher does.   YES   MAYBE   NO

3. Teachers who tell me off in front of my class mates.   YES   MAYBE   NO

4. Teachers who make comments about my family when they are telling me off.   YES   MAYBE   NO

5. Pupils who mess around in class and stop me from learning.   YES   MAYBE   NO

6. Work that is presented in a boring way making me lose interest.   YES   MAYBE   NO

7. Being given no responsibilities in school, e.g. prefect, librarian etc.   YES   MAYBE   NO

8. There do not seem to be any pay offs for coming to school and working.   YES   MAYBE   NO

9. However hard I try, it never seems to be good enough for teachers.   YES   MAYBE   NO

10. I feel as if teachers would rather not be teaching me.   YES   MAYBE   NO

11. I am made to feel that I cannot be trusted.   YES   MAYBE   NO

12. Being made to feel like a second class citizen and not really wanted in school. YES   MAYBE   NO

Any Other Comments

the schedule where they have indicated that they have not formed clear or definite views by responding 'maybe'. In this way staff can take some measures to ensure that pupils do not continue their schooling by perceiving it in negative and discouraging ways.

Relationships

Many pupils find it difficult to make and sustain relationships with peers or members of staff. They may believe that other people see them in certain ways without bothering to find out if those beliefs are real or not. It is quite common for children to think that they are unpopular, that no one wants to sit by them or interact with them by choice. These children can go through personal agonies that cause them acute distress and which can also be debilitating. Dawn, twelve and of average ability who recently moved to a new area and attended a new secondary school was convinced that she was being victimised by her class mates because she came from another part of the county. She believed that they did not want to sit at the same table as her during lunch times, and that they deliberately positioned themselves in science lessons so that she was on a bench all on her own. Her anxieties became so great that she became a chronic school refuser. Dawn would have benefitted from pastoral sessions where she could indicate what she believed to be true about herself and whether others also saw her in this way as well. From there, staff would have been able to assist her in coming to terms with adjusting to a new environment and set of people.

Another case also indicates the advantages of using self report schedules to reveal how pupils see themselves in relation to others where relationship difficulties may arise. This case involved a fifteen year old boy doing 'O' level examinations. His teachers believed him to be very bright and capable of taking up a good profession. However the boy appeared to be very depressed, and on one occasion took an overdose in school. He had previously told some of his teachers that he felt no one liked him and there was no point in living. Signs of his moroseness had been noticed ever since he began secondary education, but he seemed to get gradually more depressed, refusing any involvement with outside agencies or specialists of any sort. Pastoral work where he was given the opportunities to compare his views about himself to the way he thought his peers and teacher perceived him would have aided him in sorting out some of his difficulties in interpersonal relationships. The schedule entitled 'Comparing what I Think About Myself With What Others Think About Me' given below is an ideal tool for such cases. It is made up of a list of subheadings under which pupils simply note down their own feelings. It can therefore be used with any age group. The areas where pupils indicate that there is disagreement between what they think of themselves and how they think their teachers and friends see them are open for discussion. Where pupils believe that their peers or teachers think of them in a negative light, it can encourage an exchange of views, with all parties giving evidence for their beliefs.

With younger children or those who are less able to verbalise, it is helpful to collect a class list of adjectives and phrases that they may use to describe themselves. This is then used as a basis for pupils to think of their own responses. This task proved necessary with a mixed ability group of second form pupils. A class list compiled by the author (in the role of tutor) is presented below.

List of words and phrases to describe people devised by a second form class

Understanding	Moans a lot	Not interesting
Has stamina	Likes animals	Boring
Helpful	Tall	Nuisance
'Like a pin'	Short	Well organised
Spoffish	Kind	Has a good memory
Untrustworthy	Good at Sport	Swot
Big Headed	Friendly	Punctual
Funny	Wears Glasses	Noisy
Fit	Mature	Fast Runner

Some of these phrases were used by a boy from the class who completed the schedule, which is given as an example. Examining the responses of the pupil indicates many points of contention between himself and his friends, and a few between himself and his teachers. In particular he does not agree with his friends that he is serious, that he swots all night, that he is the teachers' pet, and that he is a big head. If these issues are left to iron themselves out, they are likely to cause the pupil some difficulties later on,

COMPARING WHAT I THINK ABOUT MYSELF WITH WHAT OTHERS THINK ABOUT ME

The things I think are important about myself	The things that my friends think are important about me	Agreement + Disagreement -	The things that teachers think are important about me	Agreement + Disagreement -
1. Openminded	I am a spoff	-	I work hard	+
2. Attentive	They like my company	+	I am active	+
3. Friendly	I am serious	-	I am conversive	+
4. Understanding	I swot all night	+	I have a sense of humour	+
5. Non violent	That I'm good at sport	-	I am a busy body	-
6. Brainy	I love school	+	I am intelligent person	+
7. T.V. addict	I'm friendly	+	I work day and night	-
8. Hard working	I'm a big head	-	I am creative	-
9. I like mods	That I'm a teachers pet	-	I am talkative	-
10. I like English	I'm a mature	+	I am a showoff	-
11. I like most subjects	I'm punctual	+	I am sensible	+
12. I get on well with other people	I like animals	+	I am childish	+
13. I am a C.N.D. supporter	I'm calm and collective	+		
14. I dislike celery	I'm modest	+		
15. I dislike travelling	I get stuck in	+		
16. I like cycling	T.V. addict	+		
17. I love animals	I'm smart	+		
18. I dislike tomato sauce	Generous	+		
19. I hate show offs	Helpful	+		
20. I like football				

as he may well be rejected by his peers, and not be able to explain to them that he does not have the same picture of himself as they do of him. Discussing it can also give the pupil a chance to find out whether what he believes his friends think, is in fact the case, and if not, what evidence he used to credit them with those views. This lad also seems to think that his teachers see him as a busybody, a show off, and a talkative pupil. He does not agree with these perceptions, and a dialogue with staff could help him give the kind of signals and messages that would make them see him as he sees himself.

Homework and revision

Complaints about the amount of homework expected of pupils are frequent. Pupils coming into the secondary sector from primary schools find the concept of homework and revision difficult to grasp. They may find out the hard way that doing homework consistently over a year contributes to their exam success and remarks on school reports. Pupils may find it very difficult to establish a routine for homework and revision time if they are not given explicit assistance in this matter. They often resent the fact that homework and revision time detracts from opportunities to do other things, some of which can in themselves be educational activities e.g. classes in music, ballet, swimming etc. Before teachers can help pupils in planning their free time to include homework, it is useful to find out exactly what type of routine the pupils are currently following. A very simple chart that pupils can fill in, almost in the form of a diary, will indicate just how much time a pupil actually spends on study as opposed to other activities. It will give the teacher an idea of how much more (or less) time a pupil ought to spend on homework, per se, and on particular subjects so that advice can be tailored to suit the pupil's needs.

Some pupils complain that they spend a great deal of time on homework but are nevertheless unable to complete their work, or grasp the tasks set for them. Others maintain that they do not find it necessary to spend the recommended time on their homework as they are able to do the work in a shorter space of time and without any major difficulties. One group of pupils in the top band of their year group were approaching their end of year exams. They were between the ages of thirteen and fourteen, and were beginning to panic because they could not organise their revision time to fit in with other activities of interest. They were also being given work by their teachers in preparation for the exams. Each pupil was given the chart below to obtain a sample of how a weeks worth of time was spent, consisting of after school hours and over a weekend.

The instructions given to the pupils when filling out the chart were, that they were to note everything they were doing within the time specified on the chart, no matter how trivial it seemed. The time bands were made up of half hour intervals so that it was possible to get a detailed picture of the way in which a pupil spent his/her time from the moment he/she arrived home from school on a week day, to eleven o'clock at night. Pupils had to account for a total of fifteen hours per day over a weekend.

The different amounts of time spent by each pupil was collated, and a class bar chart produced to represent time spent on homework and revision. Pupils were then encouraged to see for themselves whether or not they spent too much time on their work. Pupils who spent the least time on revision and homework, but who nevertheless achieved success in their work, were prompted to share with their peers the techniques they used to speed their learning. Methods of time organisation were discussed, using pupils' charts as examples. An example of one such completed chart for a five day period is provided as an illustration.

This pupil seemed to vary her pattern of homework and revision between early evening, and doing some in bed during the late evening or early morning of a weekend. The value of this exercise for the pupil is that, with guidance, she was able to determine whether she was using her time efficiently. She was also able to compare her work pattern with others in her class and better appreciated the advice offered by her teacher, since it was given in a more meaningful way.

Class discussions on the best time to revise and do homework ensued, allowing for individual differences. Some pupils found it easier to do their work immediately on returning from school, while others found that they approached their work with freshness and vigour if they tackled it early in the morning before going to school. How pupils actually used the time allocated for work was also highlighted, which was an invitation to the teacher

SAMPLE OF ONE WEEKS TIME SPENT ON HOMEWORK

Name: Jayne   Age: 13 years   Date: June 1982

TIME	MONDAY	TUESDAY	WEDNESDAY	THURSDAY	FRIDAY
4.30	Came in at 4.45. Did science home work.	Came in. Went to shop.	In bedroom.	Came in.	Did maths & R.E. homework.
5.00	Finish writing Elvis Story.	Watch T.V.	Do French home-work.	Did French homework.	In bedroom putting book in bag.
5.30	Learn maths for test.	Did maths homework.	Having tea.	Did science homework.	Write letters.
6.00	Go out back with rabbit.	Have tea.	In bedroom.	Up in room.	Tea.
6.30	Wash up.	Do needlework.	Go out.	Have tea.	With rabbit.
7.00	Watch T.V.	Do needlework.	Clean hamster.	With rabbit.	With rabbit.
7.30	Watch T.V.	With rabbit.	In rabbit run.	With rabbit.	Watch T.V.
8.00	In bedroom.	In bedroom.	Watch T.V.	In room.	Watch T.V.
8.30	Learn maths for test.	Write letters.	Watch T.V.	Watch T.V.	Watch T.V.
9.00	Watch T.V.	Go to bed and learn science.	Watch T.V.	Read in bed.	Watch T.V.
9.30	Watch T.V.	Learn science.	Watch T.V.	Read.	Watch T.V.
10.00	Bed.	Sleep.	Bed.	Sleep.	Bed.
10.30	Sleep.	Sleep.	Sleep.	Sleep.	Sleep.
TOTAL STUDY TIME	1 hour 15 minutes	2 hours 30 mins.	45 minutes	1 hour	30 minutes

49

to launch into a programme of study skills. For example some pupils claimed that they could not work without background noise of a radio or television, while others found this to be distracting. The different methods used to memorize material provided pupils with excellent examples of skills which they may not have thought of earlier. Some pupils would repeat large chunks of material to a parent, or to themselves, and others would use catchy phrases or tunes to aid recall.

This type of exercise allows teachers to give relevant advice to the many pupils they have, each of whom will do their homework and revision in a unique style. It also increases the likelihood of pupils heeding advice that is based on what they already do, as it shows that staff have taken into account their life styles and tried to give their assistance accordingly.

Rating Scales

As the name suggests, a rating scale is a device whereby pupils can rate themselves or other groups in relation to a given theme. The best known and most often used is the Semantic Differential, devised by Osgood et al (1957). Students are presented with a set of phrases or adjectives along with their opposites. There are usually seven points for the pupils to rate their feelings on the dimensions given. However shorter and longer intervals are permitted. Oles (1973) used this technique to find out what pupils thought of their schools, certain lessons, and particular teachers. Oppenheim (1966) and Cohen (1976) give other examples, and discuss the technique and its relevance in different settings. Thomas (1980) gives an account of how to use this technique in easy steps.

Pupils enjoy rating scales as it is an individual exercise and self disclosure to other children, is kept to a minimum. Rating scales have the advantage in that pupils can get an immediate visual image of their own views and begin to compare it to that of a peer, if appropriate. It can heighten self awareness by the visual feedback provided, and can increase the pupils willingness and ability to express themselves in the future. Such scales are of particular use in finding out how pupils feel in certain bands and sets. They can also be used to find out what pupils think about groups within the school, e.g. prefects, 'goody goodies', 'trouble makers', etc. In addition, rating scales can be used to find out how pupils perceive groups outside school when it is important to discuss community life, e.g. professional people, vandals, public servants, the unemployed and so forth.

Rating scales should take into account the ability level of the pupils concerned, and the structure needed by any one group of pupils when they are initially introduced to this task. The number of intervals or points that will be used in a scale should be given careful consideration. Although most scales use an odd number of intervals, such as five, or seven, there is often the problem of pupils responding by using the neutral or middle point. This provides the teacher with very little information, and allows pupils to opt out of thinking about their feelings. Using more than eight to twelve intervals is inadvisable as the meaning can become obscured.

Using the example of 'How I feel in a low set', three methods of devising a scale are given below.

Banding and setting

1. Decide on a set of bi-polar phrases that would adequately account for the range of feeling in your form. These may include:

Helpless - Powerful
Clever   - Stupid
Noticed - Ignored
Boring   - Interesting

Place five or six points in between each set of phrases, and ask the pupils to tick or circle the point that best describes their feelings about being in a low set. A set of twelve such phrases is usually sufficient to derive a profile of feelings from each pupil. This method is best used with those pupils who are of low ability, and who need all their work prepared so that they simply have to make choices without too much deliberation.

2. Ask pupils to describe their feelings of being in a low set either by class discussion or in groups of four. Extract the words which could be used for the opposing dimensions of the scale. The class may come up with phrases such as:

Embarrassing
Makes me look a fool
Makes me feel self conscious

When there are enough to make up a scale with twelve dimensions, pupils should be asked to supply the opposites that go with the first lot of phrases. This is to ensure that the meaning that pupils place on these views are incorporated. There are many possible shades of meaning that could be attached to a particular phrase, and it is only by letting pupils indicate what they mean, that the procedure will be of any value. Once this has been completed, the pupils can respond on the scale.

3. Produce about eight of your own adjectives/phrases based on your knowledge of the pupils' feelings. Give the scale to pupils, asking them to add four of their own individual opposing bipolar phrases. This technique is often a good way of helping inarticulate youngsters to express themselves.

A hypothetical rating scale that could be completed by pupils to show their feelings of being in a low set is given below. A five point scale is illustrated. All the adjectives/phrases have been compiled following the author's conversations with classes of pupils in low sets who seemed to be aware that they were being catered for differently within their school. The scale depicts a system where all the positive aspects are on the right hand side and the negative ones on the left. Sometimes pupils may respond by circling the numbers on one side, or near one side, giving an extreme representation of their feelings. If this occurs with several pupils it is often a good idea to vary the sides where positive and negative aspects are presented. However for the purposes of getting a visual representation of an overall feeling, such as indicated here, it is easier to construct the scale in the manner illustrated. A tally of how many pupils feel in a particular way is then obtained. It will suggest points of discussion with pupils. Teachers can ask pupils to expand on why they perhaps felt ashamed or not respected if that is a common response in the class. It can also provide information that staff can use in their pastoral meetings, so that more thought can be given to finding ways of enhancing the views of these students in relation to their placement in bands and sets.

ELICITING AND DISCUSSING PROBLEMS WITH PUPILS

HOW I FEEL BEING IN A LOW SET

Ashamed	1 2 3 4 5	Proud
Stupid	1 2 3 4 5	Clever
Not respected	1 2 3 4 5	Respected
Bored	1 2 3 4 5	Interested
Fed up	1 2 3 4 5	Eager
Not trusted	1 2 3 4 5	Trusted
Given the worst teachers	1 2 3 4 5	Given the best teachers
Don't feel like trying any more	1 2 3 4 5	Must keep trying
Coming to school is a waste of time	1 2 3 4 5	Coming to school is worth while
Second class citizen	1 2 3 4 5	As good as anyone else in school
Feel self conscious	1 2 3 4 5	Don't feel self conscious
Embarrassing	1 2 3 4 5	Not embarrassing

53

ELICITING AND DISCUSSING PROBLEMS WITH PUPILS

Self Awareness and Peer Relationships

During adolescent years, children often use their peers as a frame of reference. Some children unwittingly play the clown in class because it gets them noticed and accepted. They may even begin to think of themselves in that way, internalising these notions to such an extent that it becomes part of their personality. However, there are often consequences for so doing. The so called 'class clowns' may often find themselves being reprimanded by staff, as other pupils allow them to take the brunt of the punishment. These pupils may be labelled as nuisances or troublesome by staff. They may be in a helpless position having begun to play a role that was imposed on them initially by their peers, but now very much part of their makeup. It is important that these pupils be given the chance to think about their own views of themselves, to see if they correspond with the opinions others have of them. In this way the possibility of a tag given to a pupil can be prevented from becoming self fulfilling. Other pupils are at the same time encouraged to evaluate their perceptions of the pupil, and some mutual exchange of views can be helpful. One way of doing this easily is by using a rating scale.

The following is an example of an eleven point self evaluation grid used with a class of thirteen year old pupils. One boy in the class had been in some trouble in school for stealing and truanting. On interview with the author he presented as a lad who had few friends and was desperate to get in with a group within his class. He had little idea of how he perceived himself, and seemed to take his cues from those in the class whose friendship he desired. Before beginning this exercise, the author (in the role of tutor) discussed with the class the terminology they would use to describe their fellow classmates, without at this point naming any one in particular. From that interview, six bi-polar phrases were given on the scale, and each pupil had to supply two of their own to complete the grid.

Pupils had to complete the grid in three conditions. The first using a bold line was to indicate how they rated themselves. The second, using a dotted line was to rate how they felt a friend (the one whose opinion they valued most) would rate them. In the third condition, the friend whom they considered in the previous condition,

was given the grid and asked to rate the pupil
in a line of dashes. This enabled the pupil to
compare and measure the distance between his own
views of himself, what he believed his friend
thought of him, and what his friend actually thought
of him. See figure 5.

Figure 5 shows that the boy consistently rated
himself as more unpopular and having more negative
attributes than his 'friend' thought in reality.
The boy also anticipated more negative ratings
from his 'friend' than he in fact obtained. The
two phrases that he chose to include himself related
to being clever and agreeable, indicating just
how important it was for him to be seen as clever
and nice. This task if followed through could
have aided the improvement in self worth on the
part of the boy. The teacher could also have moved
on to discussing ways and means of making and maintaining popularity and recognition without resorting
to stealing or truanting. This is a clear example
of a lad who thought that doing things that were
outside the norm would raise his esteem in the
eyes of the class. But in fact his 'friend' actually thought quite well of him, and he had no need
to engage in anti-social behaviours to gain favour
with others.

School Rules and Those of Community Life

Pupils are used to being told in large groups what
NOT to do in school to conform to school rules.
These may include rules about queueing, walking
up and down stairs, going to places that are out
of bounds at certain times of the day, and about
keeping the school clean and tidy. When pupils
are told en masse it is difficult to ensure that
every pupil has understood what is being asked
of him/her and why. Pupils are probably less likely
to feel that they are being addressed personally
in such situations. They are not likely to identify
with the pupils who break all these school rules,
even though they may have actually infringed a
rule themselves at some time in the past. In many
ways the process is not dissimilar to that of adults
who are repeatedly given health or hazard warnings
of sorts, but who go through life thinking 'it
cannot happen to me', until of course it does.
In the same way pupils can and often do pay little
heed to warnings given to them about being lax
regarding school rules. Those who are likely to
pay least attention are those who do not perceive

FIGURE 5

SELF EVALUATION GRID

Thirteen year old boy in trouble for stealing

_____ = pupil rating himself.   .... = pupil rating how his friend
                                                    might rate him.

- - - - = friend rating pupil.

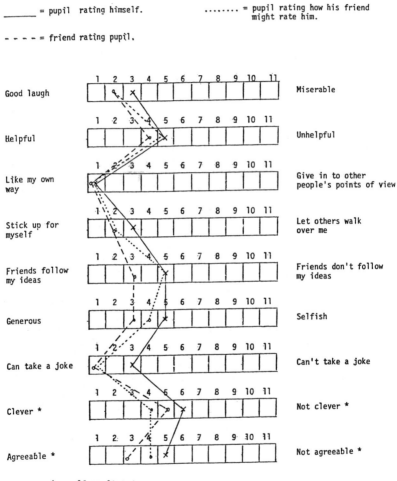

* = self supplied phrases

themselves as 'someone who is a rule breaker'.
Teachers can discover how true this may be of pupils
by using a rating scale type of instrument. By
asking pupils to rate how a typical rule breaker
would behave and what kind of a person he or she
was likely to be, teachers would be able to make
their conversations with pupils that bit more pertinent. For instance if a pupil indicated that rule
breakers were people who were selfish, then he
or she would have to see him/herself in the same
light, in order to identify with staff comments
about the behaviour of rule breakers. If tutors
said that rule breakers were 'ignorant', then the
pupil would not take it to heart and obey instructions unless he or she also thought him/herself
to be ignorant. Of course there is some overlap
in these instances, but in the main, if teachers
want to be sure of getting their message across
then they have to first tune into how pupils regard
themselves, in relation to the kind of person the
teacher is admonishing.

Many schools experience a great deal of vandalism and tutors spend much time trying to make pupils
more conscious of the consequences of vandalism
and how it relates to the moral norms of the society
in which they live. Most pupils do not consider
themselves to be vandals, and would be horrified
if such an insinuation was made. Yet unless they
are aware of how they perceive vandals, and how
similar they are in nature they are unlikely ever
to consider future actions that they may engage
in, which may include acts of vandalism. The rating
scale below was devised by the author and used
with a group of students who attended a school
which encountered many acts of vandalism. It involved twenty-two dimensions, plus two supplied
by pupils themselves. Pupils filled in the scale
after a class discussion on the social parameters
from which vandals may come. These included the
likely age group they fell into, whether they tended
to be male, female, or an equal mix, the type of
neighbourhoods they came from, and their financial
status. This discussion provided some starting
points for construction of the scale. Pupils had
to complete the scale twice, using different
colours. First they had to rate what they thought
of as a typical vandal. Next they had to rate
themselves on the same scale, and then compare
the ratings. They had to pick out dimensions on
which they were most alike, and identify on which
points they were most different. The possibility

ELICITING AND DISCUSSING PROBLEMS WITH PUPILS

<u>WHAT KIND OF A PERSON MIGHT A VANDAL BE?</u>
<u>HOW DIFFERENT AM I?</u>

_____= boy rating himself   - - - - = boy rating what
he thinks of a vandal.

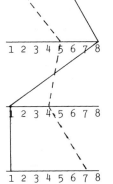

Likes to make people angry.	1 2 3 4 5 6 7 8	Likes to please people.
Easily led by others.	1 2 3 4 5 6 7 8	Makes own decisions.
Never thinks before doing anything.	1 2 3 4 5 6 7 8	Thinks about what may happen before acting.
Takes out anger on other people's things.	1 2 3 4 5 6 7 8	Takes out anger on own self or by talking.
Is normally impatient.	1 2 3 4 5 6 7 8	Can be patient.
Has few things of his/her own.	1 2 3 4 5 6 7 8	Has quite a few of personal possessions.
Has a cruel streak in his/her nature.	1 2 3 4 5 6 7 8	Is usually kind.
Has never experienced acts of kindness.	1 2 3 4 5 6 7 8	Has experienced many acts of kindness.

WHAT KIND OF A PERSON MIGHT A VANDAL BE?
HOW DIFFERENT AM I? (Continued)

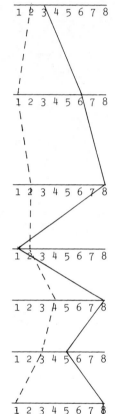

Doesn't like to do things that involve thinking. e.g. reading, talking, playing, and is usually bored.		Likes to do activities that involve thinking and playing etc. is hardly ever bored.
Wears clothes that parents don't approve of.		Wears clothes that parents approve of.
Is duller than others, and can't say what he/she wants; so expresses feeling by acts of vandalism.		Has got the ability to say what he/she wants, and doesn't need to be destructive.
Is usually young.		Usually in twenties, or older.
Didn't do well at school.		Did do well at school.
Has no plans for the future.		Has plans for the future.
Needs to be taken notice of.		Gets noticed by others.
Likes to hang around with gangs, instead of one or two people.		Can make do with one or two friends, and doesn't need gangs.

WHAT KIND OF A PERSON MIGHT A VANDAL BE?
HOW DIFFERENT AM I? (Continued)

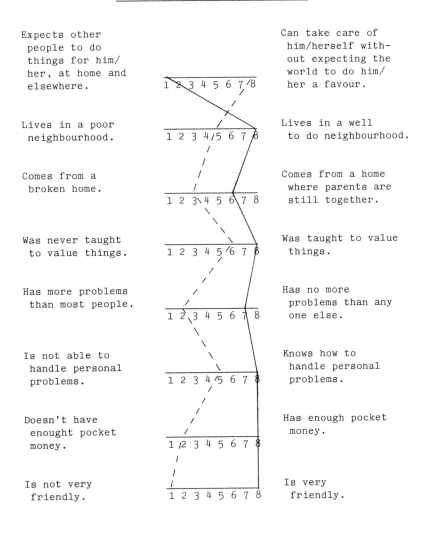

Expects other people to do things for him/her, at home and elsewhere.	1 2 3 4 5 6 7 8	Can take care of him/herself without expecting the world to do him/her a favour.
Lives in a poor neighbourhood.	1 2 3 4 5 6 7 8	Lives in a well to do neighbourhood.
Comes from a broken home.	1 2 3 4 5 6 7 8	Comes from a home where parents are still together.
Was never taught to value things.	1 2 3 4 5 6 7 8	Was taught to value things.
Has more problems than most people.	1 2 3 4 5 6 7 8	Has no more problems than any one else.
Is not able to handle personal problems.	1 2 3 4 5 6 7 8	Knows how to handle personal problems.
Doesn't have enought pocket money.	1 2 3 4 5 6 7 8	Has enough pocket money.
Is not very friendly.	1 2 3 4 5 6 7 8	Is very friendly.

of pupils engaging in acts of vandalism was brought home to them forcefully. They were also able to work out a sort of profile of a pupil most at risk from committing acts of vandalism and suggest ways of preventing it from happening.

An example of a completed rating scale by a thirteen and a half year old boy is given above.

Card Sorting Techniques

It is sometimes difficult for children to express complicated feelings and opinions about certain aspects of their personal and school life. Occasionally it is helpful for them to be able to 'sort' out their feelings by using a set of cards with ideas, feelings, or attitudes on them, into various categories. This technique is sometimes known as the 'Q' sorting method and has many advantages for the teacher engaged in pastoral work. It can reveal the attitudes of children towards various features of school. It can be used to aid pupils in revealing their attitudes towards certain lessons which they may not get a great deal from. This method can also be utilized in getting individual pupils to present the way they see themselves in relation to others who are engaged in relationships with them, be they teachers, peers, or members of their families. Insel & Wilson (1971) have used this technique to measure social attitudes in children, while Thorpe et al (1954) have used it to get a measure of childrens' interests.

The number of categories that are given to pupils for sorting purposes can be infinite. Within each category a simple two dimensional choice is sufficient to represent a view. For example, several sets of two choice categories could be given to pupils to describe their feelings about one general topic. This particular strategy is described below in relation to pupil perceptions of lessons.

Perception and Motivation in Lessons

Place the name of every subject on a separate card, so that a pack is made consisting of school subjects. Several ,of these packs may need to be produced for use with large classes so that they can work in groups. The next step is to decide on the set of categories into which the subject cards are to be sorted. These could include the following:

ELICITING AND DISCUSSING PROBLEMS WITH PUPILS

CATEGORIES FOR PUPILS TO SORT SUBJECT CARDS INTO

1. Like   Dislike

2. Interesting   Boring

3. Slow   Fast moving

4. Well explained   Poorly explained

5. New points taken   New points rushed
   steadily.

6. Have got to work   Teacher helps me all the
   on my own too much.   way along.

7. If I get something   If I get something wrong
   wrong the teacher   I have to find out myself
   shows me the correct   how to do it the correct
   way of doing it.   way.

8. Get too much home-   Get too little homework.
   work.

9. My work is marked   My work is not always
   quickly.   marked on time.

10. Too much noise in   Right amount of noise in
    class.   class.

11. I am shouted at if   I am treated sympatheti-
    I ask for help.   cally if I ask for help.

12. I am never asked any   The teacher always seems
    questions.   to ask me all the
                                     questions.

13. I am praised for my   I get little praise for
    efforts.   my efforts.

14. I am encouraged to   I am not encouraged to
    try.   try in this lesson.

   Younger pupils in forms one and two may enjoy
doing this activity in the form of a game. Pupils
could take turns to pick a card from the pack to
identify the subject in question. Two pupils could
stand at either end of a room representing the
categories for the sorts to occur. The categories
would change after every sort. The rest of the

FIGURE 6

pupils should stand in the centre of the class. When a subject is picked from the pack and called out to the class, each pupil should move to the part of the room where his/her view is represented. The teacher can then make a tally of the number of pupils feeling in certain ways about each lesson. This is illustrated in Figure 6.

Older pupils may wish to present their views on prepared handouts, each with the categories for the sort given as subheadings. Alternatively they may like to 'post' their subject cards into boxes labelled as per category. This could be done in groups, with each pupil picking a card from the pack to post in turn. This would necessitate several cards with one subject written on it so that it could be 'posted' in as many categories as pupils wished.

After each subject has been sorted according to each of the categories listed, a profile can be drawn up for pupils which would paint a very graphic picture of how they felt about their lessons, and what motivated them and why. The profile can be made up by placing the subjects under each category to represent the sort an individual pupil has made.

For the first category, one pupil could have the following list of subjects:

I like	I dislike
History	—
English	—
Games	—
—	Metalwork
—	Art
—	Science
Maths	—
—	Geography
Needlework	—
—	Religious education

Once all the permutations of subjects and categories have been exhausted, a more detailed picture can be sketched about the levels of motivation each child has in a lesson and the possible reasons for feeling as he/she does. One way of doing this is to divide all the results from the various sorting activities into positive and negative aspects of a lesson. Taking history as an example, the positives and negatives for a hypothetical pupil may look like this:

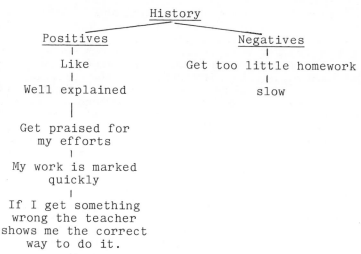

It can be seen that for this pupil, history is seen mainly as a positive experience for the reasons stated above in the profile. It gives a good indication of the features of a lesson that are important to this pupil, and what is likely to encourage him/her. A lesson perceived in less positive ways will be weighed down by many responses on the negative side and will show that, for this pupil, more stimulating ways of approaching the lesson are called for.

Role Play

There are many issues over which pupils feel very strongly but find it very awkward to express, either by talking about it, or completing schedules. These pertain to situations where pupils feel hard done by or treated unfairly. Pupils often maintain that they are rarely given a chance to explain their side of things before they are punished, or have their 'rights' and privileges withdrawn. Where pupils have experienced several such episodes they can become resentful and bitter, which could cause a rift in the relationships between teachers and pupils.

In order to allow pupils the opportunity to present their point of view, role play techniques offer a vivid and penetrating way of discovering how pupils' perceive situations in which they come away with negative and hurt feelings. Milroy (1982) gives some examples of how to set the scene for children to re-enact a scene to display what exactly produced such 'bad' feelings in them. Role play was used in the following example, when a group of pupils complained to the author that they felt trapped when they had been treated in what was to them a very unfair manner. They felt helpless and very discouraged when, during a mathematics test, one or two of them had been sent out of class for 'talking'. They knew that no talking was allowed during a test, but felt that they had actually been using words for perfectly legitimate reasons, as opposed to simply conversing for no purpose. However, they had not been given the chance to convey this to the teacher, and had left the mathematic test very disheartened, and with the attitude that trying to do well in tests was a waste of time.

The pupils were asked to 'show me exactly what happened in the lesson'. The classroom was arranged as it had been for the maths test, with one pupil opting to take on the role of the teacher, and everyone else playing themselves. No other instructions were given to the pupils and they were free to role play the lesson for as long as they chose. In practice it went on for ten minutes. During the role play it became evident that the teacher was busy marking things at his desk while the test was going on, and on hearing whispers warned certain children to stop talking WITHOUT looking up to see who exactly was talking. In actual fact, the talking involved one boy asking another to borrow his ruler, which he felt should have been allowed. The teacher then began sending boys out of the room without checking to see what was really transpiring between the children. The teacher sent children out of the class from the front rows only. Those pupils who were not doing their test and laughing at the back of the class were, according to this group of children, 'permitted to get away with it'. The boys who had been sent out of the class had their papers cancelled without being given a chance to redeem themselves. These boys therefore felt 'picked on' and treated in a very unfair manner.

The role play although used to elicit the perception of 'unfairness' nevertheless gave the children the opportunity of taking the part of the teacher, and trying to see his point of view. The situation was eventually resolved via further role play scenes and the use of the problem solving approach in social skills training, described in a subsequent chapter. Using this strategy to find out how pupils feel and why they feel unhappy opens up avenues for staff to explain their standpoint in a mutual exchange of views rather than making the children feel that the teacher is the only one who can control their lives and their feelings, as this leads to helplessness (Seligman 1975). As one of the major tasks of pastoral care in schools is to enable children to view themselves as individuals who create and solve their own dilemmas, the climate of the school has to be organised in such a way as to facilitate pupils taking the lead in managing their own lives. The use of role play exercises to help pupils express their feelings of helplessness is a positive step in that direction.

CHAPTER THREE

DEVELOPING A PARTNERSHIP WITH PUPILS

Many children experience difficulties in school,
or indeed in attending school, partly because they
are not sufficiently educated about the nature
of school, what it has to offer, and how it is
organised, so that they can get the most out of
it.   Children need to know what is happening to
them and how they can contribute in a way that
would produce positive outcomes for themselves.
Hamblin (1978) has suggested losing property, or
getting lost during the first two terms in school
are symptoms of the lack of understanding about
the school and it's system by pupils.   However,
those kinds of signs are minor examples of the
overall confusion and anxiety that pupils experience
when they are not taken on as 'partners' in the
process of schooling.
    In order to work together with pupils for
a common gain a pastoral programme should aim to
educate children about the system of discipline
a school uses, and why; about the banding and setting system used; about the manner in which exams
dictate class placement; and about the way in which
reports are written. Further, pupils need to be
helped to appreciate the system of privileges that
may operate within the school both of an official
and unofficial nature.   Pupils need to understand
actively the hierarchy of the staff, including
ancillary staff, and in particular, where the staff
with whom they come into contact most, fit into
the entire scheme of things.   Pupils should be
encouraged to understand why they are asked to
abide by rules and regulations, and why these exist
at all.   They need to be able to discuss attendance,
its problems, its value, and the consequences of
not attending school, both for them as individuals,
their families, as well as the school. Last but

not least, pupils have to be educated to learn to anticipate and deal with differential teacher expectations.

Many schools will feel that they are already tackling these subjects, and no doubt they are, but perhaps not in a way that allows pupils to feel part of the school. There is much evidence to indicate that pupils who feel that they are totally under the control of staff and have no part in the decision making processes about their lives in school learn less, and also often learn the wrong things (Rotter 1966). Other evidence indicates that when pupils are given some opportunity to exert some influence in controlling the education system they are under, they are more likely to have positive feelings towards teachers, and to be willing to work for them (De Charms 1968). If pupils are given the impression that their participation in school is voluntary they would be more strongly motivated, learn more, and have better retention of what is learned (Solomon & Oberlander 1974). It is for these reasons that it is important that students have the opportunity to understand the rules, functions and nature of a school organisation.

Many teachers try to help pupils understand why they are being asked to behave in certain ways, or dress in particular fashions. However, teachers often feel wary of going too far along this road in case pupils take advantage of this informality, and are inadvertently given the message that they should question authority. This is a genuine fear, and one which needs to be taken account of by any school when planning its pastoral programme. For this purpose a carefully worked out scheme for pupils to follow, needs to be prepared, and staff should be encouraged to exchange the information they get from pupils during their pastoral sessions, so that no one teacher feels threatened. It is vitally important that staff support each other, and in this way partnership between pupils and staff will be that much stronger, complete, and enhanced in value.

This chapter presents some ideas for facilitating the discussion about school between teachers and pupils on a selection of issues. The topics are treated systematically and in a very structured manner so that pupils think constructively, as opposed to simply questioning school and its procedures.

DEVELOPING A PARTNERSHIP WITH PUPILS

What are Schools For?

Many pupils view school in a very narrow light, often as a means to obtain jobs in the future. If they are to get the most out of school, they need to be helped to perceive school in a much broader manner. In order to do this, it is a good idea to find out exactly what children think school has to offer. This can be done by asking direct questions, or by giving a list of alternatives which may be endorsed or rejected. The latter may be more appropriate for the less able pupils, who find immediate verbal responses difficult to give.

Occasionally a class could prove unresponsive to questioning, and in this instance, the teacher could provide them with a controversial idea to provoke thought. At other times this same technique may serve to aid children who tend to be rather conservative in their views. The aim should be to help pupils move away from rigid and closed perceptions.

After the initial stimulus, the pupils should be encouraged to write down their ideas either on the blackboard, or on a large sheet of paper, covering an entire wall if possible. As many pupils as possible should take part, and be allowed to draw symbols, or cartoons to illustrate their ideas. These are collated to help them gain an overall impression of the variety of material that came from their peers, and then incorporated with tutor prepared statements such as on the handout below. Each pupil should fill in the handout with one other pupil.

A class list of priorities could be drawn up from the responses of the children, where there is agreement on certain statements. Where there are clear disagreements between pupils as to whether a particular function ought to be included in the class list, a debate should be encouraged, and a vote taken. If the votes were in favour of one statement, then it should be incorporated in the class list of priorities. Many pupils will have responded to their handout with an endorsement of the 'don't know' category. The debate should have resolved some of their doubts, but in some cases pupils will be unable to make a definite decision, possibly, because they have not experienced at first hand the implications of certain stated functions of school. This should lead pupils into talking about their experiences, and what

DEVELOPING A PARTNERSHIP WITH PUPILS

PUPIL HANDOUT ON THE PURPOSE OF SCHOOL

SCHOOLS ARE FOR	AGREE	DON'T KNOW	DISAGREE
Learning to work on your own			
Helping one meet deadlines			
Getting to know all sorts of people			
Learning to plan your time well			
Learning how to 'learn'			
Learning to pass exams			
Learning to take criticism			
Learning to live in large groups			
Learning to obey orders			
Learning how to get on with others			
Finding out what you are good at			
Finding out what you are poor at			
Teachers to boss you around			
Something to do in the day			
Learning to be independent			
Learning to be self sufficient			

they think they learned from them. For instance if pupils say they experienced criticism of their performance in school, but not at home, then this constitutes a useful experience for them. Other pupils may not have come across much criticism in school, but may receive a lot from people outside school and so on.

The class should come to realise that school has many different functions, which vary for individuals. Pupils can look at their personal relationships with the school, and its staff, and compare these to what they have learned from their relationships at home and the community at large. This can be done by giving every pupil a handout with three circles representing each one of the categories above. See Figure 7. Where pupils think that they have learned something by having experiences in more than one category, they can overlap their writing across the circles to indicate this. When pupils have completed their handouts, they should be asked to compare their responses with the following:

(a) A member of the opposite sex in their class.
(b) Their best friend in the class.
(c) Someone they did not know very well in the class.

They should be asked to make notes of the similarities and differences they come across, and then try to answer these questions:

Are boys and girls getting different experiences from school, home, and the community? If so, which ones and why? How close were pupils responses when compared to that of their best friends?

Do all children come to school for the same reasons? If not, why not?

What differences can pupils find between children who came to school having had brothers and sisters already preceding them?

Do children who come from large families learn different things at school and outside, from those who come from small families? If so what?

How do schools manage to cater for such a wide variety of needs amongst its pupils? Have they any suggestions as to improving their methods for

FIGURE 7

PUPIL HANDOUT ON EXPERIENCES GAINED FROM

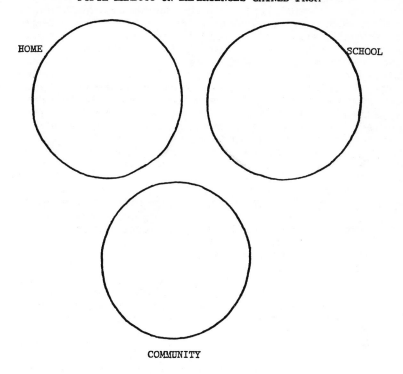

HOME

SCHOOL

COMMUNITY

so doing?

Older pupils in form three, can do a very similar task, although their perspective may well be different from younger pupils. However, if pupils took part in this exercise early in their school career, the original responses they made could be returned to them for reflection. In addition, older pupils will think about the points of view of employers, their teachers, and others. It is often at form three level that pupils begin questioning the value and effectiveness of school. It is a good time to help them appreciate that the school has a role prescribed for it by different parts of society, and encourage them to define ways in which their school goes about meeting these expectations. Pupils from form three upwards often experience some conflict about what to choose for subject options, about doing certain things merely to please their parents, and looking out for the employment market. Dealing with conflicts is discussed in the next chapter, but here it would be useful for pupils to begin to obtain a picture of what different sections of society want from schools, and fit their own ideas into that scheme.

Functions of School and How They Are Achieved

The specific functions of school and how they are achieved are frequently cloudy areas for some teachers, and pupils. For instance, pupils who believe or are led to believe that schools should help children become more mature, and learn how to undertake responsibilities often get conflicting messages from teachers who may not allow them access to certain rooms or equipment at particular times of the day. This action is, for pupils, a negation of the function of a school, which may be to encourage responsibility and trustworthiness. While the reasoning behind such rulings may be perfectly legitimate from the school's point of view, it is not always made clear to pupils. They are left with double messages that they cannot resolve, and often end up feeling very disillusioned with the entire system. Solomon & Oberlander (1974) show how students who are made to feel that they have some personal control over their own actions, respond more favourably to a school and in fact develop an internal awareness of responsibility.

Group activities can be helpful in getting pupils to think about what school should be doing, and how it goes about its task. For this exercise

DEVELOPING A PARTNERSHIP WITH PUPILS

<u>PUPIL HANDOUT FOR COMPARING VIEWS ABOUT</u>
<u>THE PURPOSE OF SCHOOL</u>

<u>My Mother thinks Schools are for:</u>	<u>My Father thinks Schools are for:</u>
1.	1.
2.	2.
3.	3.
4.	4.
5.	5.
<u>My Teacher thinks Schools are for:</u>	<u>I think Schools are for:</u>
1.	1.
2.	2.
3.	3.
4.	4.
5.	5.
<u>Society thinks Schools are for:</u>	<u>Employers think Schools are for:</u>
1.	1.
2.	2.
3.	3.
4.	4.
5.	5.

After each pupil has completed this handout, the class should discuss in groups, these questions:

Whose priorities match the pupils' most?

Do both parents share priorities?

How do the pupils' views of teacher priorities match the ACTUAL teacher priorities?

the class should divide into groups of four. Each
group should have a pack of cards with several
possible functions of school written on them. These
should have been sought by the teacher in a class
exercise preceding this task. Each group should
also have another pack of cards with possible ways
in which a school may attempt to fulfil its functions. Pupils should pick cards from each pile
until they find two that complement each other,
and enter it into the group handout given below. A possible completed group handout would look like this:

PUPIL HANDOUT ON FUNCTIONS AND MANNER
OF ACHIEVEMENT BY A SCHOOL

Functions of School	Achieved by
1. Aids communication with people of different back-grounds/lands.	1. Teaching of languages.
2. Makes people feel equal.	2. Wearing of school uniform.
3. Makes people realise their strengths and weaknesses.	3. Placement in different sets/bands.
4. Allows the practice of new skills.	4. Setting homework.
5. Makes people aware of the needs of others.	5. Teaching pupils in group settings.
6. Makes pupils self-sufficient and independent.	6. Teaching of domestic science, car mechanics, citizenship etc.
7. Makes people literate and numerate.	7. Teaching reading, writing and arithmetic.
8. Helps pupils appreciate art and music.	8. Teaching of various musical instruments, and literature.

In this way each group would come up with
a unique set of responses, which could be compared
and contrasted with other groups. Each group could
be asked to defend their responses so that their
reasoning would be made explicit. This would inform
the teacher about pupil perception and understanding. For instance, there may be functions that
pupils feel schools should be fulfilling, but are
not. In addition pupils may not agree with the

methods they think schools are using to perform a particular function. One way of helping pupils gain a greater insight into the constraints under which schools often have to operate is to set them the task of creating a hypothetical school, setting out what its aims should be, and how it would go about fulfilling them. The impetus could be provided with one of the following ideas:

(a) Set up a school within a community that has just survived a nuclear fall out by hiding underground for some months.
(b) There has been a population boom and a new secondary school is needed for your area. Set one up.

Members of the class would have to undertake certain roles within a ficticious community, to represent various interest groups, each wanting school leavers to have a different set of skills and philosophies. Other members of the class should elect a possible headteacher, as many senior and junior staff as they need, and they should sit around a table discussing the aims of their new school, and how they would try to implement them. The following questions should then be put:

What priorities did the staff give to the setting up of the school?

From whose viewpoint did they set the priorities in the main?

Could they manage to fit in all the aims of the school as they set them out? If not, what got in the way?

How did they resolve the disagreements, and what status of person won the arguments, why?

What functions did they have in their make-believe school that were not apparent in their present school?

How did they manage to achieve all the aims in ways that were different from the ones their own school used?

How did they see their imaginary school working? Would they like their own children to go there? Why?

DEVELOPING A PARTNERSHIP WITH PUPILS

As pupils progress through school they may expect different functions to be performed, to take into account their changing needs. For instance, older pupils may expect schools to offer them the chance to learn about parenthood, child management, and relationships with the opposite sex. In the author's experience with fourth and fifth form pupils, this is certainly the case. This task therefore needs to be repeated to allow for these expectations. Not only will these exercises provide teachers with feedback on what pupils needs and expectations are, but it will also indicate whether pupils are achieving a more positive attitude towards school and what it has to offer.

The responses gained from various classes can be used as stimulus material for other classes, thus assisting form tutors in their task of preparation for tutoring. It can also show whether new generations of a particular year group are continuing the trend of their predecessors, or moving onto new issues altogether. In this way, staff stay in touch with their pupils, and plan for their pastoral needs accordingly.

Teacher Expectations and Style

One of the commonest problems that pupils encounter in the first three years in a secondary school is that of trying to anticipate and cope with differential teacher style both in terms of personal discipline and expectations of work presentation, neatness and punctuality of handing in work. In addition pupils have to learn how to handle the different rates of marking and handing back of work by staff, the various types of comment and standards, implicit in the teacher's response to the work of a pupil. What might rate an 'excellent' for one teacher may only rate a 'good' for another teacher, although the pupils may feel they have put in the same effort, skills and time to the work. In some pupils this may produce symptoms of stress, especially if they aim to please all the time, and set themselves up as perfectionists. This is often apparent with especially bright children. Take the case of Malcolm a boy of superior intelligence, who came up to his secondary school claiming to have been bored in the primary school, although his teachers felt that he only worked on subjects of particular interest to him. He wasn't prepared to put in the effort for the more mechanical and routine tasks that have to

be undertaken to consolidate work. He had difficulties throughout his secondary school life
as he interpreted passing comments by teachers
as signs of interest or disinterest in him, which
directly effected his motivation to contribute
to lessons. If a teacher did not remember to ask
for a piece of work that was requested of the boy,
Malcolm became dejected and felt that whatever
effort he had put into the work was not acknowledged. Also if a teacher didn't always praise
him profusely for his work he would not want to
attempt a similar task again, as he felt that he
had to strive for perfection at all times. For
Malcolm, asking for help was an admission of failure.

Perhaps there are not too many pupils with
the characteristics of the boy described above,
but nevertheless, children do need to understand
that teachers differ in the way they control a
class, mark work, and encourage pupils. In pastoral
work, the aim is to aid pupils to come to terms
with this position, and to respond to it appropriately, rather than let it defeat them.

One of the best ways of assisting pupils to
develop an understanding of teacher style is to
explore particular types of situations that pupils
have experienced, and come across with some regularity. To begin this task each pupil should be
given a piece of paper, folded five times, to create
the impression of five strips of paper. They should
then be asked to write one situation on each strip/
fold, tear it off, and place all the strips in
a large box in the centre of the class.

The invitation to pupils for noting down situations on their strips of paper, should be as follows:

"Think of all the occasions when you have
had dealings with a teacher. Now think of
the ones that made you feel confused, worried,
afraid, discouraged, despondent, or angry.
Now write down five of those, one on each
strip of your paper. Some of these could
include things like when you are late for
a lesson, when you have forgotten to bring
your homework in, when you thought you had
done as you were told, but you still got told
off, when you went to ask for help, but didn't
feel as if you received it."

When all the members of a class have completed

this part of the programme, the children should
sit in a circle with the box in their midst. It
should be passed around for each pupil to pick
out one strip, and call out the situation described
therein. As many pupils as possible within that
circle should be encouraged to outline what experiences they have had within that situation. For
instance, let us assume that the situation is the
covering of exercise books and the maintaining
of their appearance. Going around the circle,
students should be asked to relate the expectations
of one teacher with regard to this topic. Pupils
could also discuss what has happened to them in
certain subjects if they have or have not covered
their books, or if they have stuck pictures/written
all over it etc. The teacher in this session needs
to bring out the variety of experiences that pupils
have undergone. What also comes out of this exercise is that there are probably as many different
teacher expectations as there are pupil responses,
and that they are all equally valid.

After this type of activity has been exhausted,
pupils could use the same situations to predict
what they would do if they were the teachers in
this situation. They would no doubt discover that
even amongst their peers, there would be a variety
of ways in which they would behave, were they to
be placed in the teacher's role. If there are
any common ways of handling a situation, the pupils
should be helped to explain why they chose that
particular method, as it would indicate that they
probably regarded that as the fairest method. Other
pupils too, could be asked to defend their methods.
Once pupils can see that there are good reasons
for what teachers may do or say to them, they are
less likely to feel unfairly treated or picked
on. They may not like certain methods that staff
use, but at least they will be able to appreciate
that teachers cannot all be exactly the same in
their treatments, even though they all support,
and are pillars of the same regime. The use of
role play could be useful in illustrating to pupils
the circumstances in which a teacher may take certain actions disliked by students.

A role play can be created for pupils to take
part in, with three different students selected
to take on the roles of a teacher. The situation
could be a very simple and common one of certain
pupils chewing gum or eating in class. Ask the
class to act as themselves, taking out the first
of the three pupils to act as the teacher. That

person should be told out of earshot of the class that the school policy is to crack down on eating and chewing in class. The pupil should then be allowed to conduct the class for about five to seven minutes. After that the class should give their reactions to the way in which the make believe teacher dealt with their gum chewing and eating. This activity is then repeated with the other two pupils, taking on the role of a teacher. The three methods of handling the eating and chewing should then form the basis for an understanding of how teachers can all respond differently, and with different degrees of harshness to the same behaviour exhibited by pupils.

The pupils who acted as teachers, need to explain to the rest of the class why they took the action they did, or ignored the behaviour if in fact this was the outcome. They should explain how they felt, and how the students behaviour effected them.

Additional examples to illustrate this theme to pupils might be taken from their home settings. Taking topics like table manners, getting up when asked, doing certain chores around the house etc. pupils should be encouraged to discuss the different ways in which their parents, and other relatives would deal with these issues if tasks had not been performed as expected. Do pupils always know what to expect of their parents, and if not, can they see the parallel with school?

The School Hierarchy

In large comprehensive schools where split sites create distances between parts of the school, pupils may well fail to grasp the overall chain of command. It is often the case that children in the lower school of a comprehensive think that when they move to the middle school they are actually going to a DIFFERENT school. They also tend to think that the head of the lower school is the headteacher of the entire school. Sometimes pupils have little idea as to the number of jobs within a school that staff have to undertake, or the number of personnel involved. Students in this situation are likely to lack a sense of belonging, as they do not understand who does what, in what order, and why. They fail to actively participate in the school as they remain on the periphery of what is going on because of insufficient knowledge about the staff structure and function within their school. It is important therefore that they become acquainted with the 'family' of the school, and learn where they fit in and how. Pupils will probably assimilate and retain the knowledge of the way the school is organised if the tutor begins from the pupils' present perspective, and moves on from there, as opposed to telling them about the headteacher, and moving down to other members of staff. Beginning from subjects that teachers take, it is easy to describe other functions that they fulfil in the school. When each subject has been covered in this way, as in Figure 8 then all such diagrams produced by the pupils can be fitted on to the 'family tree' of the school.

Pupils in the first form will be most familiar with relating teachers to the subjects that they teach. The tutor should get the class to compile a list of subjects they currently take. The class should then be divided into groups of not more than six pupils. Each group should be given one or more subjects to deal with, depending on the actual number of groups and subjects there are. Each group should have a very large sheet of paper with a circle drawn in the middle. In this circle the pupils should enter the name of the subject, or depict it with a symbol or cartoon to suit them. They should then think of the teacher who teaches that subject. If there is more than one teacher who teaches a subject, then the circle should be divided into half to depict this. Pupils within each group should then attempt to find out what other jobs and titles that teacher may have. They can be aided in this process, by having a list of form tutors, year tutors, heads of department, secretaries, clerks, caretaker, deputy heads, heads of sections or houses, academic registrar, youth leaders, etc. These should be on display near the tutor who can if necessary point the pupils in the right direction in their quest for information.

Pupils should attempt to discover as many jobs and/or roles a teacher fulfils and enter them outside the circle on their sheets of paper, with arrows coming out of the circle towards the duty noted down. The next task for pupils in each group is to obtain from the tutor a list of duties a role entails. The tutor should have these prepared after consultation with all the relevant staff in the school, so that all pupils get the same information about a role. A completed group activity may look something as in Figure 8.

FIGURE 8

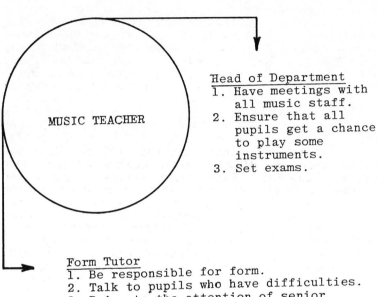

MUSIC TEACHER

Head of Department
1. Have meetings with all music staff.
2. Ensure that all pupils get a chance to play some instruments.
3. Set exams.

Form Tutor
1. Be responsible for form.
2. Talk to pupils who have difficulties.
3. Bring to the attention of senior staff any difficulties pupils may have.
4. Join in meetings with year tutor.

When each group has completed its investigations and noted down roles and duties, they should be allowed to place their contribution on a class family tree of the school, with assistance from the tutor, explaining how each contribution fits in with the entire system. This tree should generate a great deal of discussion amongst pupils and tutor, which could be further illuminated with actual examples of a situation arising in school, and working out how it would be dealt with, by whom and how long it would take. Pupils could take turns to show how a particular instance, e.g. a child feeling ill in school would deal with a variety of people, and how it would effect that pupil. See figure 9.

The role of the form tutor and year tutor should be especially emphasised in this session, so that children are constantly discovering who to approach and on what topic. As they learn about the route of actions that may follow a request, illness or misdemeanour, they will in future know what to expect, and anxiety levels will be considerably reduced. In addition pupils will be better able to use the system to its full, and avoid time wasting on the part of staff. They will be able to get responses more quickly and more efficiently.

Students in years three to five may wish to discover roles and functions of staff from a different viewpoint. For instance, who decides on timetabling, option choice, and how teachers in various departments decide on advising pupils about their strengths and weaknesses. They will want to know about careers, extra curricular activities, community service, work experience and about examination techniques. They could undertake a roughly similar exercise to that given for the younger pupils but looking at different aspects of teacher duties and roles. They could be encouraged to draw up a network of activities that they are interested in and set about finding how staff in their multi-faceted roles attempt to carry out these activities.

The use of examples from large institutions or commercial concerns can give this exercise added significance, especially for older pupils who may well be wanting to find out how other places function as part of their work in other subjects. Some examples include a large hypermarket, a hospital, a local firm etc.

For whatever age group these activities are

FIGURE 9

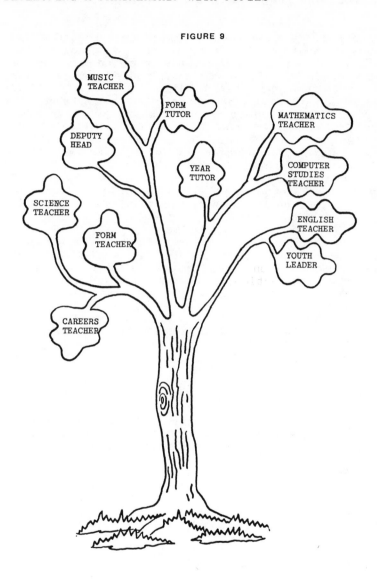

conducted, it is a good idea to check on the understanding that pupils have gained, by taking a situation, e.g. a boy missed his bus and has arrived
late in school. The other children are doing exams,
and this student doesn't know where to find his
group. Who would he think of looking for, how
would he go about it etc? Ask the pupil to trace
his procedures on the tree of the school staff.
It is also very important to provide pupils with
a visual representation of what they should do
in certain circumstances. Pupils are much more
likely to follow a flow chart than they are to
remember a sequence of activities given to them
verbally, perhaps a very long time before they
have cause to use it. With a visual chart they
can refer to it at the time of need, and follow
it more accurately.

Sometimes younger pupils cannot ask for help
when they need it because they have not been acquainted adequately with the personnel involved,
where to search for them at certain times of the
day, and the times when they are likely to be available. One example of this referred to two second
form girls who were playing in the playground,
when one girl fell and cut her knee badly. The
two girls tried to locate a member of staff during
the dinner hour but were unsuccessful. They related
how they went from one room to another, and each
time a member of staff told them to try to find
the right person somewhere else!

A possible flow chart that younger pupils
may find helpful is given below. It refers to
pupils who feel sick immediately after lunch, during
the lunch break. Where do they go, and who do
they ask for?

Banding and Setting

No matter how careful schools are in their system
of assigning pupils to bands, sets and forms with
different letters either suffixed or prefixed to
the year group; pupils still attempt and often
succeed in finding out where they stand in terms
of the academic pecking order. Even mixed ability
year groups fail to stop children and their parents
from wondering whether they are in the 'top class'
or how to get there by doing well in tests etc.
As a result of the need pupils have to place themselves in the category they think is the most
prestigious, they often get very upset when they
are moved from one band to another, or more

VISUAL FLOW CHART FOR PUPILS TO KEEP

FEELING SICK

Tell a Friend

→ Tell a dinner supervisor

Go with a Friend to Staff Room

Ask for form tutor ——— if not available

Ask for year tutor ←——— if not available

Ask for Senior member of staff

(or one with special responsibility
for children who feel ill in school)

Explain feelings clearly

If you cannot talk, ask your Friend
to explain for you

Ensure you give all the necessary information

Ensure you looked at the teacher

Ensure your speech was coherent
especially if you are in tears.

Ensure you got a suitably helpful response

If unclear about what to do ASK AGAIN

frequently, from one set to another for certain
subjects.
    It is impossible to avoid discussing this
topic without reference to different abilities
in pupils, as well as different rates of learning.
However if this task is handled sensitively, by
giving pupils the task of banding and setting a
hypothetical year group, they will come to some
understanding of how they themselves are grouped.
The class may be divided into four groups, and
each should be given one of the following tasks:

    Task one: There are 140 pupils in the second
year in a comprehensive school. Of these 60 are

boys and 80 are girls. There are seven forms with form tutors, and 4 sets for the subjects English, mathematics, and science. Girls generally seem to be better in English and the boys in mathematics and science. Allocate this year group into forms, and sets for the three subjects, giving your reasons for doing so.

Task two: At the end of year school exams, a third year group of students got a range of marks in their French from 2/100 to 94/100. There are 105 students altogether, and they need to be set for French in the coming year. There are 5 sets for French. How would you allocate the pupils to the sets, based on the marks they got in the exam, and the numbers of sets available for them.

Task three: There are 200 pupils in form one, who after their first term in school are interested in doing certain craft and domestic science lessons. There are 92 boys, and 108 girls in this year. Equal numbers of boys and girls want to do cookery and needlework, but only a handful want to do metal work or car mechanics. How would you allocate them to bands and sets bearing in mind that some of the children who don't want to do metal work, are actually very good at it, considering their marks? There are 6 possible sets for craft and domestic science for allocations to be made.

Task four: A music teacher has had to take time off school through a serious illness, and there seems no likelihood of another teacher qualified in music taking his place. This teacher taught 2 different sets of children music. Now there are only 2 teachers left, and the children have to be grouped together into larger classes so that they can all take music. The children in the high sets are good at the theory and in their knowledge of music, while those in the lower sets are better at playing modern music on small instruments, and enjoy making up impromptu tunes. How can you cater for all their interests and abilities in two sets? Can you set the children now into 2 groups instead of the 3 as was the case previously, giving reasons for so doing.

Each group requires one entire tutorial session for the completion of their task. In the following session a spokesperson is elected, who can present their actions and reasons to the rest of the class. The audience should be encouraged to react as if it was happening to them, while the group giving their results defend their actions against the mood of the class.

After each group has had a chance to present its case, the tutor should bring the class to focus on the general principles that governed the allocation of pupils into sets etc. Some of these questions could help stimulate that discussion:

Were you always able to give the pupils what they wanted?

If not why not?

Were you always able to be as fair as you would have liked, and if not why not?

What were the most difficult obstacles you faced in your task?

When pupils marks were very close together, how did you decide where they went in terms of a set?

How did the numbers of pupils effect your job?

Did the numbers of boys to girls effect your decisions about placement?

What conclusions can you draw from your own attempts at 'setting', about how you yourselves have been banded and set?

Have you got any ideas as to how your school can develop new ways of explaining what they do about banding and setting to the pupils concerned?

Are there any alternatives to banding and setting? If so what?

Visual explanations by the use of pie charts, or actually cutting up a large circle of paper to represent the composition of the sets can aid understanding of this topic, especially with forms one to three.

School Reports

Pupils will be well used to getting school reports from their days in the junior school, but the systems used for grading and the comments that accompany them, may be quite different. Sometimes pupils and their parents fail to understand what grades really mean when compared to other children

in the class. They often place emphasis on the
position they have attained in an exam however
low or high the top and bottom marks turn out to
be. Sometimes the different grades given by individual teachers cause some anxiety in pupils, and
they become frightened to take their reports home.
If pupils are to use their reports constructively
and attempt to improve their grades, marks and
comments on future occasions, then they have to
be attuned as to the function and value of reports,
as well as how they are drawn up.

A useful way to begin such a task would be
to arrange the class in a circle and to suggest
to each pupil that turns will be taken in describing
one purpose a report might serve, and one party
for whom it is written. This should take the form
of a 'quickfire' routine, with each child giving
a response very quickly and then moving on to the
next pupil in the circle. When this task has been
exhausted a tally should be made of all the categories of people for which reports were said to
be written, and all the reasons for the existence
of them. If pupils are unimaginative in this exercise, the teacher should stimulate ideas by making
one 'trigger' suggestion. This can be an outrageous
item which pupils will hopefully reject automati-
cally, but will nevertheless spur them onto thinking along more sensible lines. One such comment
may be 'reports are written for the school caretaker!'

The consensus of opinion should come up with
at least the following categories: parents, pupils,
employers, school record, heads of school. At
the next stage in this activity the tutor leads
the pupil to discover what aspects of their performance are reported on e.g. effort, presentation,
work habits, perseverance, exam results, grades
to represent a year's work, attitude toward subject,
general attitude to the school discipline, behaviour
in class, homework vigilance, general appearance
and ability to get on with teachers and pupils.

These factors may be elicited from pupils
by general questioning, and then written on the
blackboard. The class should then be divided into
six groups and each given at least two of the above
categories to work with. Pupils must note down
all the ways that come to mind regarding the manner
in which teachers make judgements about whether
a pupil has a good attitude towards a subject,
gets on well with staff and so on. Students can
then grapple with a set of questions such as those

set out below:

What kinds of behaviours on the part of the pupils could give a teacher good signals about them?

Should teachers tell pupils what they are looking for in their general everyday classroom behaviour? Why? How can this be done?

What would be likely to influence a teacher's judgement most, about a pupil's behaviour?

How could pupils be alerted to the negative aspects of their behaviour before they receive   school reports?

Should there be more interim discussions and assessments of pupil performance across the board?   If so, what form could they take?

What kinds of things should teachers be reporting on, in addition to what they already do at present?

Pupils can get a fair appreciation of how a report is written on them, by attempting to assess themselves on selected dimensions.   Apart from grading themselves in the various subject areas, pupils should make a list of the other factors that they feel would be important for them to be rated on.   These can of course be compiled from the categories already given in this chapter, or they can include new ideas from the pupils. Younger pupils may wish to include things like 'helpfulness', 'ability to share things' etc. while older pupils may be more inclined to be concerned about their level of maturity, self control, ability to see things from another person's point of view, and ability to learn from experience. An example is givew below. By using a self assessment guide such as this with some regularity, it should open up a source of fruitful discussion between various teachers and pupils, especially where pupils' self assessment indicated a discrepancy between what they thought they should get, the likely possibility of getting a certain grade, and eventually the actual grade. Pupils can then make a conscious decision to monitor their own performance and behaviour, and come to a better understanding of how teachers arrived at certain conclusions about them.
It would also be useful for pupils to comprehend how grades are allocated on the basis of

PUPIL HANDOUT FOR SELF ASSESSMENT

Subject	What I should get	What I might get	Discrepancy
English	B	A	+
Mathematics	A	B	−
History	C	C	=
Geography	C	D	−
Art	A	C	−
Games	A	A	=
Effort	B	C	−
Behaviour in class	C	B	+
Appearance	B	D	−
Self control	A	C	−
Attitude towards subjects	C	C	=
Homework vigilance	D	B	+

marks in a test or exam, as is sometimes the case. Of course they need to understand that if all pupils had the same mark, perhaps the test did not adequately measure the levels of ability of all the children. They need to understand that as in most measurements of performance and ability only a very small percentage of children achieve at the upper end of the spectrum, and similarly at the lower end of the marking scale. Most pupils actually achieve in the middle band, and when pupils realise this, their feelings about coming top or bottom will be placed in perspective. This topic actually involves some knowledge of statistics, and assistance from such a specialist would be an advantage for form tutors. However, the ideas are simple, and as most teachers use it in any

case when setting tests and exams, it can be simply
explained to pupils so that they do not get too
anxious about their work. A system such as that
below may help illustrate this:

Grade	Percentage of Pupils Getting It
A = 100 - 75	A = 5%
B = 75 - 50	B = 15%
C = 50 - 30	C = 60%
D = 30 - 20	D = 10%
E = 20 - 0	E = 10%

Attendance at School and Difficulties in Getting To School

A number of children experience problems in going
to school or in keeping up a regular attendance
at school, particularly from the third form onwards.
Occasionally pupils are not interested in what
schools have to offer them, and gain more stimulation from their exploits elsewhere. One of the
main themes of this book is making school a positive
experience for pupils. Whether or not a school
can achieve that for every pupil is debatable.
In any event, pupils should be introduced to all
the possible reasons they could have for not wanting
to attend school, its costs and consequences and
they should be allowed to make their own evaluations
as to its risk worthiness.
There is another group of pupils who for one
reason or another are afraid to face up to coming
to school. It often begins with a little act,
like not having done a set piece of homework, and
then escalates into a full blown fear, which may
need the intervention of an outside agency, such
as the School Psychological Service. Tutors can
do much to prevent such tiny episodes from developing into more serious problems. By showing a willingness and empathy with pupils over these minor
problems, schools acknowledge the difficulties
that their pupils may experience, and by assisting
them to be aware of and deal with them, they truly
act as 'partners' with their pupils.
Most pupils at some time or another during
their school lives will have experienced the sense
of wishing they could stay in bed instead of getting

up and going to school, perhaps having a slight headache or stomach ache to give some justification for not wanting to make the effort to go to school. These feelings are quite common and provide an easy way to open the discussion on 'getting to school'. No doubt tutors can add their experiences of their time at school, and the times when they as teachers occasionally do not feel like going into school. While many people may feel like this from time to time, they nevertheless manage to overcome these sensations and it is the ways in which they do so that is important for pupils to learn about and learn from.

After a general discussion about the odd times when people do not feel like going to school, pupils should be asked to call out to the tutor any incidents that they have experienced themselves, or have heard about from siblings or friends, that made them really worry about going to school. The tutor then writes them on the board, and they may include some of these items:

1. Not having a certain part of one's uniform.
2. Not having learned a topic for a lesson.
3. Not having done a set piece of homework.
4. Dislike of P.E./games.
5. Being teased.
6. Being moved out of one class into another and feeling lonely.
7. Being unduly upset if reprimanded.
8. Finding the work in general too difficult.
9. Afraid of a particular pupil/teacher.
10. Pattern of attendance disrupted after an illness.
11. Too tired to get to school if helping parents at home, or doing a milk round or other job.
12. Not having any stable friends.
13. Feeling picked on.

There are probably a host of other reasons why pupils are unwilling to come to school, and many of them rest within the family dynamics, or other circumstances not directly pertaining to school. The form tutor cannot hope to delve into all these factors. Tutors should attempt to restrict pupils to thinking about school factors that may produce in them some fear or anxiety. When an exhaustive list has been made up on the blackboard, the class should come to some agreement about which they feel are the most likely to happen to them in the future, or indeed those that they have experienced in the recent past. These should be given priority, and discussed using the following stimulus questions from the tutor:

Example: Not having learned a piece of work for a lesson.

How many pupils have felt that they didn't want to come to school when they had failed to learn some work for a lesson?

What were their worst fears?

What did they tell themselves on the morning that they were supposed to have learned their work, to give themselves an excuse for not going into school?

How did they convince their parents that they should stay home?

If they couldn't convince their parents, what did they do instead?

What did they expect their class mates would think of them if they did show up, and exhibit their ignorance?

Have any pupils done this more than once?

Does it get easier every time? Can they see themselves falling into a trap? Can it become too easy? Is that a worry?

Have any pupils decided to face up to the teacher and lesson concerned?

How did they decide to excuse their not having learned their work?

What were their worst fears? Are they the same fears as for those who decided not to go to school?

What did these pupils who opted to face the situation say to themselves on the morning of the day in question?

Were their fears borne out? If not what actually

happened?

How did these pupils try to control their fear and anxiety?

How did they talk to the teacher concerned, and what was the outcome?

What advice can these pupils give the others, who hadn't learned to control their worries, and had opted to avoid school?

This type of sharing of experiences is of value to students as they can with safety and 'permission' express their feelings quite openly, and learn from each other. The other items can be treated in a similar manner according to pupil preference. Not all the items will have an equal significance at a particular time in the school year, or career of a pupil. Tutors therefore have to plan and anticipate when the moment is opportune to introduce the topic again with new items from the list, or added to as pupils progress through the school. Many of these items will be linked to stress, dealing with authority, and trying to resolve conflicts. Tutors should therefore make themselves familiar with the following chapter of social skills, and subsequent chapters on life-skills to tie these things together. For instance the use of role play exercises to help pupils give meaning to the items that they discuss is important in this context, and full details can be found in the next chapter.

For those pupils who absent themselves from school because they do not feel they are getting a great deal out of their school experiences, it would be advantageous to have some opportunity to see truancy from other people's points of view, including those of outside agencies. Pupils could heed the costs of truancy for them, in the short and long term. This way of discussing the balancing out pros and cons of attending versus not attending school can be quite effective in alerting potential truants to thinking ahead and making informed judgements about their future attendance at school. These sessions need to be conducted at various points within the lives of secondary school pupils particularly at the end of forms two and three, as these seem to be the critical points for students developing a dislike of, and disillusionment with school.

DEVELOPING A PARTNERSHIP WITH PUPILS

If tutors are to gain an insight into how pupils begin to think of not attending school, they have to allow pupils to define truancy for themselves. This can be done by getting every pupil to join up with one other, and note down two descriptions each of the word 'truant' or any other word that has the same meaning in different parts of the country e.g. mitching, bunking etc. After this activity, couples should swap their ideas, and compare their views. The tutor then should collate all the views of the pupils and discuss with the children, from whose perspective they defined a truant. It will probably turn out that pupils have not described truancy from their own point of view, but from that of the school or the parent. This will show that pupils are not really aware of the reason why a student will want to absent him/herself from school. Even if they have been involved in truancy themselves, they may not be able to explain exactly why they did not wish to attend school on a regular basis. The tutor's task will therefore be to encourage pupils to imagine themselves as truants, and to consider how they would feel in that position.

What sort of things might be boring them in school?

What sort of temptations might they experience outside school?

Who is likely to tempt them to truant?

What are their parents attitudes towards regular attendance?

Do they sometimes feel that there are some things more important than going to school every day? If so what, and why?

Do they feel there is any point in trying to improve school life for themselves? If so how?

When do pupils first think of not going to school because they would rather be doing other things? How old were some pupils when they first considered not going to school?

The class discussion using the above stimulus questions will have made them ready to consider how other agencies and parties view truancy, and how pupils themselves relate to these perceptions.

DEVELOPING A PARTNERSHIP WITH PUPILS

The class should be divided into seven groups, and each given one of the following categories to discuss:

Parents	Children who truant
Teachers	Children who don't truant
Education Welfare Officers	The law
Social Workers	

Each group should come up with at least five points on how they think their 'party' would think of children who truant, and of truancy in general. If some pupils are unsure what social workers and education welfare officers are, then this must be explained to them in very general terms. If pupils ask what is meant by the 'law' no advice should be given, as it would bias their judgement, and in any case the whole point of this activity is for pupils to begin to discover for themselves what these various agencies do, and how they might view truancy. It is the first step in beginning to consider the implications of truancy before they take the plunge.

When the children have completed this task, the tutor should collate all the views, by asking the children to note down their ideas on large sheets of paper arranged so that they can each see at a glance the work of all the groups. The tutor should then aid the children in looking for common and disparate views from the group contributions. The following questions can then be used as aids to assist children in thinking about the implications of truancy:

Which agencies seemed to think along the same lines? Why?

Were they sympathetic towards truants, and if so why?

Did the 'parents' think in similar ways to any of the other categories under consideration? If not, Why not?

Why did some of the agencies have views that didn't match up to the others?

What were the differences between the children's views amongst those who did, and those who didn't truant? Why?

How would parents treat children who truanted? Why?

How would the law treat children who truanted?

How do those children who do not truant, feel about those that do? Do they get annoyed about being asked for books so that truants can copy up etc.?

What reasons can children have for truanting that may for them, possibly be good ones?

What other things could the truants do to solve some of their problems, or to alleviate their boredom, apart from truanting?

How do friendships influence truants to continue to do so?

Are there any right and wrong ideas about truanting?

Who decides if they are right or wrong?

Are some things right for one group, but wrong for another? If so, how can pupils try to resolve this for themselves?

Who benefits from truanting? For how long? What are the actual gains? (Examples: outwitting parents, teachers and the law, dressing as one likes, doing something more pleasurable, avoiding a telling off.)

Costs and Consequences:

What is the price that the pupil has to pay for truanting?

How does he/she have to pay?

E.g. damaged relationships with staff, and classmates; being labelled by the Education Welfare Officer; possible court attendance, losing the trust of parents and others.

What price do parents have to pay for their children truanting?

How long does the parent have to go on paying?

Are there prices to pay apart from a fine?

E.g. damaged relationships, tension and worry at home, losing their children to the Local Authority in Care Proceedings.

The long and short term effects of truanting for the pupil can then be considered, by dividing the class into four groups. Two groups should be asked to jot down the SHORT TERM effects for the pupil, and the other two groups should jot down the LONG TERM effects of truanting for pupils. The stimulation from the above set of questions will have given them much food for thought, and the tutor should leave trigger words on the board to aid recall. The groups who did the short term effects should then get together and pool their ideas, and the other two groups likewise. A master copy of all the short term and all the long term effects should then be produced by members of the class on large sheets of paper so that it can be accessible to groups later in the session.

The class then needs to divide into four groups different in composition to those formed earlier, so that more sharing of ideas can be facilitated. Each group is required to draw up a balance sheet of the benefits and debits of truanting, on the following handout.

Some teachers may wonder whether it is wise to allow children to have so much access to information and insight into a behaviour that they wish to discourage. There is very little evidence to suggest that information about a topic will inevitably lead to a child wishing to take it up. The whole point of all these activities is to warn pupils about some of the feelings and experiences that they are likely to encounter, so that they can be prepared, and act in a rational and informed manner. By giving children the opportunities to discuss and evaluate their behaviours, and possible reasons for it, they are much more inclined to be in control of their actions, and make sensible decisions in the future. We are simply giving them the tools with which to become autonomous, and self directed individuals, as opposed to becoming creatures who always need some form of external control and motivation.

The role of the school in contributing to truancy has been discussed in the previous chapter. For those wishing to read more about this, and about school refusal in general, Kahn & Nursten (1968); Carroll (1977); Galloway (1982 a, b); Turner (1974) Gregory (1980) Hersov (1976) and HMI (1977)

PUPIL HANDOUT FOR ASSESSING THE BENEFITS AND
DEBITS OF TRUANTING

BENEFITS SHORT TERM	DEBITS SHORT TERM
1.	1.
2.	2.
3.	3.
4.	4.
5.	5.
6.	6.
7.	7.
8.	8.
9.	9.
10.	10.
LONG TERM	LONG TERM
1.	1.
2.	2.
3.	3.
4.	4.
5.	5.
6.	6.
7.	7.
8.	8.
9.	9.
10.	10.

BALANCE:

OVERALL WORTH OF TRUANTING:

provide useful texts.

Relationship Between Teachers and Pupils

Pupils are unlikely to give much thought to the nature of the relationships they have with teachers. They rarely acknowledge that they are part of the process that makes for a good or bad relationship with staff, and that they too have a role to play in being partners with school. One way of introducing pupils to the notion of partnership, is to encourage them to look at more familiar relationships outside school, in the community at large. Pupils should be asked to name some 'partnerships' that occur to them. They will probably come up with 'parents' or business partners. If no others are forthcoming, then these can be used to stimulate more ideas:

Worker - employer	Shopmanager - shopper
Doctor - patient	Club - subscriber
Teacher- pupil	Builder - occupier of house

Once a list has been compiled on the blackboard children need to consider some of the characteristics of partnerships, and apply them to the above pairings. For instance, whether they are stable, or unstable; long or short term, and equal and unequal. Gradually the focus should be on the teacher pupil relationship, and these questions used for engendering thought:

Why do teachers and pupils need to have a partnership?

How would teachers and pupils achieve any goals without them?

What goals do they have in common?

What goals do they not have in common?

Do partnerships always have to be èqual? Why not?

How can teachers and pupils measure the worth of their partnerships?

Who gets the most out of this relationship and

PUPIL HANDOUT ON MEASURING THE WORTH OF A PARTNERSHIP

Good Feelings	Given by This Relationship
I feel important	
I feel special	
I feel needed	
I feel wanted	
I feel clever	
I feel creative	
I feel talented	
I get praised	
I get noticed	
I get listened to	
I get my own way with	
Bad Feelings	
I feel stupid	
I feel 'bad'	
I feel daft	
I feel cruel	
I feel dull	
I get shouted at	
I get forgotten	
I am ignored	
I feel ashamed	

why?

What do pupils give to staff, and vice versa?

After general discussion, the tutor once again leaves some trigger words on the board, so that when pupils work on their own they have some memory aids. Children should pair off to work on the above handout, with reference to their relations with staff.

When all have completed the handouts, each pair should join up with three other pairs in succession to compare responses. The tutor can check if the pupils were able to give a response to all the items on the checklist. If not, they were not really in tune with the relationships they have with staff, and the exchange of ideas with other pupils will have made them think in greater depth about this.

The discussion should be pulled together by the form tutor when colating responses. The variety of feelings that different relationships give should be pointed out, and the following questions asked when all the ideas have been collected:

Is it a good idea for all relationships with staff to be nice ones? Why?

Do we always have to get good feelings from our relationships with teachers? Why?

What can pupils learn from some of the bad feelings they get?

Why do some children get more bad feelings than good ones?

Should teachers and pupils join forces to make up common goals, and work out ways of attaining them? If so how?

The last question is a very important one, and perhaps ought to be done in a more structured fashion as follows. Pupils are placed in groups of six to fill in the handout below.

In this task it would be helpful if tutors allowed themselves to be questioned about what 'teachers' want, so that pupils can complete the first column of the handout with more knowledge. Tutors may need to move around the groups to provide them with this information, and a time limit may

PUPIL HANDOUT ON ACHIEVING COMMON GOALS WITH STAFF

Pupils and Teachers want	Teachers can do	Pupils can do
(e.g)1. To get on well.	1. Listen to pupils points of view.	1. Answer politely.
2.	2.	2.
3.	3.	3.
4.	4.	4.
5.	5.	5.

need to be set for advising a group, for instance, seven minutes, after which the tutor can move onto the next group.

When all have completed their handouts, ideas are pooled and the class should vote on the best ones, which are then set up in terms of priority. Pupils suggest ways in which they could implement the top three items in the coming year. This topic needs to be reviewed periodically, as certain goals may be more pertinent at particular points of a school year. It will also give both teachers and pupils the chance to evaluate whether or not they managed to stick to the goals set. In addition, staff could meet from time to time, and compare the responses on the handouts from various classes, so that an overall picture of how staff and students work together may be obtained. This could lead to suggestions for ways in which the school as a whole may attempt to facilitate these ideas.

CHAPTER FOUR

HELPING PUPILS COPE WITH THEIR PROBLEMS - USING
SOCIAL SKILLS

Seeking pupil perceptions about school life and
helping them express their feelings is only an
initial step in finding solutions to their problems.
Next it is important that they are given the skills
to cope with the troubles they face. Many of the
problems that pupils face occur during interactions
with other people. These include interactions
with other pupils, teachers, parents and other
professional groups who play a part in a school
system, e.g. Educational Welfare Officer, Careers
Officers etc. The skills of most importance and
value to pupils in this context are commonly known
as social skills. They are essential for healthy
living, social competence and adjustment, Trower
et al (1968), Van Hasselt et al (1979). Social
skills are behaviours which are situation specific,
have a particular purpose, are under the control
of the individual, and which to a large extent
determine the outcome of interactions between
people, Hargie et al (1981). Social skills are
made up of small component parts under the umbrella
terms of verbal and non-verbal communication.
Together these parts can influence the way in which
an individual copes with the more complex skills
of making relationships, maintaining relationships,
dealing with criticism, coping with conflict, giving
an account of oneself, asserting oneself, control-
ing negative emotions where appropriate, (self
control) taking part in interviews, and asking
for help. Pupils need to do all these things without causing themselves or others too much distress,
and it is for this reason that it is important
to teach pupils social skills.
    Most authors agree that social skills are
learned behaviours, and can therefore be taught
systematically to provide pupils with effective

means of interaction and problem solving, Spence (1980); Cartlidge and Milburn (1980); Rubin et al (1982); Priestley et al (1978) and Hopson & Scally (1980).

Pupils who are brought to the attention of staff with pastoral responsibility in schools, often lack the knowledge of when, where, and how to engage in behaviours appropriate to a certain context. They cannot therefore prevent themselves from getting into difficulties, or indeed extricate themselves from problem situations once they are aware of them. They may have inappropriate interaction skills which merely serve to exacerbate their problems instead of offering solutions. Mike was a twelve year old boy who was constantly being reported to his year tutor for getting into fights, and hurting other boys. He had been counselled by sympathetic staff who were aware that the boy had to cope with difficult home circumstances. Mike complained of being teased about his home life, and he was upset with himself for still wetting his bed every night. This would often put him in a bad mood before coming to school, and the slightest provocation would cause him to retaliate by fighting. He could not find any solution other than physical aggression to what he perceived as a stressful situation. Mike was not aware of why he was being provoked, or why the lads continued to tease him after he fought with them. The problem became serious enough for a referral to be made to the Educational Psychologist. While Mike and his family certainly needed help from an outside agency, the most practical and immediate assistance that the boy could have been given was skills training in how to deal with teasing in a manner which did not bring him a reprimand from staff in school.

The case of a fifteen year old girl who was suspended from school for being aggressive, and unmanageable also indicates the value of a social skills approach. Claire lived with one parent, and had witnessed violence and aggression within the family before it broke up. Some of her activities were calculated to bring her parents together again, and for her father to exert more direct control over her. Her behaviour in school and in the community was indicative of a lonely girl, who had few friends, and who indulged in attention seeking acts. Claire was often found to be communicating with her peers in ways which caused them hurt, both physically and psychologically. She would throw stones at them to get them to notice her, swear at them, and demand to take over games that they played in the youth club.In school she was always being sent to a senior member of staff for punishments for her misdemeanours. She responded by challenging their authority, until eventually she had to be suspended from school, and passed over to outside agencies. Claire needed help on two counts, both in relation to her modes of interaction. First she needed to learn how to respond to a telling off or punishment given by a teacher without giving the impression of being rude, challenging or 'above' the usual sanctions of the school. The skill of defusing a highly charged situation would have at least made her teachers think less poorly of her and perhaps not label her as 'unmanageable'. Secondly had she been shown the skills of making friends in more positive ways, she may not have needed to get into so much trouble by engaging in the more delinquent acts which eventually brought her to the notice of the police department, e.g. for throwing stones at another girl.

The examples above illustrate the need for a more skills oriented approach, if pupils are to transfer the knowledge and insight they have gained from counselling into real life. This would involve learning by watching others, and receiving feedback about their own behaviour in a controlled environment set up specifically for the purpose of analysing and teaching pupils to solve their problems, and adopt alternative styles of behaviour. Social Skills training practised in the school context has the advantage of utilising the group as made up by a class, which is time and labour saving for staff. Allowing pupils to discuss their problems with one another, and offer each other solutions, is a much more cost effective manner of carrying out pastoral work. This is not to argue that individual counselling is of little value. For many children it obviously is of great benefit, but for the vast majority who get into difficulties because they lack the appropriate social skills, or the knowledge of how and when to use them, role play and problem solving activities can offer them concrete help. Curtis (1982) and Frosh (1983) give examples of training children in social skills within the school and classroom setting.

In order to be able to use the social skills model to facilitate problem solving in pupils it is helpful to have an overview of how social skills can be broken down. Basically social skills can be divided into verbal and non-verbal elements. During interactions between people these two elements blend together to produce a smooth flow of communication. However for the purpose of learning and teaching social skills, it is more practical to break them down into smaller units.

Social Skills Breakdown

Verbal Skills

Content of speech
Amount of speech directed at a person
Rate of speech delivery
Clarity of speech
Volume of voice
Rhythm of voice   Paralanguage
Tone of voice
Pitch of voice
Pauses between words
Use of 'filler' words
 e.g. 'um', 'well'.

While the factors listed above apart from speech content are not strictly verbal skills, they often convey the meaning of what is said, and have therefore been included under that heading. They are more usually known as paralanguage or paraspeech skills.

Non-Verbal Skills

Body posture
Body proximity
Facial expressions
Gestures e.g. head nodding, arm gesticulations
 etc.
Eye contact
Muscle tension
Rate of breathing e.g. sighing, shallow quick
 breathing etc.
Body movements e.g. fiddling, tapping etc.

The latter three sections are not normally included as part of a non-verbal skill, but they are very powerful signals of a person's state of mind, and often the very things that annoy teachers about pupils when they are telling them off! A tense child who sighs often and audibly, and who also engages in feet tapping, or plays with a piece of their clothing can give teachers the impression

that the pupil is not heeding their comments, or
that the pupil is being rude and insolent. For
this reason it is very important to bring to the
attention of pupils all the signals they may give
and what they mean in specific contexts.
     Any communication which achieves its objectives
will encompass a combination of verbal and non-
verbal skills related to the context in which the
interaction occurs. The task of teaching social
skills to children is to help them choose an appropriate set of skills to use in particular situations. Children need to be taught how and when
to use a skill or combinations of skills to obtain
the most beneficial outcome. In some instances
it may mean learning how not to indicate anger
if the outcome will be bad for the pupil in the
long run. In other cases it may mean learning
how to approach a variety of people of different
status to make the most of life in school.
     A number of authors have discussed methods
of training children and adolescents who are already
assessed as having poor social skills, Spence (1980)
and Hayes et al (1982). However, as I have argued
elsewhere, Raymond (1982) a good pastoral care
system within a school can use the social skills
model to help prevent behavioural problems from
becoming too severe and unmanageable. Ellis &
Whittington (1981) call this Developmental Social
Skills Training, as opposed to Remedial Social
Skills Training which is offered to those who are
believed to lack relevant skills. In addition,
children are not simply skilled or unskilled
socially. They may possess the full repertoire
of social skills but lack the knowledge of when
and how to use them, which is why they experience
problems. By using situations which are common
in causing conflict to pupils in school, role play
and problem solving exercises can help pupils discover useful strategies for construing their problems, and enable them to learn from each other
a variety of techniques with which to tackle their
problems. Role play involves a re-enactment of
a situation that has posed problems for one or
more pupils. It is an illuminating way of discovering how pupils perceive their plight. It allows
pupils to re-live a scene in a safe way, when the
intense emotion originally associated with that
episode has subsided. It permits pupils to examine
their own behaviour, and to learn how to predict
how and why other people react to them in the way
that they have experienced. They learn what the

consequences are for adopting a certain stance
in their interactions with others and can judge
for themselves whether it was of benefit to them
at the end of the interaction. Pupils can expect
to find out how they are perceived by other people,
and compare that with the image they hoped
or thought they were creating. Role play provides
the opportunity for pupils to gain FEEDBACK about
their behaviour immediately after it has been ex-
ecuted, so that they can correct those aspects
of the behaviour which were maladaptive to the
situation in hand. During the role play sessions,
pupils can act as 'mirrors' for each other, and
provide information in a manner that is instant,
powerful and meaningful to those concerned.

Simulation activities can also facilitate
social learning by allowing pupils to witness a
variety of ways of behaving in a specific situation.
They can judge the effectiveness of the behaviour
in question and choose to adopt the one that best
fits their circumstances. Social learning theory
indicates that most social behaviours are learned
by 'modelling' our behaviours on others, and thus
controlled role play sessions can act as tools
in this process. In addition role play allows
a rehearsal of forthcoming situations that pupils
may be anxious about e.g. facing up to a reprimand,
so that they can begin to anticipate what type
of approach on their part will produce the optimal
outcome for them. Chesler and Fox (1966); Flowers
- Booraem (1980) and Taylor and Walford (1972)
give accounts of using simulation and role playing
techniques to aid social learning.

Preparing for Role Play

Once a problem situation has been defined, it is
vital that pupils are made aware of the aspects
of communication that will be the essence of the
role play. This can be done in a variety of ways
depending on the age group of the pupils involved.

Mime: For children in forms one and two mime is
an exercise that they enjoy and take to very easily.
Each pupil in a class can take turns to display
an emotion using their whole body, very much as
in the game charades. The rest of the class have
to guess which emotion is being portrayed. Once
a correct guess has been made, pupils should be
encouraged to give evidence for their guesses.
They should be asked to indicate what exactly they

noticed about the mime in terms of body posture, eye contact, facial expression and gesture that conveyed the emotion in question. This is especially important when similar non-verbal signals are used to indicate different emotions e.g. embarrassment and shyness. Both these emotions can be depicted by bowed heads, sagging shoulders, lack of eye contact, and a hint of a smile. Children need to be more attuned to the subtle signals that distinguish one emotion from another. It is also helpful if two or more pupils could mime the same emotion, while others in the class judged which was more effective and why. This would serve to demonstrate that not all pupils are equally adept at showing emotion, and that it is possible to learn from each other.

Where pupils are confused about what a particular mime is intended to show, the teacher can discuss the implications of this occurring in real life situations. The teacher could facilitate this problem solving exercise by asking such open ended questions as:

What would happen if you were not sure how someone was feeling when you were talking to them?

Would you be able to find out what the other person is feeling, and if so how?

What might happen to your style of communication if you did not receive any response from the person you were trying to communicate with?

How does it help the speaker to know what effect this behaviour is having on those around them?

Concrete examples of the showing of emotion and its effect on others can be brought out from class members, by asking them to think of situations at home where they have altered their behaviour because of the feelings expressed by another individual. For instance, can pupils tell when one of their parents is about to get very angry and explode? What are the trigger signals that alert pupils to the fact that mum or dad is about to become enraged? Pupils could be encouraged to discuss how they changed their behaviour in response to these signals to avert the wrath. In this way pupils can be stimulated into sharpening their skills in noticing other people's signals, and into becoming more aware of what their own bodily signals convey.

Using Photographs and Pictures: The use of photographs or pictures of people taking up a variety
of postures in different situations can also help
pupils become more alert to non-verbal communication
and its importance. Pictures taken out of teenage
magazines, or catalogues, comics etc. could also
serve as examples of how dress, body posture, gestures, and facial expressions illustrate a person's
feelings and image.   Initially pupils could be
given pictures of single individuals to analyse,
moving on to sets of couples, and lastly pictures
of many people.
    A class can be divided into groups of four,
each with one picture to discuss. They could be
asked to complete the questions below to focus
their thinking.

Stimulus picture: Person who is worried.

1. What do you think this person is feeling?
2. Look at the person's face, and give at

least three reasons as to why you think it is showing that particular feeling.
    3.   Concentrate particularly on the eyebrows,
mouth and position of head.
    4.   Look at the posture of the body, e.g.
shoulders, arms, and legs and say which of these
are showing the feeling that you have guessed.

<u>Stimulus picture</u>: Two people sitting down facing
each other, with one leaning forward, and pointing
a finger at the other. The other person is sitting
well back with head turned away and arms folded.
The body of the latter is slightly turned away
from the first person.

    1.   What do you think is going on in the
picture?
    2.   Who is the dominant one? Why? How can
you tell from the way the person is seated, and
the positioning of the body?
    3.   What is the other person trying to convey?
    4.   How does the other person do this, with
his head, arm and body?
    5.   If you could see the face of the second
person, what type of expression do you imagine
it might have? Why?

Each group of pupils in the class can exchange pictures and answer the questions. The degree of agreement or otherwise can then be pointed out by the teacher by asking each group to give an account of their views.

Another way in which photographs or pictures can be used effectively in this exercise is to allow pupils to complete a picture where a particular feature is blanked or cut out of the picture. For example in one picture the eyes could be blanked out, while in another one, arm and so on. Such pictures could once again be given to groups of pupils within a class, with a caption underneath indicating a particular emotion. The task of the pupils would be to complete the picture to match the emotion in the caption.

Pictures of individuals depicting an emotion could be cut into small pieces to form part of another game. Pupils could be asked to reconstruct a picture to indicate a specified emotion. Later they could do the same with emotions of their own choosing.

Children in the class who enjoy drawing, or producing comic type figures, could provide the stimulus material for such activities. Similar questions should be asked of the children as in the Stimulus picture section, to ensure that they are fully attuned to the language of the body.

A list of emotions that should be covered in these sessions are:

Frustration	Relief	Sorrow
Nervousness	Gratefulness	Loneliness
Worry	Embarrassment	Fear
Joy	Haughtiness	Pride
Disappointment	Aloofness	Shyness
Impatience	Submissiveness	Dominance
Anger	Excitement	Confusion
Confidence	Thoughtfulness	Humour
Pain	Disgust	Hatred
Jealousy	Humiliation	Let down

Using Extracts from Films or Television: Witnessing the flow of an emotion in time is obviously going to have a far greater impact on children than two dimensional pictures. Where possible two to three minute video excerpts from film or television sequences could be used as stimulus material in priming pupils to body language. The sound on the film should be turned down in the first few sessions so that pupils can concentrate on body posture, gestures, etc. They may find a structured schedule helpful in the early stages of this activity as given in Pupil Observation Schedule number one.

When all the pupils have completed this task, all their responses should be collated to emphasise points of agreement and disagreement. Where some pupils have noted certain elements of body language that the others have missed, this should be noted, and the film run again so that attention is drawn to such signals missed by many in the first showing.

The next step in this process is to combine sound and non verbal parts of the film. At this point children can put together what they gleaned from the previous activity with the verbal skills of voice quality, rhythm, volume etc. added. Pupils will need a more extensive checklist for this session which is given in Pupil Observation Schedule number two. Both sets of checklists can be used again when the role play sessions are in operation, to help them notice the subtitles of communication. The next film or video sequence should preferably involve an interaction between a man and a woman in a situation where they are communicating about a specific issue. Pupils will then have the opportunity to observe a flowing interaction, and relate how one character's style of communication affects the other. The film extract should be shown three times in succession, so that the pupils can note each character separately and also in unison. The instructions to the pupils should be as follows:

'The film you are about to watch will be shown to you three times. The first time you will be able to get an overall impression of what the characters are going to communicate to each other. On the second occasion, pay particular attention to the man in the film, completing your schedule as indicated. On the third occasion turn your attention to the woman and complete your schedule as indicated.'

When the schedules have been completed the teacher can use the headings within the schedule to collate the responses of pupils and channel their discussion.

When these preliminary exercises have been completed it would be helpful to construct a check-

HELPING PUPILS COPE WITH THEIR PROBLEMS

You are about to watch a very short exerpt from a film where one of the characters is trying to put over a certain emotion. You are asked to note down that emotion, and underline any of the phrases below which you think helped you to make up your mind.

THE EMOTION IS _____

I noticed:

EYE MOVEMENTS/CONTACT: staring   shifty   looking down

   looking from side to side   looking away   tearful

   widened   closed   moving up and down

BODY POSTURE: sitting up straight   turned away

   head bowed   leaning   tapping feet   fiddling with

   hands   crossing and uncrossing legs   legs splayed

   folded arms   hands in pockets   leaning forward

   slouched shoulders   hands covering mouth

   moving backwards   head in hands   hands over face

   hands waving in the air   rocking on a chair

   head almost touching knees   chin in hand

FACIAL EXPRESSIONS/GESTURES: frowning   eyebrows knitted

   smiling   clenched teeth   change in skin colour

   lips quivering   teeth showing   mouth drawn in

   pointing palms facing outwards

ANYTHING ELSE OF NOTE:

PUPIL OBSERVATION SCHEDULE NUMBER TWO

You are now going to watch a piece of film where two people
are showing their feelings to one another. State what each
is showing, and give reasons by underlining in blue what
you noticed about the man, and in red what you noticed in
the woman.
WOMAN IS FEELING _____
MAN IS FEELING _____
VOLUME OF VOICE: continuously loud   continuously soft
   changeable from loud to soft   changeable from soft to
   loud   modulated volume throughout   modulated to loud
   modulated to soft

TONE OF VOICE: pleasant   unpleasant   harsh   stern
   coaxing monotonous   acquiescent   denying   emphatic
   high pitched   questioning   lilted

RATE AND CLARITY OF SPEECH: talking very fast
   words swallowed   too many pauses in between words
   use of 'filler' words e.g. um, ah, well,   mouth not
   opened enough to make words clear   takes too long
   to make a point   searching for words   confused ideas
   unhurried   staccato speech

FACIAL EXPRESSIONS: smiling   frowning   mouth drawn in
   teeth showing   clenched jaw   change of skin colour
   chin pointing outwards   open mouthed

BODY POSTURE: clenched fists   taut and rigid body
   leaning forward   hunched   hands covering head
   folded arms   body turned away   hands moving about
   feet tapping   legs crossing and uncrossing
   leaning back   hands over face   hands on hips
   playing with tie/necklace/hair   scratching

EYE MOVEMENTS AND CONTACT: fixed stare   eyes widened
   looking down   moving from side to side   raised eyebrows
   blinking   quick glances   tearful   looking from
   side to side.

GESTURES: pointing   raising hands up in the air with
   palms outwards   moving wrists and fingers in the air
   touching   banging   throwing

ANY THING ELSE OF NOTE:

list of behaviours which includes all the aspects of communication looked at to date, under the headings of different emotions. These checklists could prove invaluable when engaging in role plays and also as guides in assessment for pupils when they are helping each other communicate more effectively. Four possible checklists are given below. They can be used as starting points for pupils to make up similar checklists for the remaining sets of emotions.

FEAR

Huddled body posture.
Trembling of hand and legs.
Looking down.
Disjointed speech rhythm.
Change in volume of voice.
Moving away from source of fear.
Change in skin colour.
Frozen body posture.

ANGER

Red face.
White face.
Stern voice.
Raised tone of voice.
Staring.
Quicker breathing.
Clenched jaws/fists.
Rigid/taut body posture.

CONFIDENCE

Upright body posture.
Head held high.
Smiling.
Keeping eye contact.
Shoulders back.
Free movement in arms and legs.
Modulated tone of voice.
Clear, modulated tone of voice.

IMPATIENCE

Shifty body movements.
Weight being moved from one leg to the other.
Long deep breaths.
Frequent sighing.
Fingers busy.
Looking around.
Face downcast.
Teeth clenched.

HELPING PUPILS COPE WITH THEIR PROBLEMS

Role Play

STEP ONE: This involves setting the stage for the role play. It can be done in any classroom with a few desks moved to make room. If desks are called for in the problem situation then they can be arranged in suitable positions. For example if the role play is to involve a teacher pupil interaction, then the teacher's desk can be used for the pupil who is to play the part of the teacher.

In the early stages of role play it is usually best to allow the pupil who has suggested the problem to play his/her own part. Class mates can then be nominated to take the part of others involved in that scene. The 'problem' pupil can either be asked to choose them, or the teacher can do so by asking for volunteers. Once the pupils who are engaging in the role play are chosen, they should be allowed to discuss the situation for about two minutes at the most. Long periods of discussion tend to be counterproductive as they stilt the scene, and deflect pupils from simply re-enacting the situation, as opposed to creating a new one. The rest of the class should then be divided into groups of two or three with a specific job to do. Let us assume that there are eight such groups. Their tasks could be divided up in the following ways as observers and commentators on the role-play:

Group 1 - To observe the problem pupil's body posture: hands, legs, way of standing or sitting, or approaching the others in the role play.
Group 2 - To observe the problem pupil's gestures: what the pupil does with the hands, episodes of fiddling, feet tapping, shifting etc.
Group 3 - To observe the eye contact between the pupils doing the role play, with emphasis on that of the problem pupil.
Group 4 - To observe the tone, pitch, and volume of voice belonging to the problem pupil.
Group 5 - To observe content of speech between problem pupil and others, with particular emphasis on the clarity with which the problem pupil made his/her case.
Group 6 - To observe body posture of other in the role play. How does it relate to the problem pupil? What message is the problem pupil receiving from it, and is it noticed by the problem pupil?
Group 7 - To observe the tone, volume, and pitch

of child talking to problem pupil. What are the intentions in using a particular tone etc.?

Group 8 - To observe the scene as a totality, and note the effect each pupil in the role play had on the other.

STEP TWO: Allow role play to begin. There are no set times for a role play to last. They vary between lasting for a few seconds to ten minutes, depending on the nature of the situation being simulated. It is important that all the groups who are observing are positioned appropriately to both see and hear the interactions.

STEP THREE: Ask problem pupil to share how he/she felt with the rest of the class. The pupil should be asked to elaborate on why he/she felt in a certain way. The pupil should be encouraged to evaluate his/her performance in the following manner:

Did it achieve my purpose?
If not, why not?
Were there any other ways I could have behaved?
What were the results of behaving in the way I just did?
Did I get my messages across to the others in that scene?

The other pupils in the scene can then provide the feedback the problem pupil will need either to confirm or deny his/her own evaluation as above. The other pupils should also have the opportunities to discuss how they felt, and why.

STEP FOUR: Each observer group should then be asked to give their report. It is often the case that although pupils were asked to concentrate on a specific aspect of the role play, they tend to get involved with the content of the speech and evaluate everything in those terms. It will be the teacher's role to remind them of their task, by asking questions related to the area of their brief e.g. if pupils say 'he acted silly' the teacher should come back with 'what did he do with his hands that made you think he was silly?'; 'What expression did he have on his face that made you think he was acting silly?' etc.

If a group are not able to give a full account of the behaviours they were asked to notice, the teacher can ask the group who were to observe the total scene if they can give any more clues. Occasionally even this is not successful in the first few instances of doing role-plays. In that event, the teacher should ask the pupils in the role-play to reproduce the exact behaviour which is under discussion. This normally serves to trigger off the responses that the teacher is looking for.

STEP FIVE: At this point the whole class should participate in a discussion about the situation, and begin to offer solutions for the 'problem' pupil to adopt in the future. This would involve the teacher in asking questions related to the outcome of the role play, what the actors in the role play think about each other in those roles, and how this would transfer to the real life situation.

The following role plays with a set of questions to channel discussion serve to illustrate steps One to Five in the sequence of conducting role plays:

1. Dealing with authority in school:
Problem: Two pupils come to school without full school uniform. One has a studded leather jacket on, the other has on the correct colour trousers, but in corduroy which is not allowed. Do they get similar/equitable treatment? If not, why not? Does it depend on which teacher tells them off? Does it matter if their home circumstances are known to the teacher? Does it matter if the teacher has a good relationship with one of them? Does it matter if one of them is particularly good at the teacher's subject?
ROLE PLAY - fourth form female pupil with a leather jacket is seen in the corridor by a male science teacher. The girl is quite attractive and looks nice, but is breaking school rules. She is good at science. Science teacher confronts her with her attire. After role play between teacher and pupil over leather jacket discuss with the class:

How did teacher address pupil? What tone of voice was used?

Did they achieve eye contact?

Did they smile at each other?

Did the teacher seem angry? How was it made

obvious?

What posture did the girl take up? Was it defiant, pleasant, non-committal, flirty, or apologetic?

What effect did her posture have on the teacher's next response?

Did the fact that the girl was good at science make the teacher treat her in a more lenient manner or not?

Did the fact that the girl was good looking have any effect on the way the teacher spoke to the girl and what he told her to do?

Did the teacher threaten the girl with any punishment if she failed to observe the uniform rules again?

Did the girl's explanation work? Why?

If the teacher had been female would the situation be different?

ROLE PLAY - Boy in form four has worn corduroy trousers but in the school colours. He looks neat and clean. He is seen by the P.E. master while changing, and taken to task. The boy likes P.E. but doesn't come to school very often. He is not very good at P.E. but makes an effort most times. He is confronted about his corduroy trousers. After the role play between teacher and pupil discuss the following with the class:

How did the teacher address the pupil? Note tone of voice, volume of voice, pitch, and eye contact.

Did the teacher ask for any explanations? If not, what did the pupil do/not do that influenced the teacher?

Is the teacher really angry about the trousers, or about the boy's poor school attendance?

Did the teacher give any signs of annoyance? What, and how?

How did the boy answer the teacher? How did he stand, look, and what tone of voice did he use?

HELPING PUPILS COPE WITH THEIR PROBLEMS

Did the boy help or hinder his chances with the teacher? How?

Did the boy antagonise or placate the teacher? How did he accomplish either?

Did the boy put his case across in an acceptable manner or not?

How could he have changed the reaction of the teacher?

If he thought the teacher was 'picking on him' because he was not very good at P.E. how did he show these feelings?

What will the teacher be likely to think of this pupil on future occasions? Why?

Sometimes it is necessary to emphasise the implications of behaving in a manner which can produce a less than desirable result for the student, by conducting two further role play scenarios. Two pupils should be chosen to interact with the student who played the teacher in the first role play. The first pupil should be instructed to deliberately behave in an antagonistic, insolent manner, while the second pupil could be asked to behave in a very submissive, compliant fashion. The checklists on Dominance, Haughtiness, Confidence and Submissiveness could be used to help the pupils take on their roles with conviction. The other pupils in the class need not be aware of which pupil is to affect which outcome. The class could be divided up into groups to watch the interaction. Four groups will be needed for this purpose.

Group 1 - To observe the first role play between boy and teacher noting the consequences for the boy of behaving as he did. They also need to give evidence as to which aspects of his behaviour in particular gave rise to the result of the inter-action.
Group 2 - To note the second role play between deliberately staged outcomes. This group should be asked to evaluate how the boy who acts as cheeky, and antagonistic makes life more difficult for himself.
Group 3 - This set of children should be requested to judge the third role play, where the boy is

to behave in a submissive fashion, and its consequences for that boy's future.
Group 4 - This group are to act as final arbiters,
comparing all three role play sessions and comment-
ing on which was the most useful for a pupil in
the suggested predicament to attend to for the
future.

The student who acted as the teacher in all
three plays should give an account of how he felt
in each situation. He could be helped to discuss
his views by the use of the following questions:

Which boy did you feel most kindly disposed towards,
and why?

What did the boy do/not do that made you feel that
way?

Who made you feel the greatest anger? Why?

What did you feel like doing to the boy who challenged your authority?

What do you think of boys who can't take a telling
off?

If you met this cheeky boy again in your lesson
how would you treat him? Why?

What did you think of the boy in the third role
play?
Did he make you have any pleasant feelings? How?
Why?
What would you be likely to say to other members
of staff about him?

How would you treat him in the future? Why?

Following these sessions the class can make
up helpful hints for the pupil who originally
suggested this as a problem situation. He/she
can then use them in further practice sessions.
The children who were observers in the previous
sessions could now engage in role play. Those
who were acting, can take on the parts of observers,
using the guidelines produced from the class discussions, and if necessary the Pupil Observation
Schedule number two. In order for pupils to make
full use of the 'hints' provided by class mates,

they need to be written down in the form of checklists of behaviours. One group of observers could
use such a checklist to monitor the pupil in question. They could assess his/her ability to learn
from the previous situations on the list, and finally give the completed assessment for the pupil
to evaluate him/herself for the future.

An example of such a checklist is given below.

2. <u>Coping with conflict</u>: choosing subject
options.
(a) Conflict with parents.
Problem: Pupil really enjoys art and craft and
would like to choose them as an option. However
parents want him/her to do computer studies as
they feel that it will enable their child to have
better career prospects. The two subjects cannot
be taken together, but even if that were possible
the pupil is not interested in computers. He/she
likes being creative, but cannot convince his/her
parents that art is worth pursuing.

Choose three pupils to enact a conversation
between the pupil and his/her parents. The pupil
experiencing such a conflict should play him/herself
and two others should take on the role of a mother
and father. In order to help the two pupils who
are to be parents, the following hints can be given
to them for a more meaningful role play:

Mother: you sympathise with your child a little,
but you are keen that your child has a useful skill
for the future. You sometimes wonder what schools
are doing these days as they don't seem to be fitting people for jobs as they should. Now here
is something very relevant on the time-table, and
you feel your child should take full advantage
of it.
Father: you found it quite hard to get a job when
you left school. You value education if it gives
you a skill that can be used to get a good job.
You think art is O.K. but not the kind of subject
that will get you far in life. You desperately
want your child to learn computer studies as it
is going to be 'the thing of the future'. You
wish you had been given these chances when you
were at school.

The class could be divided up into small groups
to note aspects of communication used by all three
pupils in the role play as suggested in the first
step of role play process. After the scene has

HELPING PUPILS COPE WITH THEIR PROBLEMS

CHECKLIST FOR HANDLING PEOPLE IN AUTHORITY

	ACHIEVED	NOT ACHIEVED
1. Avoid staring for the length of the interaction.		
2. Avoid moving head from side to side, and looking around.		
3. Avoid taking deep breaths and sighing loudly.		
4. Look at teacher at the beginning and end of the comments directed at you.		
5. Avoid smiling when you are being told off. (You may be embarrassed, but it may be taken as boldness.)		
6. Try not to stand with your hands in your pockets.		
7. Do not chew gum while you are being spoken to.		
8. Do not answer in a loud tone of voice.		
9. Do not try to defend yourself WHILE the teacher is still speaking.		
10. Do not interrupt the teacher.		
11. Explain yourself if you are given the chance without mumbling, swearing or talking too fast.		
12. Do not bring other pupils into the conversation.		
13. If you are asked a question respond immediately in a clear manner using as few words as possible.		

130

	ACHIEVED	NOT ACHIEVED
14. Try to have the position of your head just below eye level so that you are neither perceived as haughty nor devastated.		
15. Try not to clench your teeth as it may indicate anger.		
16. Watch out for trick questions (rhetorical) as they do not require an answer. If you do answer them you may be seen as very 'full' of your own self importance.		
17. Lower your voice when you are accepting a criticism.		
18. If you feel an attack is being made on you for no good reason, say so AFTER the teacher is satisfied that you have taken your telling off.		
19. Apologize for breaking a rule or upsetting someone if it is appropriate.		
20. Do not walk away until you have been given clear indications that you can go.		
21. When you walk away do not glower, stamp off, or mumble. Do not run but walk calmly, with your body upright.		

been played a discussion with the class should focus on the points given below:

How did the pupil reason with the parents?

How did the pupil deal with counter reasoning?

Did the pupil accept defeat?

If so, how was it shown (temper, frowns, sighing, banging doors, shouting etc.)?

Did the pupil present his/her case one idea at a time?

Did the pupil try to get mother on his/her side? If so how?

How did the pupil deal with negative comments?

Did the pupil keep in control of his/her feelings? How was that made obvious?

What effect did the loss/gain of control have on the response of the parents?

What were the best parts of the pupil's communication? (This question should focus on eye contact, facial expression, gestures, tone of voice, and body posture, as well as the rate at which pupil delivered speech and its clarity and rhythm.)

The pupil should then be asked to analyse his/her own performance, and judge whether he/she presented a reasonable case. Did the pupil have more success with one parent, and if so why, and how can it be capitalized upon? The other members of the class should also be invited to give some criticism of the pupil's manner of communicating with the parents, and suggest alternatives.

The pupils who acted as the parents should indicate how they felt about their child's ability to put his/her case over. They should in particular reveal which aspects of the 'child's' communication they were swayed by, and why, and vice versa. They should help to emphasise whether it was what the pupil said that swayed them, or more importantly the way it was said.

In order for the pupil experiencing this conflict to gain the maximum from this type of exercise, there are two further stages in this technique that would be valuable. First, the pupil should take on the role of one of the parents, and another pupil could take the part of the child. This would allow the pupil with the conflict to get some idea about what it feels like to be a parent and want the best for one's child. The pupil could experience the difficulties in persuading a child that a parent perhaps knows best! In addition, the class mate who takes on the role of the pupil with this dilemma could be asked to behave in exactly the same manner as the original pupil did during the first role play. This can provide the visual and auditory feedback to the pupil about his/her manner. Most pupils and indeed adults are not really aware of how they are being perceived by others, until they are shown. They will often be surprised at what others make of their behaviour, and learn a most powerful lesson in this way. Secondly, the pupil with the conflict should be set a 'homework' task. This would involve practising the aspects of communication that he/she has learned via the role play at home with other situations. His/her mastery of the art of skilful communication when in a quandary can be tested once more in a classroom situation by engaging in further role play sessions. When the pupil feels more confident of being able to present a good case to his/her parents for choosing Art as a subject option, he/she can be given the go ahead to approach his/her parents accordingly.

(b) Conflict with teachers.
Problem: Pupil wishes to do physics but recently his/her marks have not been very good. The teacher has advised against opting for this subject. However the pupil is prepared to work hard and do whatever is necessary to prove that it was worthwhile choosing physics. The parents of the pupil are encouraging him/her and would be disappointed if he/she could not do physics.

The pupil experiencing such a dilemma would act his/her part, and another pupil would be required to act as the teacher. The brief for the student acting as the teacher could be:

Teacher: you understand the pupil's desire to do physics but honestly feel that the pupil will have difficulty as the course gets more demanding. You know that the pupil is struggling and feel that the pupil's energies would be better directed in another area. However you are willing to discuss the matter with the pupil.

The role play can begin after both actors have had the above type of briefing, and the other class mates are all primed to notice specific aspects of communication between the acting pair. When the role play is over the teacher should aim to elicit from the pupil asking to do physics whether the case was argued rationally or emotionally. Did it make the teacher in the role play behave in a particular manner as a result? Did the pupil feel victimised, or treated with respect? Which ever is the case, the pupil should indicate what parts of the communication gave him/her such feelings? Was it in the way the teacher was sitting, the way the teacher looked at the pupil, or the manner of address? How did the teacher's behaviour follow on from the way the pupil conducted him/herself? How did the pupil behave in relation to the teacher's attitude?

The student acting as the teacher must also explain how he/she felt in the situation, and what action if any would have been taken if this was a genuine problem. Reasons should be given in terms of the manner of pupil interaction with the teacher, and what effect it had on the decision the teacher eventually made.

Reversed role play where characters are swapped could further enlighten the pupils as to what parts of their communication had the desired effect, and which had undesirable consequences. Other children in the class can also give hints on how to get the best out of such an encounter. One or two can be chosen to demonstrate. The pupil with this problem can then see for him/herself an alternative strategy, compare it to his/her own, and change his/her style accordingly.

3. <u>Coping with bullying and teasing</u>:
This is a common problem that seems to plague the first to third formers more than the older school population. Episodes of teasing and bullying occur in many different places and contexts. Therefore it may not be possible for pupils to be given a universal set of techniques for overcoming these unpleasant happenings. To assist the pupils solve their problems in the context in which they are currently experiencing them, it will be necessary for the teacher to make a list of all the probable places and situations in which pupils may be faced with teasing or bullying e.g. queuing up for lessons, dinner, vying for privileges to use equipment etc. Teasing may

occur when pupils cannot take part in physical education, have unfortunate appearances, are bright and called 'teacher's pet', and if they have come from another area. Let us take the case of Ian, a lad who complains of being pushed around in the dinner queue, and who has many nicknames which distress him. He has ears which stick out and that is the source of one nickname. The other is his surname itself which is like that of the name of an animal, and which is used by his peers to tease him. Ian is often brought to the attention of staff as he tries to respond to these pressures in ways that cause trouble and disturb the smooth running of the school. In addition, Ian does not seem to be benefitting from the many talks and counselling sessions he has had with his form tutor, and year tutor. Staff are also getting rather put out by his frequent complaints about other pupils, as they can do little to solve the situation after the event, or take effective steps to prevent these situations from recurring.

The role play in this situation would involve a group of children perhaps all queuing up for dinner, with the lad in question taking his part in the queue. If the children who actually do the taunting are in that group, they should be given the simple instruction of 'show us what happens when you are all queuing up for dinner'. This will of course follow the description of the problem by the pupils themselves, and more specifically the boy who claims to be bullied. Those children who are not taking part in the role play should be divided up into three groups and given the following tasks:

Group 1 - to observe the taunted boy, and how he stands, leans, what he says or doesn't say to the others, as well as how he responds to those talking to him. They should note in particular the tone of his voice, his gestures, his facial expressions, and body posture. The checklist on Fear and Anger could be used as guidelines for this group.
Group 2 - to observe the children who taunt or bully the boy in question. They should note in particular whether these lads begin to tease at any particular juncture of the interaction; whether they are provoked; whether the boy in question encourages them to go further; whether the boy's attitude pleases them and so makes them carry on. They should also stress how they came to their conclusions by discussing body stance, tone of

voice etc. The checklist on Confidence may help here.

Group 3 - to observe the entire scene, and form the basis for dicussion so to why that boy in particular got teased. They should observe how he coped, make a judgement as to its effectiveness and also be able to predict whether episodes of teasing would occur and why.

After the role play the teacher needs to ask the following set of questions, to bring out the features of the situation which are negative, and are liable to reinforce such behaviours again:

What is it about the lad in question that makes him a likely target for teasing?

Is it the way he looks?

Is it the way he behaves? If so, what does he do that makes others want to carry on teasing him?

Did the boy show fear? If so how do we know? If not, what did he show and how did we gauge that?

Did the boy face up to the other boys, or did he back away?

What effect did his behaviour have? If he backed off, did the other boys think well or badly of him, and why?

The boy himself should have the chance to explain his feelings. The others can then provide him with feedback as to his success or otherwise in indicating those feelings. For instance if the boy says he was feeling angry, the rest of the class can tell him whether or not he managed to show that. In this way the boy can learn how to show his feelings clearly, and also test out the results of so doing. The checklist on Anger would enable him to practise exhibiting anger in a safe way, with others giving him tips where necessary. The lads in the role play who engaged in the teasing should also be called on to explain what impression they had of the lad in question. They should aim to help the lad by telling him why they behaved as they did, and what they hoped to gain from it. Both parties should say what they felt at the end of the role play, and whether they got what they wanted from that

interaction. Obviously the boy who complains of
teasing will not have achieved his goal, and he
will need guidance, on how to do so next time.
One of the ways in which he can see for himself
why his behaviour is not beneficial to his own
end is for another of his class mates to take
his part in this scene, and behave exactly as he
did. Where video is available, the scene could
have been taped for instant replay. Later the
lad should be shown how to behave in a confident
manner even if he is fearful, and how to respond
to taunting in a manner that will prevent further
such episodes. This can be done in two ways.
First, another pupil could demonstrate confidence,
which the boy could imitate. Secondly he should
be made aware of the tension in his muscles that
often accompanies fear. This is a give away sign
to others that someone is afraid and is an easy
victim. Practising relaxing muscles and being
confident, together will allow the boy to reach
a stage where he can role play the scene again
and note the effects of his newly acquired skills.
Finally a homework task could be set for him with
a checklist of the procedures he needs to go through
in order to cope with bullying, which he can tick
off immediately after the event. The checklist
can be produced with a list of suggestions from
the class, and may look something like the list
shown on the next page.

Other useful hints on dealing with bullying
can be found in Lowenstein (1978a; 1978b) and
Hamblin (1978). Details of training people to
stand up for themselves, or being assertive can
be found in Hobson & Scally (1979) Liberman et
al (1975) Langrish (1981) Galassi and Galassi
(1977), and Bower & Bower (1976).

4. Making friends:
Children who find it difficult to establish
and maintain friendships often exhibit their difficulties in quite disturbing ways. They may become
school refusers or truants. Some may begin to in-
dulge in pilfering or smoking and drinking as a
means of either buying friends or being accepted
by their peers. Pupils who do not have stable
friendships are often unaware of how to initiate
conversations with their peers, and begin to label
themselves as unpopular and become quite miserable.
These children often lack a frame of reference
which they can use to judge and compare their performance to that of their peers. They will need

PUPIL CHECKLIST ON COPING WITH BULLYING/TEASING

STEP		DID	DID NOT DO
1.	When I am called a name I must avoid looking at the person.		
2.	I must take deep breaths when I feel frightened, and try to relax.		
3.	I must tell myself that they want me to react, and I will not do so.		
4.	If I feel angry I will tell them to stop teasing me, but not hit them.		
5.	If someone tries to push me around I must not let them see my face showing that I am upset.		
6.	I must keep my body upright, and my head held high.		
7.	I must smile and speak in a normal tone of voice.		
8.	If anyone speaks to me I must answer in an unhurried and clear manner, without mumbling or covering my mouth with my hands.		

assistance on two counts. First they will have to be shown the elements of a communication that other people rely on to decide on whether or not they wish to have a relationship with someone else. Secondly these children have to be taught the skill of effective communication without falling into the trap of giving an impression that they did not intend to. Many children think they are being friendly, but sadly, their attempts may be interpreted as boastfulness, snobbishness or even aggressiveness. The knack of indicating to another person that one wishes to interact with them on an equal level is a highly complex and difficult one. Most children who experience such problems will often have some anxiety on this issue, and that in itself can confuse the messages they are trying to present, which in turn can subvert the entire interaction. One prime example of this is when a shy pupil is thought of as snobby or snooty, because to those observing the child, many of the non-verbal communication behaviours are identical. The diagram below illustrates this.

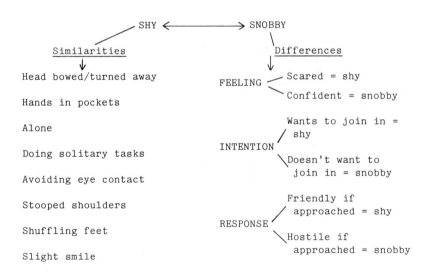

While the outward signs that an observer notices may be similar, the feelings, intention, and eventual response of a shy person and a snobbish one will differ. However, the observer will not have any evidence other than what is communicated by the body as to what a person is feeling or intending. This is why it is vital that children are made aware of how to communicate friendliness with as much clarity as possible.

ROLE PLAY: Let us take the case of a third form boy who is thought of as attention seeking by staff. Tony seems to enjoy adult company and can converse with them well providing they structure the conversation enough to suit him. He has few, if any, real friends. He is often seen in the school yard and youthclub trying to strike up conversations with other lads, or to join in their football and rugby games. However he seems unable to make any inroads into other groups of lads, and ends up spending a lot of time on his own. He occasionally indulges in a form of behaviour calculated to bring him to the attention of adults and in doing so he is achieving his objective of having contact with people, albeit in a less than positive way.

Staff feel quite sorry for Tony as they sympathise with his difficulties, but are at a loss as to how to help him other than by talking to him. He responds well to individual discussion with a teacher, but cannot seem to transfer the advice given to him to the real life situation. Teachers agree that they too find him hard work in terms of getting him to talk in more than monosyllables, and understand why other children do not bother too much with him.

The scene to role play could be the one involving the boy attempting to join in a game of football during a break time. In this case the class could be divided up neatly into girls and boys, where the boys can all engage in the role play as 'footballers'. The girls can then be further subdivided up into three groups, with a specific task to perform.

Group 1 girls - To observe the boy trying to join in a game. They should be reminded to note in particular the body posture of the lad, the volume of the voice, the length of his utterances, to whom he addresses himself, his proximity to the other lads, his facial expressions and his response to any contact made by the other boys.

Group 2 girls - To observe the lads playing football. They should watch more closely any boys
who may engage in an interaction with the boy trying
to   get   into   their   game.   They   should   focus
on whether they respond to the boy immediately
or not; whether they say more or less to him than
he did to them; whether there is any eye contact
between the boy and them; whether they seem to
like him; how quickly they get tired of him; their
facial expressions, gestures and body posture.
Group 3 girls - To observe the totality of the
interaction.   They should pay attention to the
effect the boy has on the lads playing. They should
also note what impression the boy seemed to give,
and whether the response of the lads was reasonable
in that light.   Did the boy try hard enough, or
was he expecting the others to invite him into
the game just because he was around?

After the role play is completed, the children
can all sit down again, and on this occasion allow
the boys playing football to give their account
of the outcome of the scene first.   If the result
was negative, then they should be made to give
reasons by answering some of these questions:

What did you think of the boy's chances of getting
into your game?

If his chances were poor, why?

What kind of impression did he make on you?

Did you seem to like him, and want him to join
in?

If not, what did he do OR NOT DO that made you
not want him to join in?

Did you hear everything he said?   If not why?

Did he explain himself well?   If not what effect
did that have on your decision regarding letting
him into the game?

At this stage the observer groups should be
asked to confirm, deny or elaborate on the above
points.   Then the boy in question should be asked
to indicate his feelings during the role play.
Ask him if he can at this juncture give any reasons
as to why he did not manage to get into the game

141

and be accepted by the lads. A list of 'things to do' and 'things not to do' should be made on the blackboard with contributions from the boy himself, and all the others, based on the discussion held after the role play. The scene could then be re-enacted with the boy using the hints on the board under 'things to do' to help him.

A possible set of such lists might have the following suggestions:

Things to do to get into a Game/Make Friends

1.   Stand at least three feet away/near one of the boys in the game.
2.   Try to look at one of the boys and smile.
3.   Try to keep your head upright, so that the boys can see you and so that you can be heard.
4.   Make use of your hands when talking to them so that they know you are really interested in joining in.
5.   Use a tone of voice that is pleasant, making it louder at the beginning of a sentence, and a bit softer at the end of your sentence, so that it shows some feeling.
6.   Begin talking to the boys by asking a question e.g. what are you playing?
7.   When any of the boys reply, ask another question straight away so that the conversation keeps going.
8.   Tell the boys a little bit about yourself, and ask them about themselves.
9.   Unless you get the feeling that the boys definitely do not want you in the game, walk into the game and wait for your chance to join in.

Things to avoid when trying to get into a Game/ Make Friends

1.   Do not stand too far away from the other boys.
2.   Do not ask questions in a voice that is too soft, or that is flat and without feeling.
3.   Do not wait for the other boys to start talking to you first.
4.   Do not stand with your hands in your pockets, or rigid by your sides.
5.   Do not keep too still and rigid or else the others will think you are like a robot.
6.   Do not keep a straight or dead pan face all of the time.
7.   Do not wait too long before answering

a question.

8.   Do not leave long pauses in between questions and answers.

9.   Do not wait for a specific invitation to join in the game.

After trying the scene again, the boy himself sould be called upon to evaluate his performance using the list of 'dos' and 'don'ts' on the board. The other children should provide immediate feedback as to his success.   If the lad is still having great difficulty following the advice, another member of the class should demonstrate for him. This can be followed by the lad trying once more, with the demonstrator priming and cueing the boy at every step of the process.   Video equipment would be especially useful in this case, enabling the boy to see himself progress in terms of skill learning. Several practice sessions may be needed for such a problem.   It should be reinforced by the lad having a permanent record of the lists of things to do/not do, which he can use as a reference.   His peers could be given a homework task of observing how well he put these skills into operation outside the classroom situation.   If it were feasible, one pupil from the class could be attached to the lad for a few weeks, to cue and prompt him during his attempts at interactions.

The four problems illustrated above can be adapted for use in helping pupils cope with similar situations.   A summary chart of the processes involved is provided on the following page for easy reference.

Just as with all other skills, social skills need to be learned to a stage where they become part of an individual's repertoire. In order that this happens, a few games involving role play can be set up for pupils.   Spence (1980) provides some suggestions for such games, including role play roulette, and role playopoly.   These games have a set of cards each describing a situation and place where it occurs which pupils have to role play using appropriate skills e.g. someone has just taken your pencil without asking you, and you want to get it back.   Show how you can do so without getting yourself into difficulties.   The numbers on a made up roulette wheel correspond to numbers on cards, which pupils get by spinning the wheel and waiting to see what number they are dealt.   In role playopoly, an adapted game of

HELPING PUPILS COPE WITH THEIR PROBLEMS

SUMMARY FLOW CHART OF SOCIAL SKILLS AND
PROBLEM SOLVING PROCEDURE

Choose theme for class discussion

Facilitate discussion by using open ended questions

Conduct preliminary sessions to prime pupils to
emotions and how they are communicated

Select a specific problem for analysis suggested by a pupil

Pick out those pupils who will be engaging in role play
with pupil who suggested topic to play him/herself

Divide the rest of the class into observer groups
each with a set piece of communication to watch

Allow role-play to proceed for a few minutes

Ask pupils in role play to give an account of their
feelings and to judge the outcome of the scene

Ask each observer group to give their report

Facilitate discussion so that observers can offer
alternative styles of behaviour to improve outcome

Conduct reverse role play, and allow demonstration
of behaviour by another pupil to give feedback
to one in difficulty

Help pupil with problem to practise new skills

Set homework task for pupil with difficulty

monopoly is played where names of properties are substituted with areas of a school, e.g. classroom, science lab, dining room etc. Cards with situations to role play are placed on the board, and have to be picked up as penalties for landing in a particular place.

A set of situations to place on cards to go with the games is suggested below:

1. You have come into a lesson late for the fourth time. Explain yourself to the teacher.

2. You are caught in the cloakroom looking around at the coats as if you are searching for something. A pupil in your class has already complained of losing belongings in the cloakroom. Express to the teacher who has caught you, why you are not to be taken as a thief.

3. You have forgotten to bring your pencil and rubber for your maths lesson. You have to ask the teacher to lend you a pencil explaining why you need one.

4. You are asked by a friend to truant from school tomorrow to go and watch a special video film in his/her house. You would like to go, but not during school hours. Tell your friend how you feel.

5. You would like to attend a practice session for the school band. The music teacher asked you to make sure that you get to the session on the sound of the lunch bell. In order to do so you have to leave your lesson a little early. Ask your teacher if you can be excused to get to the practice session.

6. You have given your watch to the gym teacher to look after during a lesson. He has forgotten to return it. Go and ask the teacher for the return of your watch.

7. You have been getting your mark in registration, but have not been attending all your lessons. Your year tutor has asked to see you to confront you with this allegation. Explain yourself.

8. You have been sent out of a classroom where you were taking a test. You were caught talking, but you feel it was for a legitimate purpose. After the test, you have to face the teacher, and put your case.

9. You overhear some other pupils talking and think they are talking about you and your activities outside school. However you are not entirely sure that they are discussing you. You

go up to them, and try to get in on the discussion. Do so without aggravating anyone, or making life difficult for yourself.

10. You have just given a teacher information about another pupil in what you thought was a helpful manner. At the end of the lesson that pupil threatens to beat you up. You are scared of the coming break time. As break time nears you get more threats, and you have to react. Do so in a way that can solve your problem.

11. You would like to be friends with a certain member of your class. That person seems to be very popular, and you do not think you can make him/her like you just by going and talking to him/her. You know this person collects pop posters, so you get one and approach the person. Try and engage that person in a conversation, and arrange to see him/her after school.

12. You are about to return to school after being sent home for breaking a school rule. You are frightened of facing up to your class mates. You reach the school gates and see some of your friends. Go up to them and start a conversation, coping with any comments they make that upset you.

13. One of the pupils who sits next to you in science never pays any attention during lessons. He/she has a habit of asking to borrow your notes in time for the next lesson. You don't mind doing so once or twice, but are feeling aggravated that this has been going on for so long. The boy/girl is about to ask you again, and you must refuse without being rude.

14. There are two people in your form who like bullying smaller children. They enjoy showing off, and having a laugh at the expense of others. They are now coming towards you, and are about to try and push ahead of you in the bus queue. Cope with this without resorting to physical violence.

15. You are asked to go and see your geography teacher for whom you have just done a piece of homework. You are asked for your homework, which you are certain you have handed in. Argue your case without annoying the teacher, but not putting yourself in a bad position either.

These situations can be role played quickly, and the effectiveness judged by the rest of the class. The list of such problems can be added to and subtracted from continuously with ideas from the pupils themselves. In this way pupils

can rehearse and practise their social skills.
All pupils have a chance to so do with these games,
after those with specific problems have been given
the experience of personal problem solving via
role play and discussion. A Handbook of Communication games can be found in Krupar (1973). Lorac
& Weiss (1981) also give ideas on communication
projects with adolescents.

CHAPTER FIVE

DEVELOPING SELF AWARENESS AND SELF IDENTITY IN PUPILS

Exploring the Self Concept and Self Identity

Adolescence is a time when pupils begin to develop a sense of who they are, what they are, and how other people perceive them (Wall 1968). They tend to use other people as mirrors to aid them in the developmental process of establishing a self ident- ity and self concept (Kelly 1955; Burns 1979; Bannister 1981; Bannister & Agnew 1977). Conger (1977) and Jersilds et al (1978) discuss the traumas that youngsters experience in trying to find out what sorts of individuals they are. Bannister (1981) maintains that understanding oneself is not simply an interesting pastime, it is a necessity of life. In order to plan our future and to make choices we have to be able to anticipate our behav- iour.

The influence of the school on the development of the self concept and identity can be very great (Coopersmith & Feldman 1974; Hamblin 1978). In the process of growing up, the self concept and identity can be very fluid and susceptible to change, via the constantly changing messages that children receive from adults and peers. Schools need to help children become aware of their own striving to obtain and maintain a self identity through some approach involving some moral and attitudinal evaluation (Sugarman 1973). One way of doing this is to get pupils to consider the factors that influence the way an individual forms his/her self identity. This can be done in quite a dramatic and powerful way by using the card sort- ing technique.

Two sets of cards are needed for this task, incorporating both words and pictures. These should combine to reflect all facets of life e.g.

148

DEVELOPING SELF AWARENESS AND SELF IDENTITY

<u>THE SET OF WRITTEN CARDS COULD INCLUDE THE FOLLOWING CHARACTERISTICS:</u>

Snob	Smooth talker	Enjoys food
Trouble maker	Bad liar	Efficient
Left Wing	Good at sports	Giggly
Bookworm	Careless	Big headed
Fickle	Gets bored easily	Miserable
Trusting	Likes a good laugh	Quiet
Optimist	Weighs up the pros and cons	Show off
Cruel	Punctual	Gets hurt easily
Selfish	Abides by rules	Learns quickly
Proud	Has lots of friends	Mature
Failure	Jealous type	Foolish
Impulsive	Scared to try new things	Irritating
Difficult person to get to know	Always sorry for self	Always uses big words
Runs away from things	Needs others to decide things	Shares possessions
Says one thing and does another	Gets on better with elders	Gets het up quickly
Likes plants and country-side	Has strong beliefs	Doesn't care about tomorrow
Can't take a chance in life	Will do anything for money	Helps those in trouble
Sticks up for the less fortunate	Very religious	Good listener
Never listens to anyone else's point of view	Know all	Gets away with murder
Will never grow up	Agrees with tax avoidance	Will make a good politician
Believes in life after death	Will make a good partner	Will end up in trouble

149

neighbourhood, type of home, modes of transport used, fashion etc. The written cards should depict personality characteristics, values, opinions and beliefs that a person may hold. The sets of cards need to be made up in quadruple so that a class can work in four groups. (See above)

Each group of pupils in a class should be given a set of pictorial and written cards mixed together in a large box or 'lucky dip'. Members of a group should aim to get a 'hand' which best describes the way they see themselves by playing a game akin to rummy, where each player takes a card from the deck, or from those discarded by others. When pupils have obtained a total of six cards that reflect their identity, they should leave the game. The cards should preferably include both pictorial and written examples. They should then consider why they chose the cards in their hand, and from where or whom they gained these views about themselves.

A second game can be played where pupils select cards to describe each other.

The box or deck of mixed cards should be placed in the centre of a group. Pupils should take turns in choosing a card from the pile and handing it to the person they think it fits best, giving reasons for so doing, saying "I think this suits you because....." The game should continue until all the cards are used up, and then the following evaluations can be made:

1. Who got the most cards?
2. How much agreement was there amongst the group about each individual member, to whom cards were allotted?
3. Did the group seem to know some members of their team better than others? Why?
4. Did some pupils get more of one type of card than others? Why?
5. Did the pupils who received the cards always agree with what was attributed to them. Why?

Where pupils disagree with their classmates view they should ask for clarification by the pupil who assigned a particular attribute. Others could then contribute to the discussion, as this will aid individual pupils to see themselves as others see them, which helps them form a more definite image of themselves. Following the card games, and questioning of pupils by each other, pupils

DEVELOPING SELF AWARENESS AND SELF IDENTITY

should take stock of the cards that have been allotted to them and make a list of things they agree
with and those they disagree with, using this type
of handout, having as many listings as relevant.

<u>PUPIL HANDOUT - ME AS I SEE MYSELF AND HOW OTHERS SEE ME</u>

VIEWS ABOUT ME	AGREE	DISAGREE	UNSURE ABOUT	INSIGHTS
1. Soft hearted	x			
2. Good listener		x		
3. Efficient			x	
4. Gets away with murder				x
5.				
6.				
7.				

How much did I know about myself? ....

What Insights did I gain? ....

How do I go about confirming/denying these things I'm not
  sure about?...

Am I pleased with what others have said about me?.............

151

DEVELOPING SELF AWARENESS AND SELF IDENTITY

Adolescents often use other significant people's views about them as ways of forming opinions about themselves, so beginning the process of forming a self identity. As part of their awareness programme they should discover what they know of the way they are perceived by parents, friends and teachers. One of the best ways of doing this is to use a rating scale for pupils to indicate their feelings and perceptions. Rating scales involve obtaining a set of phrases or words that can be used to describe people. These phrases and words should be obtained from the pupils themselves so that they are relevant and meaningful to the individual concerned. Instructions for constructing a rating scale are to be found in Chapter two. For the purposes of this task, it is useful to have two rating scales for children to complete. The first one should be a standard one for the class, and the phrases for the scale can be made up from some of the words given for writing on 'cards' in the previous section. To obtain additional phrases from the students, some helpful questions to ask them are:

Who can remember the first words your mother used to describe your looks?

What kinds of things do fathers say to describe their sons in terms of looks, habits, and their nature?

What sorts of words might grandparents use to talk about their grandchildren?

What kinds of comments have you received from teachers in your reports, or from them personally?

What kind of phrases would girls use to talk about boys and vice versa when discussing them with their close friends?

When the tutor has obtained sufficient words and phrases, a selection of twelve should be chosen for the class rating scale. Before the scale can be made up, pupils should be able to see the twelve phrases on the board, and begin to think of their opposite dimensions. When a majority decision has been reached as to which words will constitute the opposing dimension, this should be placed by the phrase concerned. Pupils then write in the phrases and their opposites on a prepared scale, giving at least 6 points between the polar phrases. Such a scale may look like this:

PUPILS HANDOUT ON SELF AWARENESS AND IDENTITY - PERSONALITY

Know All	1 2 3 4 5 6	Modest
Popular	1 2 3 4 5 6	Unpopular
Gets hurt easily	1 2 3 4 5 6	Tough skinned
Serious	1 2 3 4 5 6	Likes a good laugh
Flexible	1 2 3 4 5 6	Set in Ways
Will End up in trouble	1 2 3 4 5 6	Will always do the right thing
Good fun at parties	1 2 3 4 5 6	Kill joy
Will never grow up	1 2 3 4 5 6	Sensible/ mature
Can take criticism	1 2 3 4 5 6	Gets upset if criticised
lazy	1 2 3 4 5 6	Hard Working
Thoughtful	1 2 3 4 5 6	Thoughtless
Prejudiced	1 2 3 4 5 6	Open minded

DEVELOPING SELF AWARENESS AND SELF IDENTITY

The instructions for completion of the scale should be as follows:

> 'Using the colour blue for yourself, place a cross on the number that best describes your view about yourself, along each set of phrases opposite to each other. If you agree with the phrase nearer the number 1, then place a cross somewhere near that. If you agree with the phrase near the number 6, place your cross near the number that best shows your degree of feeling. There are no right and wrong answers. You have a whole six points to use to show exactly how you feel about yourself. When you have done that for all 12 phrases, join up all your blue crosses with your blue pencil.'

When pupils have completed this task, they should then be asked to complete the scale again for the following conditions, and using the specified colours, to distinguish each set of ratings.

(a) How my mother would rate me - red.
(b) How my father would rate me - green.
(c) How my best friend would rate me - yellow.
(d) How my girlfriend/boyfriend would rate me - black.
(e) How a teacher would rate me - brown.

Crosses for each colour should be joined up, and instantly the pattern of ratings will produce an impact on students. They should be asked to work out who they seem closest to in ratings, and whether that person had in fact influenced the pupils in their estimations of themselves.

Pupils can compare their ratings with their classmates, chosen at random, and attempt to find out whether there are any common elements in what parents may think of them, and what teachers may think of them.

Pupils can make up their own personal rating scale by choosing a set of phrases and their opposites from a 'luckydip' produced from the cards used in the previous section, and those contributed by class discussion. Apart from rating themselves on this unique scale, they can determine which others they wish to consider for rating purposes, e.g. siblings, enemies, neighbours etc.

Younger pupils may have difficulty deciding what other people think about them, or may not be willing to express it overtly through modesty or embarrassment. One way of helping them participate in this activity therefore, is to set them thinking about what impressions they think they give various people:

Who in school gets angry with you? Why? Why do you think you make this person angry? How do you know when this person is angry with you?

Who in your home makes you feel as if you are stupid? When do you feel this happens most often? Why?

What do you think your closest friend thinks of you as a friend? How do you know this? What sorts of things might you do to give this impression?

Does anyone make you feel as if you are good at anything? Who and what? How do they show this to you? What do you think you do to make them think well of you?

A set of reflective questions such as those above will put pupils on the right path to deciding what certain significant people in their lives think of them. It will also introduce them to the notion that other people form ideas of them based on their attitudes and behaviour. When this is fed back to the pupils in terms of comments, or some other expressed emotion, then they can assimilate and internalise some of that feedback to form their own opinions of themselves, (Wylie 1974). Other activities to help children to think about how they see themselves and how others see them can be found in Baldwin & Wells (1980, 1981).

During adolescence students affiliate themselves to various trends of fashion, music, leisure activities and beliefs about society, employment, marriage, the raising of families and sex roles. Pupils will each have a unique set of ideas on these issues which give rise to their notions about themselves, and consequently their identity. The above categories can be used to help pupils distinguish how each of them differs from others, and so has a separate identity. One method of doing this is to use newspaper headlines for stimulus material.

The tutor conducting this exercise should have ready a set of newspaper headlines about the following topics. Some possible types of headlines are given as illustrations:

(a) Youth employment - 'Youths Take Jobs From Family Men'.
(b) Behaviour at football matches - 'Teenage Lads Spoil Match Again'.
(c) Fashion - 'Boy Sent Home From School Because of His Hair Cut'.
(d) Smoking - 'Health Education in Schools Makes Youngsters Stop Smoking'.
(e) Sex roles - 'Fifteen Year Olds Still Feel That The Woman's Place is At Home'.
(f) Leisure - 'Young People Watch So Much Television That They Can No Longer Tell Fact From Fiction'.

Six topics should be enough to stimulate a class activity in this area. Taking each headline in turn, ask pupils to make a decision about whether they believe the statement, disbelieve it or are unsure, (don't know category). The classroom should have three designated areas to correspond to these categories, so that pupils can make their way to the appropriate spot. When this has been done for one headline, the tutor should note on the board the numbers in each group, and the ratio of boys to girls therein. When this has been done for a few headlines, pupils should begin to think about why they agreed or disagreed with the headline, as this is the process whereby they discover more about themselves, and so increase their level of self awareness. For each headline, the class should be divided into six groups. Three groups each should complete the handout below, for the 'agree' condition, while three should fill it in for the 'disagree' condition. Those pupils who were unable to make up their minds previously should be randomly allocated to the groups above, so that roughly equal numbers of them can listen to the arguments on both sides.

When completing their handouts, pupils will select certain characteristics that seem to fit in best with their belief system. They do not have to necessarily agree with all the issues involved, but a core of beliefs will emerge from which they form their identity. This needs to be emphasised by the tutor in the discussions that follow the completion of the handout.

To facilitate discussion, each group should elect a leader to act as their collator, and spokesperson. The leaders should take turns to inform

DEVELOPING SELF AWARENESS AND SELF IDENTITY

PUPIL HANDOUT ON INDIVIDUAL BELIEF SYSTEMS

We agree with the statement.............................

Other people who may believe this are likely to be

MALE   FEMALE   (delete as applicable)

They are likely to be in the age bracket................

They are likely to have .... type homes.

They are likely to enjoy .... in their social lives.

They are likely to have .... type jobs.

They are likely to read .... newspaper.

They are likely to belong to .... type of union.

They are likely to watch .... types of tele-
                                          vision pro-
                                          grammes.

Their personalities may have the following characteristics:

Underline as appropriate:

Racialist   Broad Minded   Insecure   Ignorant

Intellectual   Family minded   Permissive   Prejudiced

Fun loving   Stick in the mud   Trendy   Old Fashioned

Loyal   Frightened   Sensitive   Hard Working   Lazy

Thoughtful   Impulsive   Straight laced   Selfish   Open-

minded   Critical   Optimistic   Disillusioned   Articulate

Inarticulate   Calm   Fiery   Uncaring   Very caring

DEVELOPING SELF AWARENESS AND SELF IDENTITY

the class of their opinions about each statement,
one headline at a time. The others from within
a group should be encouraged to support their leader
by giving reasons and evidence for their views.
Groups who had identical handouts to fill in, i.e.
in the 'agree' or 'disagree' conditions, need to
take stock of the similarities that appear for
the same condition. However for the sake of clarity, each group with the 'agree' category should
mark down similarities in red, while the groups
with the 'disagree' condition should use blue.
Groups should then make a tally of the similarities
and differences that emerge. The tutor must then
make a very large chart in the front of the class
to accommodate all the views for each statement.
Pupils can then be asked to glean any pattern that
may be evident amongst the responses from their
work. Some questions to help them are given below:

Which of the factors on the handouts seem to distinguish between those who agreed with the headline,
and those who disagreed?

Are there any behavioural characteristics, which
distinguish the groups? For instance, the television they watch, or the papers they read?

Which of the personality characteristics separate
the two groups?

Which of the issues in the handout did pupils from
this class identify most with? E.g. type of homes
lived in.

Each individual pupil should be asked to consider
which group they come closest to in personality,
behaviour, and where they live etc. Is that what
they would have expected? Why? If not, how close
did they come to being identical to one of these
groups?

On what kinds of things do pupils differ most?
Are they matters of personality, or leisure activities, or habits at home?

Each pupil could be asked to draw up a portfolio
of themselves using all the headings in the handout,
and compare it to the responses of the groups for
both conditions.
    Those who were not able to make up their minds
in the first stage of this exercise, should next

be asked to inspect their personal portfolios and make a decision about which camp they are likely to come into, giving some reasons as to why they have been swayed one way or another. They should also be asked to give some instances of things they have learned about themselves that they were not aware of previously. The tutor can aid this process of self discovery, by placing three headings on the board, under which these pupils can make some responses:

Things Accepted   Things Rejected   Things Neutral About

Under each heading, the children in the 'don't know' group could list the issues that pertain to their judgements. The class can then witness first hand, how children of their age chose an identity for themselves on the basis of a few issues. The class should be encouraged to question the 'don't know' group about their reasons for selecting or rejecting items. The neutral category too, can provide useful information on the ways in which pupils decide to give priority to specific topics in their search for a self identity. If the class is not immediately forthcoming with questions, the tutor could begin with some of these:

Did the pupils in the 'don't know' group make rational judgements? If so, how can they demonstrate this?

Did these pupils act emotionally in their decision making? How can this be shown?

How much freedom of choice did they think they had in making a decision?

What kinds of pressures did they feel when choosing items?

How did they try to resolve their doubts, and conflicts?

How many preconceived ideas did they already have about some of these items, before listening to the rest of the class discuss and argue their points of view?

Do they like what they have discovered about themselves?

DEVELOPING SELF AWARENESS AND SELF IDENTITY

How stereotyped were their responses?

The questions above are of course equally suitable to pose to the class as a whole, although the age at which these sorts of questions are likely to be meaningful probably restricts itself to between fourteen and sixteen years of age. The activity itself can be carried out with children from form three onwards, with items in the headlines changed to suit the interests of that year group. It may be a valuable exercise to repeat these activities at least twice in the life of secondary school pupils to indicate to them that self awareness increases with age, and that identity is always changing, developing and evolving. This can be done in a way that would maintain the interest of the pupils and tutor, by alternating between the three activities presented in the preceding part of this chapter.

Where Did Self Identity Come From?

If pupils have taken part in the previous activities they should now be ready to discover details of who and what influenced their identity. At this stage pupils should be able to give some indication of WHO they think they are, WHAT they are, and WHY they hold some of the views that they do. The next step is to look at which factors have played a part in establishing that self awareness and self concept.

Basically there are four broad influences on young people in the formation of the self identity. These are the Home, School, Peers and Media. Each of these can be taken in turn by each pupil and used as a heading under which to list what aspects of their lives have been influenced by that factor. This can be done initially in four groups, each taking one of the above headings. The groups will need some topics to consider, and a variety can be given to them from the list below. These items also appear on a pupil handout for completion by individuals after group discussion. The instructions to each group are as follows:

'We all developed our ideas about things that are important to us from a variety of sources. Some of us lay more store by one set of opinions, while others of us may be more inclined to pay attention to another set of ideas, depending on where they came from.

In the end we come to our own conclusions, but they are compiled from bits of information we have received from lots of sources. This activity is to help you find out who has influenced your ideas most, about some important topics. Take at least three from the list for your group and discuss where you think you might have got some of your ideas from. To do this, you will of course have to tell each other, what it is you think about these topics in the first instance!'

FAMILY PLANNING   CIGARETTES   POETS   EUTHANASIA
THE THIRD WORLD   BATCHELORS   THE POLICE
HANDICAPPED PEOPLE   SPACE PROGRAMMES   COMPUTERS
MARRIAGE   FOREIGN PEOPLE   POLITICS
HEALTH FOOD   PROFESSIONAL SPORTSMEN
AGE OF CONSENT   DO IT YOURSELF ENTHUSIASTS

After about 20 minutes of discussion, individuals should be asked to exchange some of their ideas with one other group so that cross fertilization of views can occur. This will also help those children who tend to be quiet and who do not make up their minds until the last minute. The more they listen to their peers, the richer their responses will be when they come to filling in this handout.

The results of the responses on the pupil handout could stimulate a great deal of discussion about the role of the various sources of influence on children. Some trigger questions to channel their thoughts are given below:

How surprised are you about what type of things/people seem to influence you?

What surprised you most? Why?

Are you happy with the results? For instance, if you found that the media most influenced you, is that what you valued?

Did you try to make out that a certain party didn't have as much influence over you as the group seemed to make out? Why? What did you not like about it?

How accurate do you think your opinions really are? Did you give credit where it was due?

DEVELOPING SELF AWARENESS AND SELF IDENTITY

<u>PUPIL HANDOUT - FROM WHOM AND FROM WHERE DID I GET MY IDEAS
ABOUT MYSELF AND OTHER IMPORTANT TOPICS</u>

View	Gained From	Balance of Influence
1. About work		
2. About children		
3. About my looks		
4. About my weight		
5. About music		
6. About books		
7. About owning a home		
8. About the opposite sex		
9. About clothes		
10. About animal rights		
11. About marriage		
12. About the value of education		
13. About family planning		
14. About alcohol		
15. About cigarettes		
16. About personal hygiene		
17. About food & health		
18. About war		
19. About sexual equality		
20. About foreign people		

TOTAL MEDIA INFLUENCE =   TOTAL HOME INFLUENCE =
TOTAL PEER INFLUENCE =   TOTAL SCHOOL INFLUENCE =

Did you find that someone/something you cared for influenced you to have a view that wasn't very pleasant? For instance, did you discover that your parents may have negative views about sexual equality, and that you had taken on the same view without really realising it?

How stable do you think your views are? Do you think you have always held certain of your opinions, or have you changed some with age?

Who is the strongest influence on you at this moment in time, and why?

What topics have you changed your mind on, as you have grown older?

Do you think that young people are likely to get more staid and traditional in their views as they get older? Why?

Have you noticed anything like this in your parents, or older relatives?

On what sort of topics do people become conservative about as they grow older?

How much did the fact that you WANTED to be different to either or both of your parents, influence your views?

Are all the pupils in the class influenced in the same way about the same issue? If not, why not?

If you knew that somebody or something was influencing you at the time, would you try to counteract it? Why?

Do you think that parents should be the major influence over their children? Does it depend on the quality of parenting, or on whether their thinking was in line with the majority in society?

How would a pupil know whether they had been influenced in a good or bad way?

If you could change any of your feelings about yourself, which ones, and how would you go about doing it?

DEVELOPING SELF AWARENESS AND SELF IDENTITY

When Did Pupils Begin to Take on An Identity and Form an Image of Themselves?

At various times in their development children begin to attribute certain priorities to aspects of their lives. Montemayor & Eisen (1977) maintain that while younger children describe themselves in terms of concrete objective categories such as physical appearance and possessions, older adolescents use more abstract, subjective terminology to describe their self image, such as personal beliefs and motivation. It would be a useful exercise for pupils in their secondary school careers to trace this development in themselves so that they promote their level of self awareness.

Towards the end of their first year in comprehensive school pupils have usually adjusted well to their new setting, and begin to take on the mantle of a secondary school pupil. They will have undergone several changes of self image and identity as a result. They might find it quite an amusing and astonishing task to look more closely at what sort of perceptions they had of themselves just before they began at their new school, when they arrived and how that has changed over the year.

Some of the categories this age group might relate to are given below:

Looks	Skills	Likes and Dislikes
Too fat/thin	Sports	Food
Colour of clothes	Crafts	People
Style of clothes	Music	Places to go to
Hair styles	Domestic	Subjects in school
Jewellery		Television programmes
Make up		Music

Pupils could produce a type of biography of themselves using these categories, and complete these sentences for specified ages:

Age 9:   I used to think I was good at.............
&   I used to wear........................

DEVELOPING SELF AWARENESS AND SELF IDENTITY

Age 10	I used to like eating.....................
&	I used to like going to..................
Age 11	I used to like doing........in my spare time.
	I was a ....person with my friends.
	I used to look like.....................
	I was mad about ....pop group.

The same categories can be used again to indicate the present state of affairs, and in that way a comparison can be built up over the ages from nine to twelve. Pupils may like to complement their self histories with some cartoon drawings of themselves on a long strip of paper divided into ages, showing the difference pupils see in themselves in terms of dress, friendships, hobbies etc.

Older pupils in the fourth and fifth years probably have developed some firm views about their looks, the kind of image they want to project in terms of appearance, and activities that they excel or fail at. They may be able to indicate at what age they first began to hold views about themselves in these categories. Distinctions between boys and girls can form the basis for a useful insight into the relative maturity of the two sexes in adolescence. This task can be done using a roulette wheel on which can be placed words depicting topics to which the pupils could respond. The pupils need to be working in groups of six for this activity, each group with one wheel. Pupils should take turns to spin the wheel, and should make a response to the topic that the wheel stops at, by noting down two things:

(a) I think I am/feel/can ....
(b) I first felt this when I was ....old.

For instance, if the wheel stops at the word EXAMS, then the pupil concerned could indicate a view such as 'I think exams are only suitable for the brainy, and they don't really help you get jobs. I first began to think this at the end of my fourth year in school, at the age of 15, when I discovered that many of my mates who had recently left school with good qualifications didn't manage to get any jobs'.

Some useful words to put on the wheel include:

Shyness	Obesity	Makeup
Flirting	Contraceptives	Pets

DEVELOPING SELF AWARENESS AND SELF IDENTITY

Athletics	Smokers	Disco dancing
Bookworms	Violence	Drinking
Exams	Employment	Popularity
Karati	Drama	Acne
Junk Food	Religion	Siblings
Parents	Pocket Money	Careers

Each group should be encouraged to add some items of their own so that the task becomes as relevant to them as possible. Each individual within a group needs to accumulate at least six sets of views on different topics before the class gets together to collate its information and draw out at what ages they began to form their opinions. The teacher should categorise the topics under some broad headings, and then allow the pupils to give the ages at which they think they began to hold firm beliefs on these items. A table on the blackboard when completed, would look like this:

AGES AT WHICH WE BEGAN TO FORM OUR IDENTITIES

TOPIC	BOYS	GIRLS
Looks	10-13 yrs.	7-12 yrs.
Fashion	12-16 yrs.	9-16 yrs.
Marriage	15-16 yrs.	12-16 yrs.
Hobbies	10-13 yrs.	11-13 yrs.

The class could then consider whether boys and girls differ on any of these dimensions to a significant degree, and if so why? They could discuss whether boys and girls have different views on such issues as marriage, and looks, and how they came to hold these views. The topic can be related to previous activities on what sort of things influenced self identity. The class needs also to think about which issues boys and girls do not differ from as groups and why?

Changing Relationships

Most youngsters have to face changes in the family structure and relationships as they grow up. These range from the more usual changes such as older siblings leaving home, the addition of new babies into a household, or older relatives coming to live with a family. In addition, one quarter of babies born today are likely to experience

a separation of their parents before they reach
school leaving age (Richards 1983). Each year
there are 150,000 divorces in England and Wales,
and 60% of these involve children. Remarriage
rates are equally high, and one third of those
involve a partner who has been married before,
and who may bring other children into their new
marriage. Second marriages are twice as likely
to end as first marriages, which means that the
proportion of children with step and half siblings
must be quite staggering. Berry (1981) gives a
figure of 180,000 children a year involved in divorce proceedings, some of whom are witnessing the
break up of their second or third families. It
is not uncommon for children within a household
to have many different surnames, and the emotional
traumas that go along with these sorts of happenings
gives rise to confusions of identity, depression,
and lack of self esteem among adolescents (Walczac
& Burns 1984; Douglas 1970; Robinson 1980; Richards
& Dyson 1982).

However one wishes to interpret the statistics,
depending on demographic circumstances, schools
will have a large proportion of students who are
undergoing difficulties in their social and
emotional lives which may give rise to behaviour
problems. Richards (1983) states that adolescents
react to changes in their relationships, especially
parental separation by showing anger and finding
it very difficult to express their feelings. Holmes
& Rahe (1967) show that changing relationships
constitute one of the most serious personal adjustments an individual has to make in life. Schools
in their pastoral role should therefore provide
the opportunity for pupils to express their concerns
about changing family relationships. By doing
so, schools can lessen the likelihood of children
growing up with poorly adjusted personalities.
They can help prevent some of the usual reactions
from pupils to unbearable alterations within their
families, such as school refusal or acting out
behaviour in school.

The case of a twelve and a half year old boy
David, is an example of changing relationships
causing a breakdown in self identity, and resulting
in poor adjustment in the secondary school, leading
to school refusal. David was the second child
of his mother, born out of wedlock. He had an
older brother who was the only child of his mother's
first marriage. Both had different surnames. His
mother married again, and had two other children.

167

David's stepfather brought with him some of his children by a previous marriage, the others remaining with their mother. David never knew who his natural father was. He felt ousted in his mother's affections, and resented her for having so many men in her life, and for drinking heavily. David's behaviour at home was difficult for his mother and stepfather to control. He tried hard to please his mother by doing odd jobs for her, but never got the recognition he craved, and so behaved in a problematic manner. His mother sent him to his grandmother to be looked after from time to time. By the time David began secondary school he chose to live with his grandmother who suffered from Multiple Sclerosis. He began to show distress when in school about the health of his grandmother, and his fear of being taken into Care as his grandmother may not have been deemed able to look after him. When at home, he refused to go to school. If forced to go, he would run away, or behave in a manner that required great supervision from a sympathetic member of staff. David had no identity to speak of, and his emotional needs were so great that he could not really give priority to school. Clearly this is a tragic case, but one which is by no means unusual among the child population of today.

Another case of a fifteen year old girl called Maxine shows how disturbing a time adolescents can face when they are unsure of their identity because of changes in relationships. Maxine's mother had been brought up in Care, after being rejected by her own parents. She had Maxine and another daughter at a very young age, both by different men. Some years later, when Maxine was on the threshold of adolescence, her mother married a coloured man, and had two children by him. Maxine was adopted by her mother's husband, but never knew who her real father was.

The marriage between Maxine's mother and her husband was violent, and Maxine received little fathering from her adoptive father. During her secondary school career the relationships in her home between herself and her mother became very strained. Maxine began to run away, and incidents of disruptive behaviour in school increased in frequency and severity. Maxine had not given vent to her feelings about the relationships at home and how they effected her. She never got to grips with her self identity, and had a very poor self image. By the time Maxine was fifteen, she was

Relationship with	What it used to be like	What it is Changing into
Mother		
Father		
Brother		
Sister		
Aunt		
Uncle		
Grandmother		
Cousin		
Nephew		
Step Sister		
Half Brother		
Step Parent		

The Most Change is with ....

It seems to be for the ....

I am most Worried about the Change in Relationship
with ....

unable to express her confusion verbally, and continued to display her disturbance and lack of identity by behaving in a disruptive manner in school, which eventually led to her suspension. Perhaps if she had been given the chance to think about and express her feelings earlier on, she might not have been so uncommunicative and allowed someone to help her at the most opportune time.

Pastoral work can play a very important role in helping children discover their own feelings and come to terms with them as they grow up. It is often the secondary school who has to deal with growing awareness in its pupils, of relationships and their intricacies, and of the adolescent's quest for an identity and positive self image. This task can be made easier if it is given prominence in any pastoral programme. The tutor undertaking this job can begin by asking pupils to make a list of those within their families whom they consider important enough to warrant considering in terms of changing relationships. The people on the list should then be ranked in order of priority depending on the significance attached to the change in the relationship as seen by the pupil. Pupils should be asked to think about when the changes occurred or are likely to occur, the span of time over which it will change, and when the changes first become apparent. The handout above should aid pupils in this exercise.

The pupils should work in groups of four, each with their own individual handout. However it is important that they exchange ideas, and find out from each other what sort of changes they are experiencing. This will help those with high anxiety levels by reasasuring them that some of the difficulties they experienced or are experiencing are in fact quite common.

The people referred to in the handout should obviously be made up of the individual pupil's own list of significant people. The ones in the handout are given as examples only.

When pupils have completed their handouts, the tutor should collect a class tally of changes which pupils report. On the blackboard a list needs to be made of those relationships that seem to change often, and are the most frequently changing amongst the group of children in the class. The information can then be used to instigate a discussion. Some trigger questions for the pupils are presented below:

With which members of the family do relationships seem to be ALREADY changing?

Do these relationships seem to have changed for better or worse?

When did pupils first begin to become aware of these changes? How old were they?

Who began to institute these changes?

How quickly or gradually did these changes occur?

In what way did the changes manifest themselves? Did the people concerned talk to each other less, or more often; did they avoid each other or seek each other out more often; were remarks made to each other more hurtful or caring in nature? Were any jealousies involved etc.?

With whom did relationships change least over the years, why?

To whom did pupils seem to have been closer - the ones with whom relationships were changing now, or to those with whom little change was reported?

What kind of conclusions can they draw about personal relationships from the answers to the question above? Why?

What kind of emotions are experienced when relationships change for the WORSE with someone they feel/felt close to?

How do these emotions effect their daily lives - e.g. lack of concentration, inertia, overactivity, loss of appetite, overeating, loss of performance on tasks, tearfulness, needing to be around people, wanting to be alone etc.

With whom do relationships seem to be changing NOW? Why?

How do individual pupils feel about their current changing relationships within the family, compared to changes in friendships, and in school?

Are these changes part of young people wanting to become more independent and so part of growing up, or are they serious breakdowns in the family?

DEVELOPING SELF AWARENESS AND SELF IDENTITY

How can adolescents tell the difference between
strains in relations due to their rights in exerting
their own individuality, and genuine disturbances
between family members?

Are any of these changes part of an already deterio-
rating relationship with certain members of the
family? Do some relationships just get worse over
time? If so, which ones and why?

How do alterations in relationships with parents
compare to those with friends and boyfriends/girl-
friends? Which ones are most upsetting, Why?

Length of Time Over Which Changes Take Place

Using the same format as above, the tutor should
collect data about how long pupils feel that relationships with members of the family have been
changing, by asking these questions:

With whom have relationships been forever changing?

With whom has there been a constant and steady
change in relationship?

With whom has there been spiky and intermittent
changes? Over what period of time?

Which changes, over what period of time, have caused
the most upset or happiness?

Once these questions have been answered, individual pupils should construct a graph to depict
their own personal information. Pupils can work
in groups to help each other present the data in
the best way. An example of such a graph is given
below:

Consequences of Changes Within Family Relationships

Not all the results of relationship changes are
easy to cope with, or equally beneficial to all
those concerned. In order to increase the awareness
of pupils about the manner in which people cope
with changes, it is important that they reflect
on the consequences of such changes. Pupils also
need to learn about the different ways which their
peers cope with changes, especially those which
give rise to unpleasant emotions. Learning about
different ways of handling emotions is a

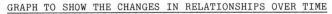

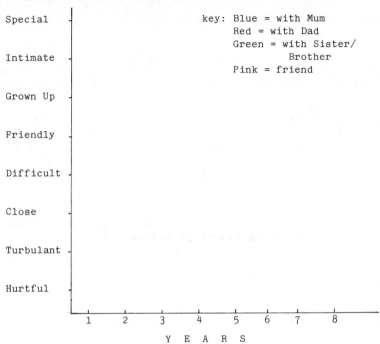

GRAPH TO SHOW THE CHANGES IN RELATIONSHIPS OVER TIME

key: Blue = with Mum
Red = with Dad
Green = with Sister/
Brother
Pink = friend

very necessary skill that youngsters should be introduced to, as failure to do so, could lead to stress and ill health (Cox 1978; Levi 1975). Stress is dealt with in more detail in the next chapter, but for the purpose of getting pupils to consider their feelings when relationships change, some useful questions to set them on the right path are as follows:

Who suffers most when children grow up, and begin to lead independent lives? Is it parents, grand-parents, siblings or any others? Why?

Does it depend on how strong or weak the people were in their natures in the first place? Can pupils give examples to illustrate their answers?

Which of the two sexes suffer the most in family relationships which go wrong?

173

DEVELOPING SELF AWARENESS AND SELF IDENTITY

How does the level of employment effect suffering
in this area? Can pupils give examples from their
own families or those that they are familiar with?

How do members of the family cope with others coming
into their midst? e.g. girlfriends, boyfriends,
in laws, step relations etc. Who has to do the
most adjusting? Why?

What kind of people find it easy to adjust, and
what kind of people find it tough to accept new
members into their families? Why? Can any pupils
give an example from their own lives?

What personal adjustments if any have pupils had
to make to additions or subtractions to their families?

How do children who have to make frequent adjustments try to cope with their feelings?   E.g. a
parent walking out, but coming back often?

        To assist pupils to consider in greater depth
how adolescents may react to alterations in relationships, some stimulus material would be helpful. The cartoon strips depicting family life
in Skynner & Cleese (1983) would provide a useful
source. In addition, two examples are given below
for pupils to work with. Both are based on fact.
The class should be divided into four groups, two
groups having case 1, and two groups having case
2 to discuss.

Case 1: Steven is a thirteen year old boy who lives
with his parents, and one sister. When he was
a baby, his parents both worked long hours and
he was looked after by his grandmother. He was
very fond of her, and thought of her as his mother,
often calling her by that name. When he was six,
his sister was born. Steven returned to his household full time, but did not like to compete with
his sister for his parent's affection. He took
every opportunity to be with his grandmother, as
she made him feel very special, and did most things
for him whereas when he was at home he had to fend
for himself, particularly when he was in the junior
school. When he got to the comprehensive school
he used to have many arguments with his mother
about going to school. He felt angry with her
for moving him from his grandmother's house. He
used to try to make his parents fed up with him,

so that they would allow him to go and live with his grandmother again. He didn't get on with his sister, and was very jealous of the affection and praise which she received from his parents. He used to try to act in a very babyish manner in the hope that his parents would do things for him, and give him some of that affection too.

Case 2: Sheila is a fourteen year old girl living with her parents and a younger sister. She likes school and does quite well in her lessons. Recently she has felt like running away from home, and has been threatening her mother that she will in fact take this action. She says that she feels unloved, and that her parents don't understand her. Her father works nights in a hospital, and her mother works for three days a week in a local shop. Sheila complains that her parents never have time to listen to her when she wants to discuss something with them, but they always have time for her younger sister who has an unfortunate illness which makes her very weak. Sheila would like to get close to her parents especially her father, but he is more interested in having a good relationship with his wife. A few years ago Sheila's grandmother died, and both she and her mother grieved a lot, getting little support from dad. The father feels deeply but finds it difficult to show it, often making Sheila angry, and gives her the impression that he doesn't love her. She wants to show them her distress, and is thinking about going into Care.

The groups discussing these cases need to consider these points:

1. How does the young person think of him/herself in the situation he/she finds him/herself in?
Does he/she think he/she is a worthwhile person, well loved and liked or not?
Why does he/she think about him/herself in this way?
2. How does the person concerned adjust to all the changes in emotions in his/her family?
3. What sort of strengths do they need to help them cope with their feelings?
4. What should each of them do in order to resolve their troubles?
5. Which of the ways pupils suggest might work best, and why?

6.   If pupils belonged to such a group of young people, how would they feel and manage those feelings?

The two groups who were looking at Case 1 should then get together and exchange their ideas and feelings about the youngster concerned. One pupil should collate all the information and present it to the other two groups who were considering Case 2. The pupils listening, should ask questions of those presenting their information, trying to discover why they suggested certain outcomes and methods of resolving the uncomfortable emotions. If they find this somewhat difficult, the tutor can help them out by asking a simple question to begin the discussion. The groups considering Case 2 should then present their case, giving reasons for their decisions and suggestions. Efforts should be made by the tutor to bring out the effects on the individual's self worth, and self image, such as how the individual concerned came to think of him/herself in terms of the place in the family, his/her 'lovability' and self confidence.

Boosting the Self Concept

In the process of partaking in some of the previous activities pupils will have indicated to their tutor whether they have a fairly good image of themselves or not. The tutor will be in a good position to discover which aspects of pupils' lives are contributing to their poor self concept, and set up some experiences for them to boost their self worth. This is a very important task for the school to undertake not just for the benefit of the pupils own personal development, but also because the school work of such children is known to suffer, (Purkey 1978).   In addition pupils who go through school thinking of themselves in a negative light are more likely to behave in ways that could be termed maladaptive in their search for a more positive self image, and so produce some management problems for staff. Phillips (1963) indicates the importance of the role of the teacher in promoting positive feelings of self esteem in young people. Some of the ways in which schools and teachers can undertake the task of improving the self worth of pupils can be found in Canfield & Wells (1976); Sears & Sherman (1964); Coopersmith & Feldman (1974) and Elardo & Cooper (1977). Most of the techniques for enhancing self

esteem and self concept involve encouraging individual pupils to focus on their positive points,
and for the pupils from within a class to make
complementary remarks about their peers on the
basis of their observations. The latter is sometimes known as the giving of 'positive strokes',
which are of immense importance for healthy personal
adjustment and interpersonal interaction (Berne
1968; 1972; Barker & Phillips 1981).

1. Focusing on Positive Self Attributes

Pupils should be asked to keep a diary in which
they could record certain events that had occurred
which made them feel good, and so help them think
of themselves in pleasant ways.

(a) The diary could be divided into various
sections under which pupils could make notes. The
subheadings may include: Things people have said
about my Looks; Things people have said about my
Taste; Things said about my Thoughtfulness; Things
said about my Humour and Personality; Something
I did which made me feel useful; Some achievement
I gained at home/school/club etc.

(b) Pupils need to be able to see that things
they once thought they could not do or were afraid
to do have in fact been done, and were coped with
when the need arose. This will make them realise
that they have got strengths which come to their
rescue when needed. They can do this task by making
a list of items they were afraid to tackle over
various spans of time, e.g. a year ago, three months
ago, last week, and yesterday. These items need
not be attempting new feats but everyday occurrences
such as having the courage to speak to someone
in authority; going to a disco; being able to say
'no' when it was necessary; moving to a new class/
house; saving money for a particular purpose; coping
with criticism or teasing and preparing for an
activity by a particular time. When this has been
done, they should take each one in turn and discover
how they managed to think positively and how they
achieved the desired outcome.

(c) Pupils often do not appreciate the value
of some of their actions, perhaps because they
do not get immediate rewards or praise. They may
as a result expect much more of themselves, believ-
ing that all their past actions have little merit.
It would be useful if once a week they could note
down any activities which they took part in that
they did not have to do, but performed out

of choice. Such acts may include being loyal to a friend or member of the family; being considerate; taking second place in something; befriending a lonely person; taking action in a crisis; buying gifts for someone; helping in the house without being asked; being polite; taking care of animals and plants etc. Pupils may need a little prompting to think of these mundane actions, but when they have made a list of their own behaviours it should boost their self opinions.

2. Giving 'Positive Strokes'

(a) Arrange the class in a large circle. Choose one child to begin the task of saying one nice thing about the person on his/her right. This can be done in several stages, beginning with looks, and moving onto courage, aptitude, friendliness, energy, talents etc. Pupils should give instances when the person on their right showed courage or displayed a talent and so on.

(b) Pair up all the pupils in the class with children of the same sex (as pupils of secondary school age often get embarrassed when working with or sitting near a member of the opposite sex). Ask each one to observe the other for a week and report in a notebook all the good points they can. Some headings under which to make these notes would include: patience, unselfish behaviour; punctuality; effort in work; sharing equipment etc. The pupils should exchange their notes at the beginning of the following week. The pairs of pupils within the class can be constantly changed, so that any one pupil is either being observed or is watching a new individual every week. The headings too can be changed to suit the pupils' perspective.

(c) Select groups of three pupils for this task. Pupils must take turns in making statements about themselves which they believe, but which aren't very complementary. The person sitting opposite this pupil has the task of contradicting every negative comment that is made, until the first pupil can no longer sustain the poor opinion of him or herself. The third pupil should sit on the side of these pupils, noting how long it takes for the first pupil to 'giveup' being derogatory about him or herself. This observer pupil should also note the reaction of the first student to being countered on all his/her remarks. Each pupil in the group must have a turn at playing all three roles described. When they have completed one session they must exchange information on reactions noticed, and times involved in the exercise. It may be necessary for the tutor and one other student to demonstrate this activity before all the children appreciate the roles they have to play.

Personal Needs and How They Are Fulfilled

Human beings have two types of 'need'. The first concerns basic primary needs for food, warmth, and shelter. The second type refers to higher order needs which involve the quest for love, self esteem and self-actualization, or to be and do what one is best fitted for. Maslow (1968; 1970) developed a model of needs hierarchy, whereby when a person's basic needs are being taken care of they attempt to satisfy their higher order needs, which are uniquely human. Most adolescents are pursuing the latter. However they are not always aware of their needs in these categories and often choose harmful ways of fulfilling their needs. Hawton et al (1982 a,b,c.) indicate that adolescents have recently taken to overdosing and other forms of self abuse in an effort to gain relief from distress, and to indicate their state of mind to others. The kind of problems that led to these incidents of self abuse related to difficulties in school (56%) quarrels with boyfriends or girlfriends (50%); and with parents (28%). The incidence of teenagers abusing alcohol, solvents, drugs, or committing acts of vandalism and delinquency is also quite high, (O'Conner 1984; Rutter & Giller 1983), and reflects largely on the fact that their needs for love, belonging and self esteem are not being satisfied in more constructive ways.
   Sometimes adolescents become DEPENDENT on the very behaviour they chose in order to call attention to a thwarted need, and their desire to continue along these paths supercedes everything else for a while. While health education in school offers an important source of prevention, the techniques often require youngsters to think of the future, which for most young people is not a realistic proposition. They often want immediate relief from their problems and the long term consequences of drinking, smoking or taking drugs are not of concern at the time they are facing their difficulties. Educating children to consider what their needs are, and how to go about fulfilling them is a much more powerful way of assisting

youngsters to lead healthy and well adjusted lives.

Youngsters will all recognise that they have certain needs, and will be able to participate in discussions involving the various means which people use to satisfy them, be they good or bad. They may not be willing or able to admit or even acknowledge that they are likely to have a drink problem, or one of solvent abuse, especially if a member of their family is known to have such a problem. However they can be made aware of the unique features of their own personalities and coping strategies that could lead them to certain harmful methods of fulfilling needs.

The task of the pastoral team in school should be to alert pupils to become more attuned to their needs, and to critically evaluate whether they go about gratifying them in the most constructive ways. The time to conduct such sessions on personal needs will have to depend on the tutor's assessment of the pupils, but it is recommended that the end of the third year and upwards is the most suitable time. Most pupils will need much structure and prompting in order to take part in and benefit from the job of examining their personal needs. A useful way to begin this process is to present them with a list of possible social and emotional needs, and let them prepare answers about how they might be catered for. Such a list is given in the pupil handout on Personal Needs.

Before filling in the chart it may be advantageous to prime pupils by having a brainstorming session, whereby members of the class call out all the ways in which people might satisfy their needs. These ideas should be written on the board in random order as they come from the students. It may be necessary to stimulate pupils by using a few trigger questions:

What do you do if you are feeling fed up?

What do you do if you are trying to make something or do something that doesn't come out the way you hoped?

What might you do if you are really unhappy?

What happens at home if one person cannot get their own way?

Some of the possible responses the tutor may receive are given below. If they are not

DEVELOPING SELF AWARENESS AND SELF IDENTITY

PUPIL HANDOUT ON PERSONAL NEEDS AND FULFILLING THEM

Needs	Satisfied by
To be popular	
To be liked	
To be useful	
To have something to live for	
To care for someone	
To feel important to someone	
To feel special to someone	
To feel part of my community	
To escape from depression	
To avoid tellings off	
To avoid being hurt	
To avoid hurting other people	
To get instant enjoyment	
To be needed	
To be missed when I'm not around	
To get attention	
To get affection	
To ease my frustrations	
To forget painful memories	
To make time go quicker	
To ease boredom	
To look handsome/beautiful	
To get in with the 'in crowd'	
To be the same as my mates	
To feel that my opinion is valued	
To have a purpose in life	
To feel that I control my own life	

forthcoming, the tutor can write these on the board
for pupils to work with:

Work   Wash   Shout   Run away   Read   Watch T.V.
Eat too much   Take tablets   Tell lies   Smoke
Play an instrument   Join a club   Drink
Go and be with other people   Smash plates
Give away money   Buy Gifts   Sniff glue/gas
Play a game   Put on the record player

When pupils have each completed their individual handouts, they can divide into groups of
four to compare notes. They should note how many
different ways each of them had of satisfying a
particular need, and if there were any common ones
among the group. Next they should make a list
of those things that are acceptable to themselves
and society at large. For instance is it acceptable
to become a 'workaholic' to fulfil one's need to
have a purpose in life? Is it harmful to run away
if you want to satisfy your need to be needed and
missed? To whom are some of these actions harmful?
Can pupils distinguish between harming themselves
and harming others even indirectly e.g. making
their parents worry if they take drugs, or sniff
glue? Have any pupils experimented with any of
the activities which the class have deemed unacceptable? What were the circumstances that led
up to it, and how far did they go? Did they manage
to prevent themselves from being harmed or badly
affected? What sorts of things did they say to
themselves to stop any undesirable actions hurting
themselves or others?
The tutor should ensure that at least four
pupils give some account of their attempts
to satisfy their needs in ways that their peers
have labelled unacceptable. The questions above
can lead the pupils concerned into giving an in-
sightful picture. The most practical point to
emphasise is how pupils managed to talk themselves
out of indulging in undesirable behaviours. If
there are any pupils who claim that they were not
able to exert any self control, and for instance
got drunk 'to be the same as my mates', then the
differences between the first set of pupils and
this second set should be drawn up and used by
pupils to help them in the next part of the task.

DEVELOPING SELF AWARENESS AND SELF IDENTITY

Discovering Risk Factors For People Who Might
Satisfy Their Needs in Harmful Ways

From the previous discussions pupils should be
able to construct a checklist of factors that would
indicate an 'at risk' individual. This activity
can be done in groups, with each group taking one
heading under which they can list between six to
ten risk factors. The class should be divided
into six groups, and each should be given one of
the following categories with one or two factors
written underneath, just to start the group off
on their task. Instructions to the pupils are:

> 'Some people are more likely to choose actions
> in order to indulge their needs which we have
> decided are probably harmful to themselves,
> and to their families. These people are at
> risk from hurting themselves and those close to
> them. There are many factors that influence
> whether or not they will have a greater likeli-
> hood of taking up dangerous habits. We can
> call these "risk factors". Let us see how
> many of these risk factors we can isolate
> so that we can make up a checklist for people
> at risk.'

Headings:

Type of Neighbourhood		**Wealth/Affluence**
Leisure facilities		Pocket money/wage
Housing		Own transport
Family Relationships		**Personality**
Numbers in a family		Gets bored easily
Copying a parent		Impatient
Violence/frequent rows		Loner
Employment		**Skills/Attributes**
Availability		Imaginative with materials/or not
Level of employment in the family		Needs things done for him/her

When each group has completed its list, they should pin it up on a large sheet of paper in the front of the class, so that all the work of the pupils is visible to the students. The next task for the pupils is to imagine that they are community workers trying to discover all those young people at risk in their neighbourhoods. They are to work in teams of three with one as the leader. Can each team draw up their own checklist of 'at risk factors' to help them in their search for the young people? When each team has made up their list, they should compare it with others, and the class as a whole should choose the best to be properly printed or typed by the school. The pupils can then use that list to suggest ways in which they could help individuals at risk. They could do this by making up advertisements to warn young people against the dangers of using drugs, smoking etc. But part of their task MUST be to offer alternative advice for those people who need to fulfil some of their aspirations, but who are not sure of the constructive ways of so doing. Other activities which perhaps classes and tutors can join in on are the formation of 'advice teams' and 'agony aunt' figures for those in trouble. They would have to be chosen by the members from the relevant classes, where two or more classes had joined forces for these sessions. Pupils who were not part of the teams, could go to them with real or imaginary difficulties. The team should question these customers using their checklists to determine how much at risk their customer was, and offer advice accordingly. The pupils can all take turns in offering and asking for advice in their various roles. After that type of activity had been exhausted, the tutor should close the topic by asking the pupils what they had learned from the exercises, and what they had learned about themselves. Stress should be laid on the personality characteristics, as these are the factors that are probably most under the control of the individual. By becoming aware of their own natures, adolescents are more likely to attribute cause to themselves and so begin to take appropriate action (Duval & Wicklund 1973) rather than see themselves as victims of fate or external circumstances beyond their control.

The National Children's Bureau produce excellent summaries of research on Solvent abuse (1981); Smoking (1980); Violence, Disruption and Vandalism in schools (1977); Juvenile Delinquency (1977);

Children and Alcohol (1979), which would be helpful
to tutors when presenting children with relevant
information for their pastoral work.

Discovering Personal Attributes

Part of developing a sense of self awareness and
positive self image is to concentrate on
the attributes one may possess. Youngsters have
to learn to maximise their good qualities, and
turn their weaknesses into strengths. This will
serve them in good stead when they are considering
careers, going for interviews, deciding on how
to serve their community or indeed in coping with
unemployment when necessary. By knowing what their
good points are, pupils will think of themselves
in a positive way, and communicate this to those
around them. Their self confidence should be enhanced as a result, which will in turn have beneficial effects on their overall performance both
in and outside the school setting.
     The kinds of qualities which will be important
to pupils will vary according to their age. Some
will be constant across age, and there will be
many others that pupils fail to consider, as their
ideas of good attributes may be restricted to those
that parents and teachers stress. Youngsters may
have many other qualities that are not evident
to their teachers and parents, and therefore it
is important to give them as complete a list as
possible of personal attributes. First, the tutor
should conduct a brainstorming exercise, where
the class call out as many attributes as they can
think of in five to ten minutes. When they can
contribute no further, the tutor can add to the
list others that are felt to be of importance.
A collection of between thirty and forty
such attributes should be the final outcome. A
pupil handout can then be made up so that individuals can examine which of the qualities they definitely have, those that they may have and those
that they are unlikely to possess.
     If pupils have difficulty filling in the hand-
out, the tutor should aid them by asking them to
consider what sources of evidence they could use
to help them make their minds up. For instance
if a pupil is unsure about having a sense of humour,
the tutor could ask 'Can you take a joke? Do you
see the funny side of things? Can you make witty
remarks?'
     When pupils have finished completing their

185

DEVELOPING SELF AWARENESS AND SELF IDENTITY

<u>PUPIL HANDOUT - PERSONAL ATTRIBUTES</u>

Attributes	Definite	Probable	Unlikely
Well dressed			
Articulate			
Punctual			
Cheerful			
Polite			
Sense of humour			
Reliable			
Trustworthy			
Careful with money			
Get on well with people			
Help those in trouble			
Good listener			
Patient			
Can make people welcome			
Full of good ideas			
Can take orders			
Enjoy being part of a team			
Can work on my own			
Enjoy travelling			
Like meeting new people			
Like dancing			
Like solving problems/ puzzles			
Like drawing/sketching			
Can persevere on tasks			
Don't get easily frustrated			
Well motivated			
Can keep a conversation going			
Don't panic in crises			

handouts, they should be asked to choose five of their best qualities, and give reasons as to why they were chosen. They should give some suggestions as to how these qualities can be best put to use in some of these situations:

Meeting someone for the first time.

Being given a task of responsibility at home or in school.

Going on a camping trip with a group of students

Spending a long time on your own e.g. on a single handed sea voyage.

If youngsters could use their five best qualities for managing all the above four situations, what does that tell them about their best qualities? Are they diverse enough? What do they think they are best fitted for? What additional qualities would they need to be able to cope in all the above situations? Can they find out which members of the class have the qualities they are missing?

All the attributes that were thought of at the start of the session should be written on cards and placed in a large bag or box. This should be done in quadruple, so that the children can work in groups of four. Pupils within a group should make a note of those attributes they did not think they had, but wish they did. They should attempt to obtain cards from the box that represent their qualities, and aim to obtain the others by making a 'bid' for them. They should offer some attributes in exchange for ones they already possess, if they feel that they should buy new qualities. If no one in a group has or claims to have a particular talent, then members of that group can request bartering terms from another group. When individuals think they have got as many desirable qualities as they wish, the class should consider which were the most popular ones, and why?

Pupils who would genuinely like to possess a particular talent should find a class mate who definitely claims to own that quality. The owner's task would be to teach or coach the other pupil in how to develop that skill. The pair of students need to be given two or three weeks to achieve this goal. This system is known as 'peer tutoring' and is known to be quite successful in helping youngsters develop social skills and talents (Rubin

& Ross 1982). The 'tutor' student should elect to serve the partner during the entire school day for the entire two to three weeks, by prompting and reminding the ward to practise the skill in question. For instance if the pupil made a request to learn how to persevere in tasks, then the peer tutor should note signs in the protoge of frustration, boredom, and defeat. The peer tutor should talk to the pupil and give relevant advice wherever possible emphasizing alternative strategies for dealing with difficult or monotonous jobs. Students and tutors should change roles if they have something to learn from each other. If not the form tutor should pair pupils in such a way, that all the pupils in the class get a chance of taking on both roles.

Those youngsters considering careers, should evaluate which of their skills and talents are relevant to particular jobs. They can do this by getting together a list of at least three careers they may seriously contemplate. From the careers department, or local library etc. they should then discover what the job involves, and from that work out which skills, talents, and personal attributes would be of most use to a person working in that post. They can then check off on their handout, whether or not they have the requisite attributes. They can make an estimate of how close they come to having the necessary talents and whether in fact it is worth acquiring a few more. Those who found that they were quite far off the mark should think again about the careers they thought of pursuing. Every pupil should double check the list of attributes he or she compiled for a job with at least two other students and the form tutor. If at all possible, youngsters ought also to check with someone already doing that job. This will ensure that they have come up with a reasonable estimate of the qualities needed for that post.

Some students may need additional guidance and thought development about what 'kind' of people they would like to be, before they can pick out jobs that may interest them. The following handout may assist them in that process.

Following the exercise of discovering which qualities are most needed for certain jobs, pupils need to research the value of five key attributes that were chosen for most jobs e.g. punctuality, getting on well with people, trustworthiness, politeness and having a sense of humour. Why are these the most valued, and by whom? What would

DEVELOPING SELF AWARENESS AND SELF IDENTITY

<u>PUPIL HANDOUT - THE KIND OF PERSON I WOULD LIKE TO BE</u>

WHAT I WOULD LIKE TO DO	YES	NO	MAYBE
Like to make things from materials, e.g. wood, metal, cloth, plastic etc.			
Like to plan and design projects e.g. buildings, factories etc.			
Like to help animals			
Like to use different languages			
Like to help elderly people			
Like to be outdoors a lot			
Like a title before/after my name			
Like to tell other people what to do.			
Like to look after children			
Like to increase my knowledge on a topic			
Like to be in the media			
Like to go to several different places			
Like to have things done for me			
Like to work with new technology			
Like an easy life with no responsibilities			
Like to entertain people			
Like to preserve old things			
Like to make quick and easy money			

be the consequences if employees did not have these talents?

A final activity which the class could do would be to examine the pool of talent within the class and suggest ways in which they could serve their community. This would probably mean most to children in the fourth and fifth forms, as they may be more aware of the needs of their community. For those pupils who may be leaving school in the near future, the purpose of life may be in question particularly if employment is difficult to obtain, and the students wish to remain within their own communities. Discovering skills and talents before leaving school can help pupils think of ways in which they can make use of their time and give them something to aim for. Pupils need to make up a talent and skill list doing a brainstorming activity. This should include all the resources a community would need as perceived by the pupils. They should then consider which groups within a community are likely to need help, why and what kind of help they may require. These groups include the elderly, mothers and toddlers, homeless, teenagers, mentally ill and handicapped, the business community, pet owners, physically disabled people, retired individuals and school leavers. The pupils may like to consider the needs of one of the above groups, according to their interests. Pupils could work in teams, perhaps taking turns to discuss one group, and passing on their notes to the next team who may add to it.

The class may elect to prescribe roles to various individuals within their midst to replicate community officials. The chosen team of officials should take the notes made earlier of the needs of the various groups in the community, and 'advertise' for volunteers to provide for those needs. The other members of the class should 'apply' for these posts, and be interviewed by the team. The form tutor should act as chairperson of the team giving advice to the 'officials'. The skills of being interviewed are of course important, and they can be found in the next chapter. The class should then be able to discover what they have to offer a hypothetical community, and discuss ways in which they could do this. Being interviewed for posts will have made them very conscious of the type of skills they would require, and present them with ideas for their own benefit when they are in fact out in the community.

The form tutor would be well advised to make

available a list of volunteer agencies in the local community which pupils could use for research purposes or in fact to ensure that their time was suitably occupied during leisure hours, and to help cope with the threat of possible unemployment.

CHAPTER SIX

LIFE SKILLS

Dealing with life itself and being able to cope
with its many vicissitudes is fundamental to the
welfare of every pupil. Social and life skills
therefore play an important part in a pastoral
programme. Experiments in 'social education' have
taken place in some schools (Rennie et al 1974)
and centres for further education (Lee 1980) but
schools have not really taken on board the systematic teaching of social and life skills, which
is now much needed and long overdue.

Many teachers who are given specific pastoral
duties are faced with pupils who get themselves
into difficult situations because they cannot plan
their time effectively, or who suffer so greatly
from stress in particular situations that their
behaviour gives rise to concern. For most tutors
these situations present them with very little
time or opportunity to help pupils cope better
in the future. They may be able to lend a sympathetic ear, but can do little in the way of deliberately 'teaching' the pupils how to manage their
lives better. As a result tutors find, much to
their frustration and annoyance, that the same
pupils are referred to them time and time again
for a 'talking to'. It would make more sense to
include life skills and techniques of self management in the pastoral programme starting with pupils
in form one, so that the tutor's time can be used
more efficiently and with more chance of success.
By making pupils aware of what they need to accomplish in the way of life skills, they are far
less likely to get into as much difficulty as they
do at present, and thus take up less tutor time
after they have encountered problems. In addition
pupils who learn from an early age how to manage
their lives, stand a better chance of developing

good coping skills rather than depend on poor ones formed by habit and ignorance.

Making Plans and Planning Time

Phillip a lad in the fourth form complained that after a school holiday such as a half term or summer break, he would worry greatly about returning to school. When asked why, he said that he would have no plans for doing any homework during the holiday, and at the last minute he could not organise himself well enough to do it. In addition to homework given for holidays, he would also have some left over from the previous term. These bits of work became ever increasing in amount because he could not plan his time effectively. This often made him so worried that he became ill, and had to avoid going to school, which of course only served to exacerbate his problem. Phillip had a similar problem when trying to plan his evening and weekend activities. He would toss up between doing weight lifting, watching television and working on his computer. He was so torn that he just opted out of them all, and began to feel more and more guilty, until he became completely debilitated. School was not aware of his difficulties, and his parents seemed powerless to help him, as all advice was taken as 'nagging'.

Phillip is by no means an isolated case. Many pupils encounter similar difficulties which indicate a lack of self management and knowledge of how to plan ones life to maximum advantage. What children like Phillip would benefit from are regular opportunities to discuss their life styles and make provisions for improving their plans and for carrying them out. Some suggestions for tackling this during tutorial sessions are presented below.

Most youngsters unless they are extremely mature and self disciplined are not going to take kindly to the idea that they should examine their lives and plan everything. That for them would take the spontaneity and excitement out of life. One of the first tasks for the tutor beginning on this task is to somehow demonstrate to the pupils concerned that their lives could be improved if they were planned better. Pupils have to begin by noting down all the things that they want to do, have to do, and feel they should do but are not compelled to do. They have to give some indication as to the type of lives they wish to lead, and whether in fact their current life styles reflect their wishes.

A useful way to begin pupils thinking about the kind of lives they lead is to allow them to split up into groups according to how they perceive their existence currently:

Boring   Exciting   Varied   Lonely   Too much choice
Too little choice   Full of worries   Full of
Pleasures.

The class can take any two combinations of the above until they have all been used up, and express which of these dimensions they see themselves in. The tutor can ask the children either to move to a spot in the room that is designated for one of the above categories, or simply to raise their hands to indicate their responses. The first idea will appeal to younger pupils while hand raising may be more appropriate for older children. In both cases the tutor should make a tally of how many pupils chose each category. Naturally pupils may choose several categories that may be complementary to each other.

When all the groups have been counted for the numbers of pupils in each, the tutor should indicate on the blackboard which categories were the most frequently chosen. The categories need to be listed in order of choice, with the actual number of pupils choosing it by its side. The tutor can draw this to the attention of the pupils, and ask what conclusions if any the class can draw from this.

Was there anything surprising about the results?

What kinds of lives do these pupils seem to be leading?

Would their feelings be reflected in their activities and moans?

Did pupils expect their peers to choose as they did? If so why? If not, why not?

Can all pupils feel totally happy with what they are doing in their lives? Why?

After this brief priming session, the tutor should pair up pupils according to their responses. One pupil who claimed to have a boring life should be teamed with one who said he/she had an exciting life and so on. They should be paired where possible with pupils who gave a response opposite to their own. If numbers within the class do not allow for this, because one category was over subscribed, then larger groupings can be made, but ensuring that the two opposing poles of view are present. The pupils who represent each category should take turns in questioning each other as to what makes them view their lives in the manner they subscribe to. For instance, the ones who felt their lives were full of worries could ask those who thought their lives were full of pleasures what made it so.

Younger pupils may be at a loss as to what questions to ask and how to keep the session going. For this reason, it may be advisable to give them a sample of questions, that they can tick off as they get asked, and answered. See example below.

Similar handouts can be made up for the other categories so that pupils can use them to some effect. When all groups have questioned each other, they can swap groups, until all pupils have completed handouts for each category. Following this the class can be divided into four groups. It should be possible to get a reasonable variety of categories with responses that give material for discussion. Each group nominates a leader who then conducts members to consider whether those who complained of being bored, worried etc. had done enough to change their ways of life, and also suggest ways of altering for the better.

It will probably be very difficult for pupils to give their peers constructive help without some guiding and prompting in the early stages. The tutor can aid them by asking the pupils who claim to have exciting, and happy lives to give an account of a 'day in my life'. They can do this by drawing a cartoon strip, putting their experiences on a cassette tape, making up a little play to illustrate their lives, or simply writing about it as a type of biography. Pupils should have as much choice as possible about the way in which they elect to describe their lives, so that no one method acts as a barrier. It will of course also add to the interest of their class mates, to see several varieties on a theme. At least half a dozen of such 'days in the life of.....' is required for the class to use as stimulus material. This material should then be distributed to groups of four to six pupils. The groups can then attend to certain aspects of that information:

LIFE SKILLS

<u>PUPIL HANDOUT ON DISCOVERING LIFE STYLES</u>

QUESTIONS - FOR THOSE THAT WORRY   ANSWER

---

1.   What sort of things do you
worry about?

2.   Do you worry about yourself
or other people?

3.   What happens when you feel
worried?

4.   Do you get any help when you
are worried? From whom?

5.   Can you do anything to feel
less worried about minor things?

6.   Who do you blame for causing
you to have so many worries?

7.   What changes would there
need to be in your life, in order
to lessen your worries?

8.   Have you ever tried to make
any of these changes happen?

9.   What changes do you find most
difficult to make happen? Why?

10. What do you find gets in
the way of you making changes?
How much of it is you, and how
much those around you?

1. Does this person do things as he/she pleases?

2. Does this person have time for everything in one day?

3. Does this person have a lot left over to do the following day?

4. Does this person try to plan things out in advance?

5. How do you think this person has organised his/her time?

6. Do you think at the end of the day, this person is pleased with him/herself or not? Why?

7. Does this person get into a lot of scrapes? Why?

8. Does this person make sure that all the things needed for the day are obtained well before hand, and if not, what does that mean for the way he/she lives her/his life?

9. What are the good points about the way this person has planned his/her day?

10. What are the weak points of the way the person has planned his/her day?

11. What do you think are the advantages of having a plan?

12. What happens if you have a plan but don't stick to it?

Each group should communicate its findings to all the other groups by electing a spokesperson. The tutor needs to make some general points on a large sheet of paper as they crop up from group to group. These can then be used for future sessions. Pupils should now be ready to consider how they organise their own time, and begin to make plans for improvement. The first task in this process, is for individual pupils to complete the following handout, where they have to estimate how much time they spend on suggested activities, and any others they wish to add.

When pupils have completed the handout, they should attend to the following questions:

Did I waste any time?

Was there anything I wanted to do that I didn't get round to?

What goals and targets do I need to set myself?

Did I have any plans that were not working? Why?

LIFE SKILLS

ACTIVITIES	I THINK I SPEND ABOUT hours & minutes
Eating	
Sleeping	
Washing/cleaning myself	
Household chores	
Homework	
Watching T.V.	
Shopping	
Looking after pets	
Visiting relatives	
Sports	
Out with friends	
Babysitting	
Helping Mum	
Helping Dad	
Hobbies	
Travelling to places	
ANY OTHERS:	

I would like to spend more time doing:

I would like to spend less time doing:

198

LIFE SKILLS

Pupils should then attempt to work in pairs to construct a checklist of plans that they can use for themselves over the next few days. Each pupil should act as advisor to the other, and question his/her decisions. A sample handout should be given to each pair so that they have something to model their efforts on.

<u>PUPIL HANDOUT - SAMPLE CHECKLIST</u>
<u>FOR PLANNING MY DAY</u>
<u>MAKING TIME FOR WHAT I WANT TO DO</u>

I spend about 2 hours a week on sport. I would like to spend 3 hours a week on sport.

My plan of action for each evening is:

CHECK

4.00	Come home from school	_____
4.10	Wash and change	_____
4.30	Have my tea	_____
5.00	Watch T.V.	_____
6.00	Decide on homework topic	_____
6.30	Do set exercise	_____
6.40	Check over work	_____
6.50	Get books and clothes ready for tomorrow	_____
7.00	Go to sports club/swimming bath/judo etc.	_____
9.00	Have supper	_____
9.30	Watch T.V.	_____
10.00	Get ready for bed	_____

If some pupils still find it difficult to construct a checklist then they need to begin by jotting down on scrap paper all the things they may wish to do in a week, in random order. These should include items of minor significance, such as eating,

FIGURE 10

travelling, and other routine items. Next the pupils with the help of their partners, should place these items in some order of priority, and space them out for seven days of the week. Then, they can take one of those days, and use it to make up their checklist. For some pupils, it may be essential for them to have their days represented by some visual and concrete means. A ladder made of card, where activities can be slotted in, and taken out could be a useful tool. The gaps between the steps on the ladder would act as 'windows' for pieces of card with activities written on them, which can be inserted or removed to suit the pupil. The top rung of the ladder would represent the item of highest priority, while the bottom rung that of lowest priority. See figure 10.

To ensure that pupils see the purpose in planning their time, the tutor should set each student a homework task of following their plan for a week. Each partner in the construction of a checklist should act as monitor to see that the other pupil made some effort to do so. The pupils observing each other should try to make some notes on what part of the plan didn't work and why, so that when the class evaluate their plans, they will be better able to do so constructively.

Pupils should learn to get into the habit of evaluating their plans and schemes, if they are ever to learn to correct their own errors, and manage themselves with the minimum of stress and worry. At the end of the first week of trying to keep to their plans, the tutor should encourage self examination, with the aid of the following handout.

PUPIL HANDOUT ON SELF EVALUATION OF PLANS

Tick the ones that you think apply to you

I was able to keep my plan because:

(a)   I checked each activity as I went along.
(b)   I did not let anything get in the way of my plans.
(c)   If someone upset me, I did not let it make me loose heart and give up.
(d)   If visitors came I explained politely to them that I had already made other plans.

ANY OTHERS:

The benefits of keeping to my plans were:

     (a)   I felt very proud of myself.
     (b)   My parents were pleased with me.
     (c)   I got all my chores out of the way early.
     (d)   I did not panic in the morning as everything was ready for the day.
     (e)   I was not worried or frustrated as I had organised myself well.
     (f)   I was cheerful the next day as I have achieved my target.

ANY OTHERS:

I was unable to keep to my plans because:

     (a)   I mislaid my checklist.
     (b)   I couldn't be bothered to follow it strictly.
     (c)   I wanted to watch T.V. instead.
     (d)   Someone called round to see us.
     (e)   My parents asked me to do something else.
     (f)   I was punished.
     (g)   I hadn't completed my homework.

ANY OTHERS:

The costs of not keeping to my plan:

     (a)   I felt really awful the next day.
     (b)   I was upset when I went to bed.
     (c)   I felt useless.
     (d)   I felt angry with myself.
     (e)   My parents shouted at me.
     (f)   I got in a panic the next day.
     (g)   My friends did not think much of me.
     (h)   I've given myself more work to do in the long run.
     (i)   I've made life more difficult for myself.

ANY OTHERS:

LIFE SKILLS

It is vital that pupils who did not do well when they had the chance to examine themselves on the previous handout, should be given guidelines for improving performance. They should be given a reference sheet or flow diagram to keep so that they can use it as and when necessary. Such an example is given below.

<u>PUPIL HANDOUT ON DOING BETTER NEXT TIME</u>

First decide whether you did not keep to your plan because it was mainly your own fault, or because circumstances arose which prevented you from going ahead as planned.

———————— IF ——

MY FAULT   UNAVOIDABLE
   ↓   ↓
I didn't really care.   I did care but let other
                               people's needs come before
                               mine.

   ↓   ↓
I need to make my checklist   My plans were too rigid.
with my parents so that they
can remind me to use it.   ↓
   ↓   I need to make alternative
I need to make a more   plans.
detailed list.
   ↓   ↓
I need to keep my mind   I need to inform people of
on course and not allow   my plans in good time so
myself to get diverted.   they cannot be disrupted.
   ↓   ↓
Then I will feel pleased   I need to see this episode
which will make me want   as not a typical one and
to care next time.   still have faith in myself
                               that I can carry out my
                               plans.
                                    ↓
                               I will try very hard next
                               time and allow myself
                               room for manoeuvre.

Pupils need to practice making plans and evaluating their efforts if they are to get into the habit of doing this exercise with any degree of regularity and success. Therefore the tutor needs to reinforce the previous sessions with tasks set for the class every now and again. They can be asked to make plans for specific weekends, holidays, time in school, or simply on how to conduct themselves in certain lessons if this is relevant. Similar evaluations as before should be made, and each individual should always end the task having experienced a positive outcome, either because they did well, or because they know what to do in the future.

Planning Time for Revision and Study Habits

One of the tasks which pupils of all ages find most difficult to plan for, is the time for revision, and planning and evaluating their study habits. Unfortunately study skills does not form a subject in its own right worthy of inclusion on the school time table. Teachers use their own subject lessons to give pupils some advice on how to study for exams, but all too often this is done in a very haphazard manner, and much too late for most pupils. Pupils need to learn right from the time they start life in the secondary sector, what it means to study, revise, and plan their work and time effectively. It may well fall to those with pastoral duties, such as form tutors to reinforce what their colleagues are doing in other lessons, and help students learn the techniques of planning and evaluating their performance, before they have developed poor habits. In addition, pupils tend to compartmentalize what they have been told in one lesson, as relevant only to that lesson. It is up to the form tutor then to aid pupils in transferring their study skills and developing useful ones across all subjects.

Once again it is a better tactic to start from where pupils are at present in terms of their plans and schemes, and work outwards from there, rather than train children to adopt new strategies in which they are unlikely to see any purpose. Pupils could begin by charting their usual routine for a total week including a weekend, and then evaluate whether they spent enough time on studying, and also whether the time they did spend was used economically. The chart used for this purpose was first described in chapter 2, for looking at

LIFE SKILLS

homework patterns.

<u>PUPIL HANDOUT TO DISCOVER TIME SPENT ON</u>
<u>STUDYING AND REVISING</u>

<u>How I spend my time</u>

<u>Weekdays</u>

TIME p.m.	Monday	Tuesday	Wednesday	Thursday	Friday
4.00					
4.15					
4.30					
4.45					
5.00					
5.15					
5.30					
5.45					
6.00					
6.15					
6.30					
6.45					
7.00					
7.15					
7.30					
7.45					
8.00					
8.15					
8.45					
9.00					
9.15					
9.45					
10.00					
12.00					

LIFE SKILLS

The same procedures should be used for the weekends, with periods of time still divided into fifteen minute blocks.

PUPIL HANDOUT TO DISCOVER TIME SPENT ON
STUDYING AND REVISING

How I spend my time

Weekends

Time	Saturday	Sunday
8.30 a.m.		
8.45		
9.00		
9.15		
9.30		
9.45		
10.00		
10.15		
10.30		
10.45		
11.00		
11.15		
11.30		
11.45		
12.00 noon		
12.15		
12.30		
12.45		
1.00		
1.15		
1.30		
1.45		
2.00		
2.15		
2.30		
2.45		
↓		
Midnight		

The instructions given to pupils should be that they must fill in EXACTLY what they were doing over the past week for every block. They should then total up the time spent on studying, revising, thinking time, time wasted etc. The students should then consider the following:

(a) Did they spend enough time on their studies?

(b) Did they spend their time efficiently?

(c) Did they do their work at peak energy times?

(d) Did they check off their work on a prepared list so as not to miss anything out?

(e) Did they give all subjects equal time, if not why not?

(f) Did they ask for help when they needed it? From whom?

The tutor should collate all the information from the responses to the above questions and try to draw out the differences between individuals in their habits. Where possible this activity should be linked up to the previous ones on making plans and planning time. For instance if pupils had made plans to spend a certain length of time on a subject, but did not manage to do so then the 'evaluation' sheet given before can be given again, but this time for the specific purpose of looking at study habits. The use of material from different sections of tutorial sessions should help students see the relevance of topics over a much wider field, and begin to use them without prompting.

The next step in the process is to get pupils to underline what they consider to be their good points, and those which they wish to retain. They should also make a separate list of those activities which they consider to be their weaknesses for future discussion. The pupils should then be placed in groups of four. Within the groups, each pupil should have the chance to pair up with the other three and get some advice on how to alter weak points to more helpful strategies. By asking at least three others, each pupil should end up with a reasonable set of ideas. The tutor should ensure that groups are constituted with this aim in mind.

First form pupils will probably have the most difficulty in helping their peers, and the tutor may need to visit each group and give some hints and stimulating questions for them to ask each other. It is crucial that the tutor does not have any pre-set ideas about how pupils should organise their study time and technique. Too often, teachers say to pupils that they should aim to spend 1 hour or some other period of time on a subject, when, for that individual student, it could either be totally inadequate or far too long. Students vary a great deal in the amount of time they take to do an exercise, or revise. The actual time therefore is probably the least important of all the aspects of studying and making plans for revision. It is the strategies that are used for aiding recall, understanding, marking out important points etc. that need emphasis. The main task of the tutor should be to help the children verbalise about the techniques that they presently use and find helpful. Pupils are more inclined to listen to their class mates, and try to adopt some of their techniques if they are seen to work. This will also cancel out the conversations that occur about who is the cleverest and who is the dullest. The tutor needs to stress that some people have better ways of learning and remembering things than others, and this session is all about sharing those skills, after each pupil discovers what his/ her failings are.

Some of the points that the tutor may need to bring out whatever age group is being taught, are as follows:

(a) Do people try to remember facts 'by heart' or do they have other systems? If so what? e.g. diagrams, key facts etc.

(b) For what kinds of subjects does each method work best?

(c) Do pupils use 'rehearsal strategies'? E.g. repeating items to themselves? If so, how is this done? E.g. using a tape recorder, using your parents or friends to listen, or saying it yourself under your breath/sub vocally? Which is best, and for whom?

(d) Do pupils use the system of underlining, or putting asterisks near key facts?

(e) Can pupils scan their material for relevant facts?

(f) Which pupils use a lot of charts, diagrams, and annotated notes to give themselves visual pictures for ease of recall, and which use mainly words and figures? Do they work well for everyone? Can those who use a lot of pictorial images show the others what they do, and vice versa?

Following the exchange of ideas and skills, pupils should have benefitted in two ways. First, they will have been introduced to some techniques which they had not previously considered, and secondly, they will have had the chance to make decisions about which ones they would like to try out. Pupils should be asked to make a PLAN detailing which strategies they aim to experiment with in the next few weeks. Copies of these plans should be lodged with parents, the tutor, and one friend; so that while at home, parents can help and encourage their children to use their plans, and the tutor can check on the value and detail of the plan, giving advice where necessary. Friends can motivate pupils as they can check on each other when they assemble to discuss their results. By checking, it is not suggested that they pass judgement, but when pupils monitor each other, they develop an increased sense of desire to complete their tasks, and the sense of camaraderie spurs them on to participate and criticise each others work constructively.

To help pupils especially in forms one and two to see what a plan can look like for revising, the handout below can be given as a reference. However, they must have been introduced to scanning, for key facts in prior discussions.

The handout on revision, if given early enough to pupils in their school careers can identify good habits for studying. The pastoral programme then builds in success for pupils from the very beginning, thus preventing children from experiencing failure through a lack of knowledge of study skills.

It would be an interesting exercise to allow pupils to construct their own such flow diagrams for different subjects, and for themselves as they get older and evolve new skills. If practised on a regular basis pupils should anticipate that they should always be aware of exactly what strategies they use, and evaluate their effectiveness.

To reinforce these techniques and encourage students to think in terms of making and checking on personal plans, older pupils from forms four onwards could be given the job of acquainting first form children with the format for studying and revision. Obviously this is a fictitious exercise, but if done in this way, students see it as having some purpose, and can identify with younger children, having been through those years themselves. Hopefully, this will prevent fourth and fifth

PUPIL HANDOUT - VISUAL REPRESENTATION
OF REVISION TECHNIQUE

Select a topic from within a subject area
↓
Divide topic into its component parts, e.g.
in biology - digestion, reproduction etc.
↓
Read own notes/text by SCANNING
↓
Read own notes/text again and underline or mark key
phrases. If you are not allowed to mark your books, write
down those phrases on a piece of paper, a maximum of one
sentence.
↓
Take each key phrase and put it in its correct order in
relation to the others, so that one follows on from the
other.
↓
By the side of each key phrase draw, write (or both) something to pad it out, to make it stand out in your mind.
This should be an ASSOCIATED fact/phrase, i.e. something
that goes with your first fact.
↓
Use a REHEARSAL STRATEGY to learn your facts.
This can be silent or audible. E.g. SILENT = saying the
facts 'in your mind' or writing them out again. AUDIBLE =
saying the fact out loud to yourself; saying the fact into
a tape, or saying the fact out loud to another person.
↓
Check how many you remembered
↓
Slot in the ones you forgot
↓
Repeat process of rehearsal
↓
Put key facts on a card for easy access
↓
Refresh your memory by looking at the card from
time to time.
↓
As you are looking at the card, bring to mind all the other
facts that go with the key ones.
↓
Write out the facts in the form of a flow chart/
diagram, every so often to help you recall.

formers from getting bored and claiming that they are just going over ground already covered. The instruction for these pupils is as follows:

'Can you think back to when you were in the first form? Imagine how much help you needed to study, and revise for tests and exams. In order to help your first form colleagues now, can you write a booklet for them, using language which you think they will understand. You should put down all the things that you felt was important at the time, and things you now realise are necessary, but did not appreciate at the time. You can use some of the following headings to help you in your task, and you can work in groups of four

Headings to help you:
Rooms to use in the house.
Equipment necessary.
Ways of remembering things.
Planning your free time.
Getting enough food, sleep, and breaks.
Finding out what you don't know.
Allocation of time to techniques.'

To ensure that pupils of all ages are getting into the right habits it is important that every so often they complete an evaluation questionnaire, on the strength of which they can plan to improve their self management in the future. (Hamblin 1981)

<u>PUPIL EVALUATION QUESTIONNAIRE FOR</u>
<u>REVISION AND STUDY SKILLS</u>

	Tick as appropriate	
	<u>YES</u>	<u>NO</u>

A. <u>Revision Timetable</u>

1. I have produced a timetable to cover evenings/weekends.
2. I have allowed sufficient breaks.
3. I have got all my books and equipment to hand. List these.
4. I have my plans ready for answering questions, and revising.

B. <u>Techniques for revising</u>

1. I have made use of colours, asterisks, and underlining to emphasise key phrases.
2. I use headings to sub-divide notes in a topic.

	YES	NO

3.   I use diagrams to help me
remember.
4.   I label diagrams clearly.
5.   I use flow charts to organise
and put together all the information
on one topic.
6.   I have got index cards to use as
memory aids, and to refer to things
quickly.
7.   I use symbols and abbreviations
to help me revise. e.g. (pupil to
insert own symbols).

C.   Coping with Stress

1.   I am aware of my level of worry.
2.   I talk about it to parents/friends
3.   I practice my relaxation exercises.
4.   I check off my work as I go along.
to help ease my worries.
5.   I make contingency plans to avoid
panic if things go wrong.

D.   Difficult Topics

1.   I ask the teacher for extra help.
2.   I try to read other accounts of
the topic.
3.   I try to put the topic into my
own words.
4.   I spend more time on such topics.

E.   Checking my progress

1.   I tick off items on my plan as
I've completed them.
2.   I do mock questions at home using
my handouts on revision, and answering
questions.
3.   I use a tape recorder to help
me remember and check how well I'm
doing.

Using the answers pupils put down on their revision evaluation questionnaire, ask them to jot down their strongest and weakest points in two columns, and draw up a balance sheet as in the example below:

A REVIEW OF MY STRENGTHS AND WEAKNESSES IN STUDYING AND REVISING

STRENGTHS	WEAKNESSES
a. I spend a lot of time with books in front of me and try to put all the information about one topic into a diagram with notes.	a. I try to remember everything instead of salient points.
b. I use symbols and abbreviations when taking notes, or recalling facts.	b. I do not allow myself adequate breaks and so get tired and inefficient.
c. I have made a timetable for myself.	c. I do not keep an easy reference list, and spend a lot of time searching.
d. I ask the teacher for extra help.	d. I regurgitate information by heart without fully under-standing it.
	e. I allow myself to get distracted often.
	f. I do not plan my time well enough to do all the things I wanted to do in addition to studying.
BALANCE 4	6

When pupils have identified their strengths and weaknesses, they should then make PLANS for changing their weaknesses into strengths, a point made with force by Hamblin (1981). However, pupils, unless they are of average or above average ability are going to have extreme difficulty in so doing. They will also have problems with identifying their weak and strong points, even with the aid of their questionnaire responses. Tutors should then set up a sort of panel within the class, to which others can come for advice, bringing their completed questionnaires with them. The tutor can act as consultant to this panel, bringing in guest members constituted from pupils from other classes, and or other teachers. If this is not practical, then pupils should be allowed to go outside the classroom for about a week to discuss their strengths and weaknesses with relevant members of staff.

What ever methods are employed to help pupils of low ability, all pupils would benefit from a model to work from, and it is suggested that the previous handout be given to them to use as such. They will also need a model for the task of changing their weaknesses into strengths in the form of a plan, and it is recommended that this next handout be used as a further 'model'. Pupils should work in pairs for this task, one helping and advising the other, and then changing over roles. The tutor should give a demonstration with a hypothetical list of strengths and weaknesses, showing pupils how to take each weakness in turn, and devise a new coping strategy.

When pupils have with the help of the panel, partners, or other expertise completed their PLAN, they should exchange it with other groups, who can give it a rating out of ten, and above all give hints for improvement. It is essential that the tutor tell the class that there are no right or wrong ways of studying which can be universally applied. For instance, some people actually NEED to have the radio on while they work, while others find it a distraction. Finally, the tutor should ask pupils for PLANS such as those above at various intervals of school life, to ensure that pupils have mastered the technique. For those who obviously cannot, the tutor will probably have to give individual guidance. At least these types of exercises encourage autonomy within the individual pupil, and serve to identify very early on, which pupils need personal attention.

It is difficult not to overemphasise the need

LIFE SKILLS

CHANGING MY WEAK STUDY HABITS
INTO GOOD ONES PLAN

Weaknesses	Converting into a strength
a. Trying to recall everything instead of just salient points.	→ Use underlining with coloured pencils to stress key facts.
b. Insufficient breaks.	→ Keep an alarm clock on desk, set to go off every half hour, when I can take a 10 minute break.
c. No easy reference list.	→ Keep an index card file with source, dates, quotes and other relevant facts.
d. Not understanding information.	→ I try to summarise paragraphs in my own words.
e. Distracted often	→ I choose a quiet room and do not allow radio to come on until my break.
f. Inefficient planning of time.	→ I draw up a timetable with a detailed estimate of time to spend on my work, spread over the week, and discuss it with a teacher or my parents.

for tutors to get together from time to time, so
that they make themselves familiar with the techniques that pupils use, in an effort to assist
each other in helping those pupils who are having
great difficulties. Perhaps tutors will not agree
with one another at all times, about the best plans,
and strategies, but this is not the issue. Tutors
have to facilitate the use of ANY useful method
that pupils find work for them. They should help
their colleagues to assist students in planning
their time, strategies, and evaluating their performance.

Coping with Stress

All pupils experience stress at some time during
their time at school, and during their adult lives.
Stress can be a very debilitating occurrence and
without some access to coping mechanisms, students
may enter adulthood having acquired poor methods
of handling the stress they encounter through life.
They may get locked into these inefficient systems
of coping and suffer more than they need, as well
as passing on these maladaptive coping skills to
their children, without perhaps being aware of
it. Children therefore have to learn actively how
to recognize signs of stress within themselves,
identify the situations which trigger it off, and
devise ways of handling the stress that are acceptable to those around them, and actually serve their
purpose.
Phillips (1978) reviews the factors that can
lead to anxiety and stress in schools, amongst
which he lists crowded rooms, teacher expectations,
and pupils' own reaction to mildly anxiety provoking
situations. They perceive them as more stressful
than they actually are because they have not the
appropriate skills with which to cope with such
situations. Thus stress creates more stress in
pupils who do not have the requisite mechanisms
for stress control. Triggers which induce a person
to experience anxiety and stress may be highly
personal and unique to that individual. They nevertheless have certain common features that are known
to precipitate feelings of stress. These include
factors in their environment, such as neighbourhoods, employment situations, family difficulties,
and psychological factors e.g. criticism, failure
to get a post, lack of recognition by those whom
one regards as important, and lack of perceived
control over one's circumstances. Dobson (1982),

McGrath (1970); Gray (1971); Spielberger & Sarason (1975); Cox (1978); Lazarus (1966) and Levine & Scotch (1970).

Most youngsters in school experience fear, anxiety and stress all as a total package, and cannot differentiate between them. As a result they cannot control any of them. Let us take an example of Andrew, who complained of feeling very frightened, worried and stressed in two different situations. The first was to do with a peer who Andrew thinks talks about him to other boys. He gets very angry, and then because he feels powerless to do anything, he experiences stress and helplessness. In the second situation Andrew is asked a question in class by his teacher. He gets so anxious about getting the answer wrong that he completely dries up and cannot execute any behaviour at all. He is immobilized. This is known as 'freezing' or sometimes as 'flight' behaviour, to indicate that the individual cannot face up to the problem and either runs away or fakes a type of 'death' to prevent the other party from pressing its case.

Yet another boy, Richard gets very upset when his class mates tease him about his poor work in the classroom. He already thinks of himself as not good at school work, so that any instruction by his teacher to do his work brings back that sense of failure, and he reacts to his stress by loosing his temper, and getting abusive. On some occasions he throws chairs about, and has to be restrained, or sent out of the room to calm down. Richard reacts to his stress by using what is known as 'fight' behaviour. His emotions run away with him, and after the episode he is unable to recall anything which he felt or did a few minutes earlier.

Both these cases illustrate the need for pastoral programmes to embark on a planned scheme of teaching stress control to pupils BEFORE some of them become so set in their ways, that they need even more intensive and professional help. There are several methods to teach stress awareness and control, and they range from altering thoughts and feelings, using problem solving strategies (Cartledge & Milburn 1980), to learning to relax and using relaxation skills in future situations (Benson 1977). Other methods include self control and cognitive behavioural control (Goldiamond 1965; Goldfield & Meraum 1973 and Meichenbaum 1974). Still others have outlined more behaviourally orientated strategies where specific skills are taught to individuals (Poitras-Martin & Stone 1977 and Beech et al 1982). Most of these strategies involve self management and self awareness, as unless the person concerned makes a conscious effort to alter some of the factors in the environment, and how they are perceived, then it is unlikely that they will ever be able to cope with stress appropriately in the future (Kanfer 1980).

Awareness of Stress

The first step in helping pupils with problems of anxiety and stress is to help them become aware of what happens to their bodies, thoughts and feelings when they experience stress. Unless they tune in on themselves and find out what they are actually going through, they will have no targets to aim for when it comes to control and management. The best way of beginning this topic is to collect a list of situations which pupils would rate as stressful. The word stress may be unfamiliar to a lot of pupils, and some alternatives in the form of questions are given below:

In what situations do you, or have you felt nervous?

What situations make you feel anxious?

When do you feel angry?

What situations make you feel afraid?

When do you worry so much that you cannot do anything else but worry?

When do you feel that you just cannot face up to something?

These questions should generate several situations with which most pupils within the class will be able to identify. These may range from being made conspicuous in front of a large group of their peers, having a test, being misunderstood, getting a piece of bad news, being rejected by a loved one, being left in the dark about something, having to face up to a telling off and being challenged to conduct a feat of minor or major significance. The tutor needs to list all these situations, on the board or large piece of card, and by taking each one in turn, ask how many pupils have experienced anxiety or stress in that particular case. This will allow those pupils who were not forthcoming during the previous informal session to make some valid contribution. The situation which gets the most votes is a good place to start exploring the thought, feelings and other signs of stress which go with that occurrence. It is also the first stage in stress control using problem solving and cognitive strategies.

Taking the example of Andrew, these are the procedures which were adopted to get him to reveal his thoughts and feelings: He is describing the situation in class where he is asked a question by his teacher. The tutor asks him to describe how he feels, and encourages him to use words describing actual emotions. He is then asked to describe what the implications are for him in answering the question. In other words the thought that he has in his mind that is preventing him from carrying out the task. Then Andrew is taken through the steps of what he actually does, which is to 'freeze up', and the final outcome of that for him, and how he then feels. As the tutor directs Andrew through his thoughts and feelings, another line of enquiry is made to increase the awareness of the pupil. He is asked to indicate at each stage what is happening to various parts of his body - the physiological signs of stress. These are signs such as increased heart rate, that one can 'hear', sweaty palms, change of body temperature either to hotter or cooler etc. Cox (1978) maintains that people realise that they are under stress when they experience these changes in their physiological parameters. Thus it is important that pupils learn to recognise them, and try to control them in order to reduce the effects of anxiety.

Following the journey through the pupil's thoughts, feelings, and bodily signs, the tutor needs to construct an alternative way of perceiving the same situation for the person concerned. At the same time, the boy, in this case Andrew, is asked to imagine how he would feel, what the implications and outcome for him would be, and what would happen to his bodily signs. Both these series of interviews need to be presented visually, so that the boy has a record of his effort at cognitive stress control, and can use it when necessary. The two situations about which Andrew felt anxious, are presented below in a flow diagram together with the suggested change in thoughts and feelings.

In both situations with Andrew, he was assisted

LIFE SKILLS

Situation one – Andrew feeling stressed in class

Questions asked by tutor:	Andrew's responses:

1. What happens in class which makes you feel anxious?

Teacher asks question.

↓

2. How do you feel then?

Feel afraid to answer.

↓

3. What happens to your body, for instance your hands, heart-beat, legs, stomach etc.? Do you get butterflies, sweat etc.?

Heart beats faster
Feel hotter
My hands shake

↓

4. What would happen do you think, if you did answer the question?

The others might think I'm stupid.

↓

5. What happens next?

I don't answer.

↓

6. What happens then?

Teacher asks another pupil.

CHANGE THOUGHT: THAT OTHERS MIGHT THINK HE IS STUPID

1. Are there any other ways in which the pupils might think of you, e.g. brainy, and that you just don't want the others to feel bad, so you don't answer ?

Others might think I'm brainy, not silly.

↓

2. How do you feel now, and what happens to your body?

I feel confident.
My heartbeat stays the same, my hands don't shake, and I don't feel hot.

↓

3. What can happen then?

I can answer.

↓

4. What could happen next?

Teacher will tell me if I am right or wrong.

↓

5. Then what might happen?

Teacher will be happy that I have answered and ask me again.

LIFE SKILLS

Situation two - Andrew thinks his friends talk about him to others

The procedures are the same as that for the first situation. The tutor asked the same questions:

1. What happens to make you feel so awful?
2. How do you feel exactly?
3. What do you feel like doing, but can't do?
4. Why do you think you cannot do anything to him?
5. So what do you do next?

The actual flow chart of what was worked out, and the suggested change is presented below. Note that alternatives are given so that the pupil doesn't choose to take anti-social actions, by working out the implications of so doing.

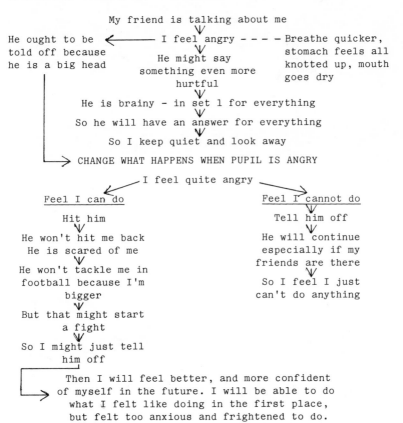

My friend is talking about me
⋁
He ought to be ⟵——— I feel angry – – – Breathe quicker,
told off because ⋁ stomach feels all
he is a big head He might say knotted up, mouth
something even more goes dry
hurtful
⋁
He is brainy - in set 1 for everything
⋁
So he will have an answer for everything
⋁
So I keep quiet and look away
⟶ CHANGE WHAT HAPPENS WHEN PUPIL IS ANGRY

I feel quite angry
⟵ ⟶
Feel I can do   Feel I cannot do

Hit him   Tell him off
⋁   ⋁
He won't hit me back   He will continue
He is scared of me   especially if my
⋁   friends are there
He won't tackle me in   ⋁
football because I'm   So I feel I just
bigger   can't do anything
⋁
But that might start
a fight
⋁
So I might just tell
him off

Then I will feel better, and more confident
⟶ of myself in the future. I will be able to do
what I felt like doing in the first place,
but felt too anxious and frightened to do.

in thinking about carrying out a behaviour which he wished to do but felt too stressed to do. He was given help in imagining how he would feel if he did execute his chosen behaviours, and that the implications would be advantageous to him rather than disabling as he had originally envisaged.

Children like Richard may not respond as readily to such a verbal and cognitive technique, as he is of lower ability and his ability to express himself could perhaps be poorer. For such pupils, a more visual technique may be helpful, where they pinpoint without using words how anxious they feel, and set themselves targets for reducing their fears and worries. It involves children colouring in the hypothetical mercury level in a thermometer to represent how stressed they feel in different situations. The only way they can do this is to compare what happens to their bodily signs in each situation, and then make a judgement on their level of stress. It has to be a relative judgement, as there are unlikely to be any absolute levels of fear for pupils. An example of this schedule is given in Figure 11.

Richard, the boy who responded to his stress by exploding was asked to complete one of these schedules. He appeared to be unaware of what happened to his bodily signs, and so was not really able to give his view of how stressed he was. He rated himself at a very low level indeed, at about 20 degrees, when his actual behaviour, would have suggested that he was probably up to the maximum. This brings up an important point when helping children to think about what factors are involved in stress, before trying to control it. It indicates that pupils do need a great deal of priming about physiological signs.

Tutors can do this as a class exercise with pupils of all ages by using the thermometer schedule to get pupils to carry out some observations on themselves. Learning about one's bodily signs, and how one feels at the time is merely a matter of self awareness at two different times. One has to know how one feels in a pleasant non stressful situation to appreciate the difference between that and how one feels when under stress. Therefore the tutor should give pupils a variety of situations to observe and discuss to draw out the comparisons. Some are given below:

1.   Missing the bus for an important appoint- ment/destination.

FIGURE 11

STRESS THERMOMETER

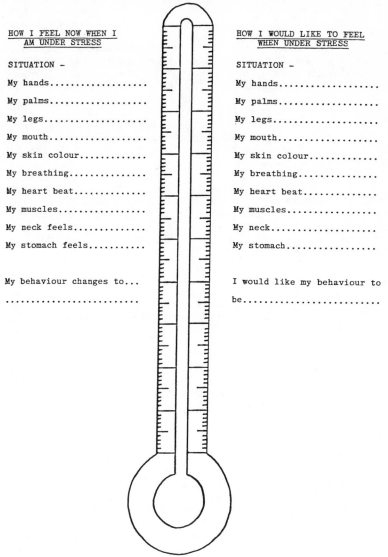

HOW I FEEL NOW WHEN I
AM UNDER STRESS

SITUATION -

My hands.....................

My palms....................

My legs.....................

My mouth....................

My skin colour.............

My breathing...............

My heart beat..............

My muscles.................

My neck feels..............

My stomach feels...........

My behaviour changes to...

....

HOW I WOULD LIKE TO FEEL
WHEN UNDER STRESS

SITUATION -

My hands....................

My palms....................

My legs.....................

My mouth....................

My skin colour.............

My breathing...............

My heart beat..............

My muscles.................

My neck.....................

My stomach.................

I would like my behaviour to

be.........................

2.   Being given a compliment.
3.   Being ignored when you think you deserve acknowledgement and praise.
4.   Wanting to talk to someone but feeling very shy.
5.   Getting a nice letter from a friend.
6.   Having a surprise from your parents.
7.   Waiting for news of a loved one, letter of application etc.
8.   Having an argument with someone, and wondering how and when to make up.

The above can be given to pupils according to their age and likely experience. They should fill in their thermometer schedule for each of the above items, but if none of them are relevant, then they can supply alternatives. When pupils have observed themselves in at least two pleasant conditions, and two stressful ones, the class can join up and discuss them. Pupils need to be paired up, one partner having a pleasant experience to relate, the other an anxious one. They should compare the things that they noticed about their bodily signs, and level of stress or excitement. There may be some similarities in bodily signs, e.g. heart rate might increase for both conditions. Pupils are to be encouraged to then seek out what exactly makes one situation perceived as nice, while the other one is seen negatively. When both pupils have had a chance to discuss one good and one bad feeling, they should then join up with one other pair. The group of four should have a leader, and be asked to think about the different ways their members coped with the stress. They need to focus on the part of the schedule that relates to 'My behaviour is.....'. They are to find out whether their group used very different or very similar mechanisms for coping, and then they should make a group list of ideas on how to tackle stress in the situations that they looked at. Each group should then feedback their results to the rest of the class.

When all the groups have finished their deliberations the tutor should take in any of their schedules which were used in the discussions. They will be useful later on when stress control is reviewed and reinforced at regular intervals. The tutor could take some examples of good coping behaviour, and bad coping behaviour, and put them in the form of problems for the students to tackle at a later date. Such a task may look like this:

'Julie has been told several times by her
parents that they do not like her to mix with
a certain crowd. She doesn't agree with her
parents, but nevertheless tries to keep a
low profile. She is afraid of what her father
may do when he finds out, and tries very hard
to make sure that he never finds out. However,
Julie's younger brother has discovered that
she is still hanging around with this group,
and tells their parents. Julie is aware that
her parents have found out, and now has to
face them.

How do you think Julie feels the day
before she is confronted by her father? Make
a list of all the things that might be going
through her mind, and what happens to the
following: her breathing, her hands, legs,
stomach, colour of skin, and anything else
you may think important.

Now do the same for the two hours preceding the interview with father. Does she get
worse or better? What sort of things get
worse and what type of things improve?

Have you ever been in such a position?
If so, can you describe how you coped? What
were your worst fears, and how did you try
to overcome them? Did what you attempted work
for you, or are you in just as bad a way for
similar incidents in the future? Did you
prepare for it, or just tackle it as and when
it happened? Can you now write down some
hints for those who may have to face this
kind of thing in the future? What sort of
things should they think, and feel, and how
should they try to control all the body signs
that make them realise that they are nervous.
You can do this by drawing a cartoon strip
or some other picture to explain yourself
if you prefer. You can also work in pairs
if this will help.'

Situations can be varied for pupils to prepare
them for impending stressful situations such as
examinations, going for interviews, undertaking
a challenging project, changing relationships
especially for those in the third, fourth and fifth
forms. They probably more than most will be suffering from changes of friends, taking on and dis-
carding of boyfriends and girlfriends etc. all
of which are likely causes of stress.

Relaxation Training and the Use of Imagery

Being aware of ones thoughts and feelings as well as the physiological signs which accompany stressful experience is still not enough for many people. They need one other string to their bow, in actually doing something positive to reduce their bodily stress symptoms. The best and easiest way for the tutor to help pupils help themselves is to train them in the skills of relaxation, and the use of positive visual imagery. This technique rests on the assumption that if a person can control the physiological signs of stress, then the situation is perceived as less stressful, and the person is not debilitated. This is a form of biofeedback (Brown 1974; 1975) but without the technical equipment that is used by experts in the field. Those who advocate relaxation training tend also to value positive visual images, such that the person involved in relaxing actually imagines the body resting, and more importantly, the individual uses that experience to REHEARSE what it would be like to act in a stressful situation without feeling awful (Bernstein & Berkovec 1973).

Practising relaxation training with a class of students need take up a very small amount of time for the tutor concerned. In fact between five to ten minutes in any one tutorial session should be quite sufficient. Obviously if these sessions are conducted with the more disruptive and active elements within a school as part of their programme of treatment, then more time would be advantageous. However it is recommended that tutors attempt to do relaxation training with all pupils. The reason for this is that many pupils are extremely tense, and without warning may behave in ways generally out of character. When done as part of a regular pastoral programme students not only learn how to control symptoms of stress in future instances, but get some immediate benefit. They may be able to give time to those thoughts that make them worried and anxious, and try to imagine themselves getting rid of them in acceptable ways. In this way pupils are more inclined to approach their school days with better spirits and be less troubled by the everyday vicissitudes, that they meet.

Many tutors are constrained by their form rooms which may be laboratories, drama studios and the like. While these are not ideal conditions for learning to relax, it really does not matter

where the tutor conducts the sessions. So long
as pupils can get comfortable somehow, it makes
little difference what the surroundings are like.
Pupils can use the walls to lean against, or get
comfortable on their chairs. If at all possible
they should move desks and chairs and place something on the floor to lie on. However it is perfectly possible to do these lessons with pupils
simply resting back on their chairs. Pupils may
find the first few sessions very strange, and many
will giggle and disrupt the session. This should
not be taken as a bad sign. It simply indicates
that pupils are trying to adjust to a very novel
experience, not just in school, but probably in
their lives to date. If children are exposed to
this sort of self control and learning from form
one, they will soon accept it, and many will enjoy
and actively demand it. Of course, there will
be a number of students who have heard about relaxation for pregnant women and the like. If discussed
in class, the tutor can use these experiences for
the advantage of the session.

Most of the pupils when first practising the
art of relaxation will have difficulty reaching
a state of relaxation because they may have no
idea what it feels like. This is very common in
youngsters, but there should be at least one student
who can relax, and who can therefore be used for
demonstration purposes.

For the tutor beginning this task, it is as
well to discuss what pupils know of relaxation,
and what their perceptions are of trying to attempt
it. If responses indicate to the tutor that the
pupils think it is 'stupid' etc. then some back-
tracking to the social skills and stressful situations is called for. It is of great importance
that the tutor does not undertake this exercise
unless the children have some motivation to participate, and that they see some value in it. Situations which pupils indicated previously that caused
them to worry and made them afraid can quite quickly
show them the value of having a tool at their disposal to use when needed.

When the tutor is satisfied that relaxation
is going to be given a chance by the majority of
pupils, and that they can all get reasonably comfortable, the following instructions can be given
to assist in relaxation, using a modulated tone
of voice:

'We are just going to try and relax for a

few minutes. I want you to try and get as comfortable as you can. If you have the room, just put your arms and legs out from the rest of your body so that you feel no strain in any part of your body. You have already learned how when you are anxious, scared or worried about something, you start to breathe much quicker, and your breath is quite sharp and short. Now I want you to practice taking some slow and deep breaths. Try to breath slowly, steadily and deeply. Can you feel how calm you are now? Just take in how it feels to feel quite safe and not anxious about anything. Lets see if you can relax some of the muscles in your body that get all knotted up when you are stressed. What about your head and face first? Just imagine all the area on your skull. Just let it relax. Perhaps you would like to see it floating or sinking into something soft. Imagine whatever makes you feel happy and relaxed. You know that for some of you when you are particularly worried your head feels trapped and you may get headaches. Now just tune into the feeling of relaxation with no worries. Now let us move to the muscles in our faces. Often the muscles around our mouths feel very strained and tired when we are anxious. Just relax them now and feel how good that is. Continue breathing slowly and deeply. If you hear lots of noise outside this room, just try and let it stay in the background. It cannot disturb us.

Now focus on the muscles at the back of your neck. Remember how tired this part of your body feels when you are on edge? Just relax that part of the body, and then imagine yourself relaxing all the bones of your back, going downwards from your neck. When you reach the part which gives you the most trouble when you are worried, spend some time there, and try and imagine yourself taking all that strain away. Imagine something wiping it away, or whatever image suits you best. Now can you move to your stomach? This part of our body is one that suffers a lot when we are feeling tense. Just as when you laugh a lot, or when you are especially impatient, it feels all knotted up, or you may get 'butterflies'. Just try and relax your muscles now, continuing to breathe slowly and deeply.'

Similar instructions can be given for other parts of the body, although the areas outlined above are the ones which generally cause tension. Just as when looking at the awareness of stress it was important that pupils distinguished between episodes of stress and those that were stress free, so when learning to relax, it is valuable for pupils to be conscious of the difference in their muscles between tension and relaxation states.

Instruction for this type of exercise is as follows:

'We all get tense from time to time, and often we are not aware of it until we give ourselves a chance to relax, and then we suddenly discover all sorts of strains and aches that we didn't know existed. Some of us never give ourselves that chance to unwind, and we may not know what it means to relax. Lets try now to see if we can find out what it feels like to tense up and relax.

Lets start with our feet. Imagine your feet in your mind's eye. Now tense them up as much as you can. Can you feel all your muscles working overtime, and how awful that feels? Thats what happens when you are nervous, or anxious about something. Now relax your muscles, and take some deep slow breaths. Feel how nice that is. How about trying with our calves now. Tense them up as much as possible, and then relax, breathing deeply. Focus on how good it feels when you relax. Now move up towards your thigh, and try tensing them up. Now relax, and enjoy being relaxed. Now can you try tensing up all those parts, from your feet to your thighs. How does that feel? Relax now, and take a few breaths, and enjoy your feelings of relaxation. This is what you should aim to do when you are uptight about something.'

Similar instructions can be given for the rest of the body, moving upwards from feet to head, always emphasising the breathing.

These exercises need to be practised until all pupils are able to perform the task at will. Where the odd pupil cannot achieve relaxation, it may be helpful if that pupil was allowed to get up and feel the arm of a relaxed person. With a hand on the arm of a relaxed pupil, tension and relaxation attempted one after the other, will

give the pupil the kinaesthetic impression of both
sensations, so that he/she can try them out. This
may need to be done several times before a pupil
with difficulties gets the hang of the task. If
the tutor is with a group of pupils who may feel
embarrassed by one touching another, the tutor
can overcome this, by building into the training
sessions, all pupils touching their neighbour.
Once it becomes an accepted thing, for the purpose
of learning, pupils will soon settle down, and
be more than willing to help their peers. However,
it is important that early experiences are attempted
with pupils in forms one and two so that no undesirable overtones can be cast on the exercises
of touching.

When pupils have mastered the art, tutors
merely need to reinforce the skill at intervals.
It would be particularly helpful if pupils had
the chance to conduct practice sessions in rotation,
as they will then see the experience as even more
meaningful. Just before certain stressful school
events the tutor should step up these sessions,
encouraging pupils to imagine themselves coping
well with the impending situation. It would be
as well for the tutor to encourage the pupils to
indicate what they perceive as likely to be nerve
racking, as it will be impossible for the tutor
to anticipate all such instances. A 'STRESS BOX'
can be left on the tutor's desk, so that pupils
do not have to disclose their personal fears to
all their peers if they do not wish.

After training in relaxation skills, it would
be useful for pupils to complete their stress ther-
mometers again for situations which they used to
feel very concerned about. This will be a sort
of check for them as well as the tutor about whether
they are benefitting from the training, and what
if anything is needed to enhance it.

Handling Interview Situations

Schools have been preparing students for interviews
for quite some time now. The focus has however
been on appearance in terms of style of dress,
filling in application forms, and answering tried
and tested questions. Rarely are older pupils
taught the skills of communication during an interview, and the interaction skills that are necessary
to conduct a good conversation. Furthermore, interviews are stressful experiences, and with all the
requisite skills, if a person cannot cope with

the anxiety that accompanies an interview, all may be lost.

Training pupils to prepare themselves for future interviews should begin in the fourth form, as it will take many practice sessions for students to acquire a level of skill that they feel confident in using. The training sessions should combine those aspects of social skills and stress control that are applicable to this skill. These are:

1. Communication and interaction skills:

(a) Verbal –
Content of speech.
Length of phrases and sentences.
Keeping on the path of the question.
Use of words that are not really part of one's normal repertoire.
Answering the question you think you heard.
Pauses in between answers – uh, ah, etc.
Using redundant words e.g. 'well', 'you know', 'really', 'of course'.
Putting across one idea at a time.

(b) Non-verbal –
Body posture – sitting up straight, to one side, hunched, position of head, legs crossed etc.
Body proximity – if there is any choice about how close one can sit to the interviewer in an interview, this becomes an important issue.
Eye contact – perhaps the most vital of all aspects of the style of communication. Does one keep one's eyes fixed at one point, look at everyone, look up or down?
Listening skills – another vital component of an interview. It is necessary to listen carefully, and show it.
Response skills – nodding at the right place, smiling when appropriate.

2. Stress control:

(a) Controlling ones breathing rate so as not to indicate undue anxiety, and to have enough 'steam' to complete sentences.
(b) Relaxation exercises to control trembling of hands and legs.
(c) Relaxation and breathing exercises plus visual imagery to help control sweaty palms, blushing or loosing colour, increased heart rate,

and muscle control in area of face and mouth.

Role play and simulated interviews are usually the most effective ways of helping pupils to acquire the complex range of skill necessary for good interviews. It would be of advantage if a video camera and play back facilities were available, so that students can get some feedback about their performance, and develop some strategies for changing the parts that did not work too well. A taperecorder could also be used to some effect, especially with pupils who use a lot of pauses in between words, and or who use words redundantly.

However if neither is available, pupils can role play each other to provide any feedback that is required. Before simulations can take place, it is probably worth while for pupils to think about what they might be asked, and what type of answers they are likely to give. Often pupils are staggered by questions about their personal views and preferences, and can end up with long silences, disjointed speech, and a fumbling for ideas. They therefore need to complete a sort of biography about themselves, which provides information not only about their school history and performance, but also about their views on current issues on employment, sexual equality etc. An example of one is given below, which pupils should familiarise themselves with before attempting to take part in role play or genuine interviews.

PUPILS BIOGRAPHY HANDOUT FOR INTERVIEWS

Use Block Capitals:

1. Name (in full):   Surname........................

                           Christian Names...............

2. Address...

    ....

3. Date of birth.....................................

4. Name of Parent or Guardian........................

5. Address of Parent or Guardian.....................

    ....

6. Schools Attended:

    Name of School   Date attended

7. Examinations you have taken or intend taking:

    Subject   Exam and level

8. Positions of Responsibility held (prefect, team captain, librarian etc.)

9. Awards you have gained or hope to gain: (sports, Duke of Edinburgh, life saving, computer electronics etc.)

10. Hobbies and interests:

11. Clubs, or societies you belong to:

12. The type of work you are interested in: Tick as appropriate.

    (a) Indoor   (b) Outdoor   (c) Alone
    (d) With others   (e) Office   (f) Factory
    (g) Shop   (h) With Children (i) Shifts
    (j) With animals (k) Nights only   (l) Days
                                             only

13. Any jobs you have already had:

14. What are your skills: (e.g. gardening, carpentry, catering, hairdressing, computers, typing, helping people, personal attributes etc.)

233

15. Any voluntary work undertaken:

16. What do you think about:

    (a) Married women working......................

    ....

    (b) Leisure facilities for young people........

    ....

    (c) Youth training schemes....................

    ....

    (d) Men and women having equal pay.............

    ....

17. My referees are................................

    ....

18. What is your health record like?..............

    ....

19. What would you like to know from an employer?...

    ....

    ....

    Pupils need to complete these biography sched-
ules at least three times during their fourth and
fifth years, so that they can continually update
any information such as new hobbies, or change

of opinions etc. For the first completion, pupils can work in pairs, to ask each other the questions and stimulate thoughts which perhaps one pupil may not have considered. It may also be a good idea for pupils who cannot complete a section of the schedule to think about why no responses are forthcoming. Could they carry it off in an interview? How would they manage if they were asked point blank why they did not fill in every section? Students may find it helpful to use tape recorders to answer some of these questions, and play it back before participating in role play sessions. The tapes should be retained by pupils so that they can compare their first efforts, with hopefully more polished versions by the end of the fifth form.

When tutors feel that students are ready for simulated interviews, they must go over the aspects of body language first introduced in social skills training. (See chapter 4) If pupils had been well versed in the body language, and verbal skills of communication, this should involve only a short recap with the tutor perhaps prompting where necessary. Some useful prompts involve asking pupils to give a meaning to the following:

What might the following convey in an interview situation?

> No eye contact.
> Continuous stare.
> Continuous grin.
> Shifting positions often.
> Slouched shoulders.
> Bolt upright position.
> Arms folded.
> Facing away from interviewer.
> Fidgeting.
> Sprawled legs.
> Sighing.
> Shrugging shoulders.
> Raising eyebrows.
> Touching a part of clothing/body continuously.

Pupils also need to rehearse what it feels like to be nervous and anxious, by discussing the various symptoms this could take. This could be done with some meaning, if pupils discussed with the tutor the kinds of instances during an interview that they may be dreading, that may put them off, or throw them completely. If they can learn to anticipate these occurrences then they could teach themselves to use their skills of relaxation, breathing, and changing a negative thought and feeling to a positive one. All these skills were outlined in detail in the preceeding section of this chapter for easy reference. The tutor should encourage students to practice the breathing and other relaxation techniques when they mention a threatening part of an interview. They should be asked to imagine themselves reducing their heart rate and any other unpleasant symptoms that they may feel, while at the same time rehearsing in their imagination, how they could cope without falling to pieces.

Simulated Interviews

The first role play sessions should concentrate on weekend or part time jobs, which some pupils may have already experienced. For instance, being interviewed for a job in a shop, garage, farm, stables, and such like. Two pupils chosen at random from the class should take on the roles of interviewer, and interviewee. The pupil playing the candidate for the job should have the biography completed earlier for reference.

The rest of the class should be divided into two groups. One group should concentrate on the verbal skills of the prospective candidate, while the other group should focus on the non-verbal elements of the interview, as well as any symptoms of stress. If they are needed, the pupil observations schedules presented in the chapter on social skills can be used as props for the two groups. Alternatively, pupils within the groups, may like to make up their own checklists for observations following the recapping session held earlier with the tutor.

The pupils playing the interviewer may be primed as to what questions to ask, as it is difficult for students to emulate roles for which they have no direct experience. The tutor can draw up a sample list of questions relating to general characteristics, and a few specifically to do with the job in question. However it will be of greater value to children if they get together in groups before the role play begins and produce a list of possible questions an employer may ask. If they come up with a reasonable variety of questions, the form tutor can proceed. However if the questions lack variety and depth, it

will indicate to the tutor that pupils are naive
and that they need some assistance in this task.

Ask the two pupils doing the role play to
begin the interview, including features such as
entering the room, being seated, and leaving the
room when the session is over. The rest of the
class should be given their tasks as mentioned
above but in addition a video recording and/or
a tape recording would be of added advantage. The
role play should take no more than ten to fifteen
minutes, and then the tutor should first of all
ask each participant how they felt about the interview. What sort of things had they noticed about
the way questions were asked and answered? The
interviewee also needs to be given the chance to
indicate what if any stressful points there were
during the interview. It is necessary for the
two pupils concerned to have the first chance to
discuss their performance, so that they can unwind,
and be open to assimilate the views of their peers.

Next each group from within the class should
make their comments, giving the two role play pupils
the right of reply. This will give the necessary
feedback to the pupils conducting the role play
as to whether others observing their behaviour,
perceived intentions or emotions that were not
intended.

The tutor should ensure that the following
points are discussed at the opportune time after
the role play and group feedback sessions:

1. What kind of questions did the interviewer ask? Were they skill orientated or more
personal?
2. Were the answers satisfactory to the
interviewer? How do you know? Were the rest of
the class pleased with the answers? Why?
3. Did the interviewer ask for the applicant's opinions on any matter? If so, how did
the candidate manage to cope with them?
4. Did the interviewee do anything with
regard to body posture, actions, eye contact that
made the interviewer think less of that person?
5. What sort of picture did the applicant
present to the employer? How do you know? What
signals were given out for you to make that judgement?
6. Would you have taken that person on for
the job? If so why? If not, why not?
7. Did the applicant seem interested in
the job? How do you know?

8. How can you tell if an applicant is hedging, lying or unsure of him/herself?

9. Was it easy to understand what the applicant was trying to express? What evidence is there for your answer?

10. Did the candidate appear nervous? How do you know? Did he/she control it or let it get the better of him/her?

Where a video tape was made of the interview, pupils can watch it again to check the validity of their observations, or in fact to emphasise a point. Pupils who did the observing should try to give helpful hints to the pupil who acted as the applicant, using the video as an example. If the session was taped on a tape recorder for the quality and content of the verbal messages that passed between the couple, then this too can be used to point out observations, and suggest improvements.

It may be necessary for pupils to take turns in acting out the role of the candidate for the purposes of 'teaching or modelling' the original applicant. This can be done in two ways. First, if no video is available, another pupil should 'mirror' the one who took on the role of applicant. This will provide feedback to the pupil concerned and give some information about how others perceive the behaviour in question. Second, another pupil can give another version of how that interview could have gone, and comparisons of the effectiveness of both can be made.

Future sessions of simulated interviews should vary the scene, and number of people involved. For instance, pupils could practice being interviewed by a panel, by two people, and by same sex individuals, as well as those interviews carried out by members of the opposite sex. Pupils will have much more difficulty relating to two or more people who may all be quizzing the individual, and not always verbally. A lot of summing up by panel members is done on the basis of non-verbal issues, such as how a person sits, their appearance, stress factor, where they put their hands, and general level of self composure.

Pupils may respond differently to being interviewed by members of their own sex, and to those who represent the opposite sex. For instance women interviewing girls may be far more intimidating as elements of competition may creep in. Men interviewing girls may be less critical of appearance when it comes to detail, but may wish to explore

the views of the candidates on marriage, children
and work. Obviously these are generalizations,
but are still worthy of discussion with pupils
who have quite definite views about what men are
looking for, and what women are looking for, however
misplaced. Some questions to stimulate discussion:

Does physical appearance and style of dress matter
more for girls or boys, or neither? Why?

Does it make any difference what type of job you
are going for when it comes to dress and appearance?

In what kind of situations is dress going to be
important? Why?

What about accents of speech, e.g. having a local
dialect?

Are all interviews sexist, or are certain ones
more likely to be so? Why? Give some examples.

What might happen if a panel of men interviewed
a girl, or a panel of women interviewed a man?
Are there any real differences? Can you outline
them?

Are men and women likely to ask different types
of questions? If so, what? Why? Do you agree
with this?

Which kind of interview would pupils prefer, why?

The tutor should select about four to six
members of the class to act as an interview panel
for a job nominated by the form. They need an
interview schedule so that they can rate the interviewee on how 'smoothly' the conversations flowed.
At least six different pupils should take the roles
of candidates. The remaining students should once
again be split up into two groups. One group to
observe the verbal elements of the applicants,
and the other to concentrate on the non-verbal
and stress parts of the candidates. The observers
should swap tasks with the onset of each new applicant being interviewed so that they do not get
bored, and so that they all get a chance to dwell
on the totality of the candidates' performance.
The groups should have at their disposal separate
observation schedules for each applicant, three
to note down verbal skills, and three to note down

non-verbal skills. Pupils in each group may work in pairs, taking turns in observing and noting down.

The interview schedule that members of the panel have to rate the interviewees could be prepared by them as a team, with the one below to be used as a guide only.

Each member of the panel should rate each applicant. At the end of the interviews, the panel should conduct a mock briefing session, where they compare notes, and give their choices and reasons for so doing. This should be done in full view of the candidates and the observers in the class. When the decisions have been made, the observers should be asked to comment on the deliberations of the panel, giving evidence for any disagreements. The same questions as for the previous simulation may be asked, with a few additions to cover the applicants response to a panel, and the specific questions on the schedule. When the panel and the observers have had their say, the applicants should give their impressions of what it felt like to be interviewed by a panel. They should also comment on the results, giving reasons for views that indicate unfairness, undue stress etc., or simply having poor interviewers.

Members of the class can all take turns to play the various parts in these simulations and each time, the tutor needs to facilitate discussion on the effectiveness of the applicant's coping strategies, giving particular emphasis to the non-verbal signs of interaction, and levels of stress. There will be moments when the pupils playing the part of interviewers will 'dry up' as it will be a strange role for them. The tutor should step in at these times, and ask follow up questions if it seems likely that an interview is going to end in disaster. Pupils should also be encouraged to engage in role reversals immediately after playing one part and discussing it, so that no one pupil gets into a set pattern of behaviour which cannot be broken.

From time to time tutors should also take on the part of an interviewer to 'model' the role for prospective players in the class. They can learn a lot in this way. In addition, tutors should also give children the opportunity of interviewing them. Occasionally it would be appropriate for tutors to exchange classes so that the stress factor for pupils is increased when they are being interviewed by their 'exchange' tutors. If possible

MODEL INTERVIEW SCHEDULE FOR INTERVIEWERS

	Good answer	Poor Answer
1. Why do you want the job?		
2. What have you got to offer us?		
3. How do you get on with a large team?		
4. Can you work unsupervised?		
5. Can you take the initiative? Give us some examples.		
6. What experiences have you had in this field of work?		
7. Have you ever been in trouble with the police?		
8. Do you have any other jobs at the present time?		
9. Do you live on your own, or with parents? What does that mean for your life style?		
10. How many jobs have you tried for? Were you success-ful in any?		
11. What would you do if you didn't get this job?		
12. Do you enjoy good health?		
13. Do you have elderly/sick parents to care for?		
14. Would you be prepared to go to college part-time?		

senior staff who do not normally conduct pastoral tutorials, should be recruited for this task. These will be the nearest for pupils in terms of simulating a genuine interview.

Further information on helping students get jobs and interviews can be found in Dowding & Boyce (1979) Webb (1978) Hopson & Scally (1979; 1982). Further details of communication and decision making skills can be found in Hargie et al (1981) and Russell & Thoresen (1976), while more general works on life skills may be located in Stanton et al (1980), Conger (1973), Cheston (1979), and Ellis & Barnes (1979).

CHAPTER SEVEN

DEVELOPING AND IMPLEMENTING A PASTORAL CURRICULUM

For many educationalists the idea of having a pastoral curriculum is a contradiction in terms. They
believe that pastoral care is an integral part
of the process of schooling and as such is carried
out at all times of the school day. They would
argue that to separate pastoral care from other
aspects of the school routine would defeat its
purpose. However, if pastoral care is viewed as
a vehicle for building up skills in pupils and
preventing them from getting into personal difficulties, then some well thought out framework has
to be produced for staff to work within.

The Need for a Pastoral Programme

Any work undertaken with and for pupils needs systematic planning, so that teachers know what they
are supposed to be doing. Many tutors dislike
pastoral periods simply because they have no definite plan to follow. This can make some tutorials
fall flat, and cause the pupils to take
less interest in future. Pastoral work often involves using a variety of teaching methods that
may be unfamiliar to some tutors, and it will certainly involve content that is diverse and not
subject to the restrictions of a discipline or
body of knowledge. As such, pastoral sessions
can sometimes create feelings of insecurity in
both staff and students. A carefully set out curriculum which included content and methods would
act as a much needed aid for the tutor embarking
on a long term pastoral programme.
    The needs of each year group within a school
are variable. Pupils within the same year group
will have differing views and needs from one year
to the next. Therefore it is important that staff

take the trouble to evolve their pastoral programme to take into account the changing needs of their populations. In order to do this, there has to be a skeleton of topics and methods that staff can adapt for their pupils. Teachers have to get together in the first instance and decide what their objectives are for the welfare of their pupils. This will then give rise to the fabric of the tutorial sessions that all tutors can use. Much of that core curriculum will be relevant to pupils at different stages of their school lives, and staff should be aware of what has gone before so as to build on, and extend the awareness and level of skills in students. This cannot occur without a fully planned programme, as pupils are likely to get an unbalanced and uninteresting pastoral diet.

As pastoral work involves the development of personal and social skills within the individual pupil, it should reflect the standards and values of the pupils themselves, society at large, the parents and the school staff. This can only be done if schools devise a pastoral curriculum which can then be added to, subtracted from, and mixed in such a way as to incorporate the views of all those who have an interest in the future generation of adults. By listening to the pupils regarding their problems, both in school and in the community, schools can take action almost instantly by adapting their pastoral programme to help pupils before the difficulties become serious. Similarly, when teachers are involved in continuous curriculum development, they too can highlight problems which can then be tackled systematically in the pastoral sessions.

A curriculum is needed in pastoral work as with any other type of work, so that a proper evaluation can be made. In fact, it is even more important to evaluate pastoral work because many of the objectives are long term, somewhat nebulous, and do not always lend themselves to immediate examination. This feature alone can act as a disincentive for teachers to carry on with their programme. If however, a curriculum was developed with a set of agreed objectives that could be checked on at certain points of a pupil's career, then teachers would get some feedback about their efforts.

Evaluation does not only involve assessing pupils to see whether they have actually developed personal and social skills, or become more aware of their needs, it also means evaluating the content and methods used within the pastoral sessions. A curriculum has to change continuously to ensure that it's purpose is being achieved. For this reason it is essential that teachers meet regularly to discuss the effects of certain methods of getting a topic across, to learn from each other, and to revise content and style where appropriate. None of this can be done without a detailed and well planned curriculum in the first instance.

Getting involved in curriculum development enables teachers to review their topics and methods. It provides them with the opportunity to further their own education, and encourages them to develop new skills and improve existing ones. It can have the effect of motivating them as they have an input into curriculum planning, and are therefore more likely to give it a fair trial. They have a vested interest in making it work, and will be more inclined to share their experiences with their colleagues. They can then extract useful points, and include them in programmes for the future.

Putting pastoral care on the same footing as other subjects by having a planned curriculum, gives it a status that it may not otherwise have. It no longer gets stuck with the label of 'the hidden curriculum', and a consequent low priority in terms of time allocation. There are many subjects fighting for inclusion on the school timetable. If the pastoral programme is well planned and is shown to have a meaning for pupils and teachers, it stands a better chance of gaining a significant place on the timetable, without which pastoral work becomes a second class topic, and discourages commitment from staff. By showing clearly what is intended, how it is going to be undertaken, and what forms of assessment are used, those who have the power to make decisions about timetabling will be forced to consider it seriously.

Reporting on the social, emotional and behavioural aspects of pupils' development is becoming an ever increasing demand on schools from employers, statutory agencies and parents. By having a detailed pastoral curriculum with well set out objectives, pupils can be judged according to those criteria and reporting can then become more standardized and skills orientated.

Planning a Curriculum

There are several factors that need consideration

when planning a programme for pastoral work. These are listed below and developed at a later stage.

1. Who plans the curriculum?
2. When is the curriculum planned and re-vised?
3. Who co-ordinates the planning?
4. Who monitors the implementation of the programme?
5. How can the implementation be monitored?
6. When should pupils' responses be checked, and by whom?
7. When should staff evaluate their methods and topics?
8. How should pupil problems brought to light in tutorials be included in the programme?

Curriculum planning should be undertaken by those who have the task of conducting pastoral sessions. In most cases this means form tutors in consultation with year tutors, and school coun-sellors where they are in post. It is quite well known that tutors do not take kindly to curricula being forced on them, when they have had no part in devising it themselves. In a study of how form tutors perceived their role, Raymond (1982a) found that 59% wished to develop their role. Methods endorsed included regular discussions with col-leagues, joint planning of curricula, and school based in-service training. This suggests that in schools where pastoral care is given a high priority rating, year tutors need to foster positive atti-tudes among form tutors by giving them the chance to devise the content of their sessions. The frame-work must be agreed by all concerned, with year tutors and other relevant staff giving direction, and advice on methods of approaching certain topics. As in-service training appeared a popular method for form tutors to develop their role, then outside agencies could be brought in to present details of particular techniques or topics. Youth workers may have a great deal to contribute on methods of working with groups of young adults on personal issues. Intermediate treatment officers from the Social Services Department could contribute some of their expertise on educating youngsters to use their spare time more constructively. The Edu-cational Psychologist has much to offer on aspects of social skills training, stress control, self identity, emotional growth, and the schools part in nurturing the development of adolescents. They can also give valuable advice on how to go about seeking the perceptions of pupils which is vital to an effective pastoral programme.

Programme planning needs to take place before the start of each academic year. This should involve setting down the basic topics that tutors feel ought to be covered in each year group. The experiences of the preceeding or current year should give some indicators as to timing, and style of approach that is needed. For those schools starting from the very beginning, some trial and error will be inevitable. From whatever base tutors are planning for the next year, some guidelines have been provided in this chapter. Each year group is taken separately. Using the headings of Partnership with Pupils, Life and Social Skills, and Self Awareness and Self Identity, ideas for topics are presented in sequence allowing three terms per year group. The ideas in these guides are by no means exhaustive. The substance of the pastoral programme for each year group is given together with suggestions for techniques that may facilitate the implementation of the topics. Where they are covered in some detail in previous chapters, then the reference is given for the ease of tutors. It has not been possible to cover every topic in detail in this book, but techniques for so doing are listed, should tutors wish to tackle them. See tables 1-5.

Further detail for the curriculum must be planned after the first half of the autumn term. This is to allow tutors to get to know their pupils, and to seek out the perceptions of the students as to what particular problems they encountered in school. This then needs to be fed into the curriculum for each year group, with staff discussing the most appropriate methods of handling them so as to aid pupils in resolving their difficulties.

Towards the end of the autumn term, the first check needs to be carried out to ensure that the curriculum reflects the intentions of staff, and the needs of pupils. Some discussion on the difficulties encountered by staff, either with a topic or in using a certain technique should be held. Sometimes talking to colleagues will be sufficient for tutors to feel reassured and to gain hints on aspects of the work that they found stressful or difficult in some way. Methods of supporting these tutors is given in chapter one. These can be put into effect at the beginning of the spring term. However, it may be the case that discussions may not be enough for some staff. A few may feel a little inhibited, and would benefit from a slightly more structured method of expressing their grievances, or problems. Using the curriculum for the year group concerned, individual tutors may be asked to mark the topics which they felt did not get off the ground and why. If several tutors marked a topic as unsuccessful, then plans would have to be made for some in-service training in the following term. This ensures that tutors do not lose confidence, and shy away from tackling that item again. Where many form tutors have shown a dislike for a topic, or have found it difficult to develop, it is essential that a check is made with the pupils about how they perceived that same subject. It could be that tutors were worrying unnecessarily, and year tutors would then have to boost their morale. If however, pupils also found the topic uninteresting and of little value, then a REVISION of the curriculum needs to be undertaken. This can be done on two levels. Either the topic failed because the methods used to get them across were unsuitable, badly done, not understood by staff, or the subject itself was inapt. It may need dropping altogether, re-scheduling, or a complete new plan of attack.

The two checks made in the first term, both of pupil responses, and tutor perceptions serve to evaluate the effectiveness of the programme in sufficient time to support tutors, and to alter the programme where necessary.

Additional monitoring should be carried out at around the end of the spring term, and half way through the summer term. These checks should focus more on the skills that pupils are building up and putting into use, as well as the reinforcement of certain issues so as to increase the likelihood of efficient learning and consolidation by students. This can be done in two ways. One way would be to ask the pupils themselves to rate their own ability to cope with difficulties that they outlined in the beginning of the year, and subsequently. The other method would take into account staff views about the skills of their pupils. It is important that all teachers who have dealings with a particular set of students get the chance to remark on the kinds of problems that they face. These should be compared to the kind of issues that arose in the beginning of the year, and an assessment made on that basis. For instance, if several staff noticed that a small group of pupils had great difficulty in coping with stress in personal relationships, and were always in trouble as a result, then the same staff should reflect on whether the pupils are better able to handle their stress and so come to the attention of teachers less often. Objectives for such evaluation are given later in the chapter.

The overall responsibility for monitoring should rest with the year tutor. However, in some instances this may be seen as a negative role both by the year tutor, and the form tutors. It may be useful for the year tutor to allocate certain parts of the curriculum to interested form tutors for assessing, developing and evolving. For instance if one form tutor had an interest in 'time management' then he or she would have the task of ensuring that pupils had learned the skills taught at each level, and would also have the job of seeking staff comments about the pastoral sessions when that topic was tackled. In this way, all members of staff can get as involved as they wish and make a real impact on the pastoral system of their school.

Towards the end of the summer term, the cycle begins again, with planning for the following year being reviewed. It is at this point that form tutors, previously given specific responsibility for a topic, should advise on what needs to be reinforced the following year. If a certain aspect of social skill had not been adequately consolidated at the end of the year for which it had been planned, then staff should consider whether they ought to continue with that before moving on to the next stage in social skills. At this point too, form tutors need to discuss the problems indicated by pupils over the year such as getting to grips with aspects of school routine, or understanding the school, levels of motivation and problems with relationships, be they with staff or other pupils. The topics that seem to be prominent with many pupils and tutors should be considered for inclusion into the programme for the same year group in their curriculum for the next academic year. It is important that tutors discuss why pupils were continuing to face these problems, as if they do not, then it is quite likely that similar methods would be used in the forthcoming year. A new approach with advice from tutors who felt their groups had coped with a similar set of difficulties should be put down in the programme for the coming year.

Time Allocation and Timetabling

The amount of time that should be spent on pastoral tutorials causes staff much consternation. Some schools have tried to deal with this problem by allocating the first fifteen to twenty minutes before the first lesson for tutorial work. Form tutors feel that this is not the best time, as they have certain administrative duties to perform, which do not allow them the opportunity to conduct a meaningful tutorial. With pupils coming to school late, getting organised for their lessons, this time in the morning does not appear to be conducive to effective pastoral work. Other schools have tried to obtain a lesson on the school timetable for 'form period', and these occur at times when no one is greatly motivated or energetic, for instance the last lesson on a Friday afternoon. Staff are not going to perceive such a time slot as being important, and are more likely to use that time to send pupils on messages, mark work, or simply tie up loose ends for that week.

The only way that teachers are going to take on pastoral work with any enthusiasm and energy is if it has sufficient time on the normal timetable, and when they are not expected to be doing several other things at the same time. The ideal would be at least two double lessons during a week, slotted in during the morning session during the first part of the week, and the afternoon session, during the latter part of the week. In practice schools may not feel that they can afford this time for pastoral work. In that case, a minimum of two lessons a week needs to be given over to pastoral work. Much of the work involves a gradual building up of awareness, understanding and motivation within pupils. This requires carefully planned units per term for which a regular set of lessons is needed. A haphazard allocation of time by senior management would only serve to illustrate a poor conception of what pastoral care is all about. Under these conditions, they should not blame staff for not carrying out their duties. As well as putting pastoral work on the pupil timetable, staff must simultaneously make a timetable for year tutors to meet and work out how best to help form tutors. Time must also be set aside for meetings between form tutors and year tutors for discussing problems, and evaluating the curricula. These two parts of the timetabling dilemma have to be considered in unison, as neither will have much significance without the other.

A Guide to the Curriculum for the First to Fifth Year Groups

When considering the content of any curriculum, three points need to be borne in mind. The content should be relevant, it should be interesting and it should be 'learnable', (Nicholls & Nicholls 1978). Taking the issue of relevance first, the topics covered within each year group must be seen by both staff and pupils as having a purpose. Pupils will see a purpose behind learning about the school, its organisation, its timetables, and routines as early as form one. Therefore these topics have been placed in the first term for the first form. Many authors refer to such topics as 'induction' for first formers. It is rare for schools to give time to these same topics later in that year, or in subsequent years. This is a false economy. As with all other kinds of topics and learning, revision needs to be carried out. Pupils cannot, and will not, absorb the entire induction programme in the first term, and some time must be set aside for recapping, both later that year and some time in the second year. The most opportune time for the reinforcement of these topics can be decided by staff when they carry out their checks and evaluations during the year.

Time management is something that all pupils will find relevant when they come to developing habits for doing homework and carrying out their sporting activities. In form one this exercise can begin with making plans for homework, and the first introduction of self evaluation can be made. In form two, pupils can discover how they actually spend their time, and improve their routines. In form three these two elements need to be brought together, as third years begin to become more independent and autonomous. They need to ensure that they can fit in all the things they want to do in the time available, and they must begin to make plans for revising and serious studying. Staff should recap on these skills at times during the fourth and fifth years, to maintain the performance level of the students. The exact time for that could be discussed at evaluation meetings.

When we come to issues of stress control, relationship building and social skills training, it is unlikely that pupils will see the relevance of these exercises immediately. However, if begun

at the first year level, by the fourth and fifth
years, students will be able to assess the worth
of skills training. They will find these sessions
concentrating on their personal attributes and
views interesting and enlightening, and eminently
learnable because they learn by doing. They will
have the chance to practice these skills in their
everyday life, and their incentive to learn therefore becomes greater.

In the first year pupils experience a lot
of stress when they are criticised, are reprimanded,
and have to learn by trial and error what is expected of them. They also begin to have relationship difficulties with teachers. Their pastoral
curriculum should include these topics together
with the learning of how best to communicate their
problems. They need also to consider perhaps for
the first time what their personal attributes are,
and compare them to what their peers think. These
exercises set the scene for continuous self assessment and self evaluation as they progress through
school. As motivation needs to be built into the
pastoral programme from the earliest possible time,
the curriculum for the first form should have in-
built a system of discovering what encourages and
discourages pupils at this age so that adaptations
can be made in the second form. See table 1.

In the second year, pupils have come to understand their school somewhat, and they begin to
question authority, and want to behave in more
assertive ways. They question the banding and
setting system, uniform, and school reports. These
topics therefore need an airing at this stage.
Although the curriculum guide for form two (table
2) is the only place where these issues receive
prominence, it is expected that staff will take
up relevant points again in later years, and include
it in the curriculum, where appropriate, after
discussions with pupils and colleagues.

Form two should see the continuation of the
self awareness begun the previous year. Where
personal attributes were looked at in form one,
the second year pupils should extend this to a
discovery of their skills and talents, by linking
into personal needs and the kind of people they
think they are.

Form three is often a watershed for pupils
in secondary schools. They wonder about the purpose
of school, and often begin a pattern of non-attend-
ance. They think about the rights of children,
authority, privileges and exerting their influence

on what is going on around them. The curriculum needs to reflect these issues. In addition, third year students begin to experience a great deal of personal unhappiness in relation to their looks, their self image, and they strive to be the kind of people of which they have idealised images. It is a very important element in the pastoral programme that enough time is spent helping youngsters grapple with their difficulties. In the fourth and fifth years, the same themes should be brought up again as they are ongoing problems that cannot be solved in a few sessions during one term. See table 3.

In form four, certain topics deserve greater emphasis. One of the most important aspects of the curriculum of this year is that of equipping pupils to deal with problems that they will face for the rest of their lives. Leaving it to the fifth form is too late, as there is insufficient time for efficient learning at that stage. Such topics as interviewing skills, dealing with institutions, coping with conflicts, and the taking on of personal responsibilities need to be tackled during the fourth year, and developed during the fifth and/or sixth years. Previous themes such as privileges, school attendance and personal needs can be reviewed from the point of view of the students who are now older than when they first discussed these topics. Revision skills need to be gone over again as pupils plan for examinations. See table 4.

In form five, students cope with the need to obtain qualifications of one sort or another AND with their growing need to self actualise through relationships with the opposite sex, in addition to taking control of their own lives. The curriculum for this year group should reflect these points. Many disillusioned youngsters once again question the purpose of school and the whole issue of discipline. Some pupils will be reflecting on a life of unemployment, while others will be considering parenthood simply as a means of giving their lives some purpose. All these topics need a prominent place on the pastoral curriculum. Revision and interview skills need to be reinforced. Coping with endings and beginnings of relationships as well as changing one's, needs full discussion. The role of youngsters in their communities could be given some time, especially for those that have poor chances of finding long term employment. This should be linked to their self discovery of personal attributes, skills and talents. Pupils should leave their fifth years feeling that they have something of value to offer their communities, and the pastoral programme is the best place to ensure that this occurs. See table 5.

Objectives for the Evaluation of the Pastoral Curriculum

Assessing pupils on the skills they have learned is one way of evaluating whether the pastoral programme has had any effect. In order to do this, objectives have to be written in a manner which describes what pupils do in a selection of situations. These are known as behavioural objectives. Teachers can only come to a reasoned judgement about the skills of pupils by observing their behaviour. By writing behavioural objectives, all members of staff will be observing pupils in the same way, and assessing them on the same action. This does away with differences of opinion or interpretation which so often plague teacher reports on students. A set of objectives for monitoring pupils under different skill areas is given below. They are not meant to be a complete set, but a base from which staff can add to and build up their own evaluation procedures.

Objectives for Assessing Self Control and Stress-management

1. Can anticipate a stressful situation (for example, argument with a peer, telling off from an adult) and adapt by controlling breathing, relaxing muscles, and controlling voice tremor.
2. Is able to predict a stressful situation (for example, being teased) and engage in a behaviour which would remove the opportunity for stress to occur.
3. Is able to devise alternatives to a particular behaviour which may bring stress with it.
4. Is able to think of a previously anxiety provoking situation with calmness, and so reduce its stress value; by altering the things that he/she says to him/herself about the situation.
5. Is able to rehearse behaving calmly when thinking about an anxious situation, by imagining a better outcome, and a change in heart rate, muscle tension, and general feelings of well being.
6. Is able to control his/her anger in a group setting by not raising his/her voice; not

254

TABLE 1 - A GUIDE TO THE PASTORAL CURRICULUM IN FORM ONE

	PREVENTIVE →	SKILLS BUILDING ←	→ DEVELOPMENTAL
Term	Partnership with Pupils	Social & Life Skills	Self Awareness and Identity
1	Role of tutor. Buildings-nos, functions. Timetables-introduction. Homework-role & function. Hierarchy of staff.	Stress Management - coping with criticism and tellings off.	Relationships with teachers and learning to make them better.
TECHNIQUES:	Visual flow charts, analogies. Ch. 3.	Role play, stress thermometer and relaxation exercises. Ch. 4,6.	Role play and discussions of problem situations. Ch. 2,3,4.
2	Teacher style. Buildings. School Organisation	Communicating my problems and learning to ask for help.	Personal Attributes- how do they link in with the kind of person my peers think I am?
TECHNIQUES:	Role play, maps, tours, simulation activities. Ch. 3.	Self Report Schedules, role play, visual flow Charts. Ch. 2,3,4.	Self Report Schedules, rating scales. Ch. 2,5.
3	Motivation-what encourages me, what discourages me? Evaluation of subjects and teaching style.	Making Plans - for homework, studying, and evaluation of my strengths and weaknesses	What I used to think about myself when I first started secondary school, compared to what I think of myself now.
TECHNIQUES:	Self Report Schedules, card sorting, and group discussion. Ch. 2.	Self Report Schedules, rating scales, group discussions. Ch. 6.	Card sorting, rating scales Ch. 2.

TABLE 2 - A GUIDE TO THE PASTORAL CURRICULUM IN FORM TWO

Term	PREVENTIVE → Partnership with Pupils	SKILLS BUILDING → Social & Life Skills	DEVELOPMENTAL → Self Awareness and Identity
1	Banding & setting. Feelings about my worth in school.	Dealing with authority - Fairness as perceived by pupils. Methods of punishment and reprimand. Role play, group discussion. Ch. 2.	Personal Needs (1) - how can I find out what they are, and attempt to fulfil them in constructive ways. Self Report Schedules, group exchange of ideas. Ch. 5
TECHNIQUES:	Group problem solving, card sorting, rating scales, group discussion. Ch. 2.		
2	Measuring the value of a partnership between teachers and pupils from the student perspective.	Assertiveness - coping with teasing, bullying, threats, and extreme shyness. Role play, with emphasis on non-verbal communication. Ch. 4.	My skills and talents - what they are, and how can I put them to best use, at home, in school and in the neighbourhood. Self Report Schedules, group bartering. Ch. 5.
TECHNIQUES:	Rating scales, group discussions. Ch. 3.		
3	Uniform-purpose, pros and cons, and its effect on individual self image. School reports and what they mean. Attendance.	Time management - exercises in discovering how pupils spend their time. Evaluation of project, and exchange of views on improving allocation of time to various activities. Self Report Schedules, group problem solving. Ch. 2,6.	What I think of myself and how others see me. In classes, in the school yard and outside school. Rating scales, group exchange of ideas. Ch. 2,5.
TECHNIQUES:	Visual charts, making own reports. Ch. 3.		

TABLE 3 - A GUIDE TO THE PASTORAL CURRICULUM IN FORM THREE

Term	PREVENTIVE → Partnership with Pupils	SKILLS BUILDING → Social & Life Skills	DEVELOPMENTAL → Self Awareness and Identity
1	Purpose of school- functions as seen by teachers and pupils, and how they are achieved. School as a community.	Time management-making sure I can do all that I hope to do.	What impression do I give of myself to: teachers, pupils, family members.
TECHNIQUES:	Self Report Schedules, group discussion, and production of class ideas in booklet form. Ch. 3.	Self Report Schedules, group problem solving. Ch. 6.	Rating scales, discussions. Ch. 2, 5, 6.
2	Attendance at school- problems faced, methods of overcoming them.	Making plans - revision; techniques, evaluation scales, changing weak- nesses into strengths.	Self Concept - assessing self image and boosting pupils with low self worth.
TECHNIQUES:	Role play, group problem solving. Ch. 3.	Self Report Schedules, group exchange of ideas. Ch. 6.	Self Report Schedules, card sorting, group boosting of peers. Ch. 5.
3	The rights and needs of children and teachers in school: balancing them.	Stress management - examinations, tests, giving an account of oneself.	Kind of person I would like to be - subject and job choices linked to personality.
TECHNIQUES:	Group production of balance sheet.	Stress thermometer, Self Report Schedules, relaxation, and discussions. Ch. 6.	Self Report Schedules, rating scales. Ch. 5.

TABLE 4 - A GUIDE TO THE PASTORAL CURRICULUM IN FORM FOUR

	← PREVENTIVE	SKILLS BUILDING →	DEVELOPMENTAL →
Term	Partnership with Pupils	Social & Life Skills	Self Awareness and Identity
1	Privileges of age in school. Privileges within the staff group, related to those in pupil population.	Dealing with institutions - Consumer services, government departments, voluntary agencies. Role play with use of verbal and non-verbal communication.	Exploring self Identity - Where did it come from? What influences it? How does it alter in time?
TECHNIQUES:	Card sorting, group discussion, rating scales.		Self Report Schedules, card sorting, group discussions. Ch. 5
2	School attendance - as viewed by various agencies, the implications of those perceptions, and their costs and consequences.	Dealing with conflicts - situations with teachers and parents. Recap on revision skills.	Personal Needs (2) - What are they and how different is my list to that made in Form 2? Do I still meet them in the same ways?
TECHNIQUES:	Group problem solving: production of balance sheet of pros and cons. Ch. 3.	Role play, discussions and suggestions for resolving conflicts without undue stress. Ch. 4.	Self Report Schedules, group problem solving. Ch. 5.
3	Who controls my life in school, at home, in the community? What aspects of my life are controlled externally, and how do I take on personal responsibilities?	Interviewing Skills (1) - Biographical details, functions of interviews, aspects of importance.	Relationships - which ones are the greatest influence on personal belief systems, and help to form self image?
TECHNIQUES:	Card sorting, balance sheets and group problem solving.	Self Report Schedules, group discussions. Ch. 6.	Self Report Schedules, group discussions, card sorting. Ch. 5.

DEVELOPING AND IMPLEMENTING A PASTORAL CURRICULUM

TABLE 5 - A GUIDE TO THE PASTORAL CURRICULUM IN FORM FIVE

Term	PREVENTIVE — Partnership with Pupils	SKILLS BUILDING — Social & Life Skills	DEVELOPMENTAL — Self Awareness & Identity
1	Purpose of school - as seen by teachers, employers, pupils etc. Compare to responses in form 3.	Dealing with unemployment - and/or poor living conditions. Using time, developing new skills and crafts, capitalizing on positive aspects of self. Self Report Schedules, card sorting, group bartering exercises. Ch.5,6.	Relationships with the opposite sex; why they exist, what qualities do people seek out? What keeps a couple together? Ending relationships in least hurtful and damaging ways. Card sorting, Self Report Schedules, group discussions.
TECHNIQUES:	Self Report Schedules, group discussions, Ch. 3.		
2	Discipline - types of: self, parental, courts, schools. Effects on personal needs and relationships.	Interviewing Skills (2) - Communication - verbal and non verbal. Evaluation by class. Recap on revision skills.	Feelings experienced at the beginnings and endings of relationships. Controlling unpleasant feelings- linked up to personal needs and how they are fulfilled. Group exchange of views, Self Report Schedules.
TECHNIQUES:	Self Report Schedules, group problem solving.	Role play, hints on doing better. Ch. 4, 6.	
3	Balancing control - teachers and parents controlling ones life, versus self autonomy.	Parenting Skills - needs of parents and children, and issues of management, using pupils' own experiences.	Changing relationships - in a family over time-splitting up and reconstitution of families.
TECHNIQUES:	Role play, balance sheets, group problem solving.	Role play, card sorting, group problem solving, projects which produce pamphlets of best ideas.	Role play, Self Report Schedules, card sorting. Ch. 5.

259

making threatening remarks or gestures, and without hurting anyone.

7. Is able to control his/her sadness in a group setting by remaining in the group (i.e. without walking out), and by not crying, and explaining him/herself in an articulate manner.

8. Is able to think ahead of possible alternatives/solutions in times of crisis or panic, and put plans into action.

9. Is able to act swiftly and appropriately when faced with a crisis by not crying, screaming, running around or becoming indisposed.

10. Is able to show an awareness of his/her own level of stress by accurately predicting his/her behaviour and physiological symptoms - and attempting to put it under control.

Objectives for Assessing Problem Solving and Decision Making Skills

1. Is able to solve a problem with a member of staff by using logical arguments.

2. Is able to solve a problem with a member of staff by presenting his/her case cogently, without getting stressed and upset.

3. Is able to solve a problem in relationships with peers without resorting to physical means.

4. Is able to solve a problem in relationships with peers without using staff authority as a back-up.

5. Is able to solve a difficulty in peer relationships without the support and protection of staff.

6. Is able to solve a difficulty in peer relationships without the support and protection of stronger peers.

7. Chooses appropriate and suitable times and places for solving personal problems in relationships - i.e. not during a lesson, or during assembly times.

8. Chooses appropriate times to discuss a problem with a member of staff - before or after a lesson, designated break times etc.

9. Is able to make a decision by weighing up the pros and cons of a situation beforehand.

10. Is able to make a decision by weighing up pros and cons, and stick to is unless circumstances alter.

11. Can seek the help of adults and/or peers in discovering the pros and cons of a situation

before coming to a decision.

12. Seeks advice from both camps of an argument before coming to any conclusions.

13. Can change a decision to suit altering facts or circumstances.

14. Makes contingency plans if one plan based on a set of decisions breaks down.

Objectives for Assessing Assertiveness and Self Confidence

1. Is able to say 'no' to a person who requests him/her to do something that he/she does not wish to do, or cannot do.

2. Is able to present his/her case fully without being put off by negative remarks.

3. Can express own opinion even when others disapprove or disagree.

4. Will ensure that his/her rights are not undermined by others, for example, being pushed to the back of a queue.

5. Is able to adopt the appropriate procedures for making complaints.

6. Continues to press a complaint even though unsuccessful the first time.

7. Makes complaints to the right people, and asks for a reply.

8. Is able to ask for favours to be carried out by peers.

9. Will make an effort to contribute to a group discussion when others are dominating the conversation.

10. Will seek advice when needed and use it, without waiting until he/she is in a predicament.

11. Maintains upright posture in interactions with people in power, or of status.

12. Maintains sufficient eye contact to conduct the interaction with a person to show confidence.

13. Speaks clearly, in a modulated tone of voice when trying to give an opinion, or make a point.

14. Keeps a calm exterior and does not show fear when confronted with a threat.

A second way of evaluating a pastoral programme is to assess staff reactions, the techniques used, and the breadth of content that has been covered each year. Behavioural objectives can also be written for this section, although staff may

find it easier to use a form of checklist for pin-
pointing areas of weakness.

Objectives for Assessing Content and Methods

(a) CONTENT
     1. All teachers tackled topics under the
section entitled Partnership with pupils.
     2. All teachers tackled topics under the
heading Social and Life Skills.
     3. All teachers tackled topics under the
section entitled Self Awareness and Self Identity.
     4. All teachers allowed pupils to bring
forth problems for discussion at least once every
three sessions.
     5. All teachers took note of pupil problems
by using them in the pastoral programme.
     6. All teachers spent at least a third of
each term on skills building - social, study skills,
and those on self knowledge.
     7. All teachers set practice/homework tasks
for students in the personal and social skills
areas.
     8. All teachers faced issues of school organ-
isation, teacher style and teacher expectations
where they were relevant for pupils, and gave pupils
advice to assist them.

(b) METHODS
     1. All teachers used role play when dealing
with social and life skills training.
     2. All teachers used role play techniques
to help pupils resolve pupils' conflicts with
teachers and parents.
     3. Self report schedules were used by all
teachers to elicit pupil perceptions.
     4. Self report schedules were used by all
teachers in group discussion work.
     5. A variety of techniques OTHER than simple
oral discussions were attempted by all teachers
in pastoral sessions.
     6. Team teaching was used by at least half
the staff within a year group to share skills.
     7. Teachers made a note of useful hints
in review meetings, and put them into operation.
     8. Themes that needed continuity from one
year to another were carried on by successive members of staff.
     9. Staff reinforced topics at different
times of the school year by including items in
their curricula.

DEVELOPING AND IMPLEMENTING A PASTORAL CURRICULUM

10. Form tutors with the responsibility for co-ordinating certain topics did so, and passed on their findings to other members of staff.

Staff response to the whole package needs some scrutiny. A year tutor, or someone with senior management responsibility may wish to use a checklist to highlight which members of staff need extra guidance and assistance in the classroom. Similarly a check needs to be kept on which techniques are proving the most difficult, and whether in fact regular review meetings are held for teachers to air their problems and get support. Such a checklist can be designed as below.

Techniques and their use	Frequent	Infrequent	Not at all
Interviewing			
Eliciting pupil perceptions			
Card sorting			
Group discussions			
Group problem solving			
Role play - discussions			
Group projects			
Group bartering			
Production of booklets			
Self report schedules			
Balance sheets			
Rating scales			

Review meetings and their usefulness

TIME HELD   EXCHANGE OF VIEWS (+ = good
                                                - = poor)

Term one-half term.

Term one-end of

Term two-end of

Term three-half term

The use of these monitoring devices and pupil objectives should provide information for staff to adapt their support systems and the curricula

263

DEVELOPING AND IMPLEMENTING A PASTORAL CURRICULUM

for an interesting and effective pastoral programme.

REFERENCES

BALDWIN, J. and WELLS, H. (1979; 1980; 1981) Active
    Tutorial Work. The first to fifth years.
    Oxford. Basil Blackwell in Association with
    Lancashire County Council.
BANNISTER, D. (1981) Knowledge of Self. In HERBERT
    M. (ed.) Psychology for Social Workers. London.
    McMillan in Association with the British Psy-
    chological Society.
BANNISTER, D. and AGNEW, J. (1977) The Child's
    Construing of Self. In LANFIELD, A.W. (ed.)
    Nebraska Symposium on Motivation. Nebraska
    University of Nebraska Press.
BARKER, D. and PHILLIPS, K. (1981) Transactional
    Analysis. In COOPER, C.C. (ed.) Improving
    Interpersonal Relations. Some Approaches to
    Social Skills Training. Aldershot. Gower Pub-
    lishing Co.
BEECH, H.R., BURNS, L.E. and SHEFFIELD, B.F. (1982)
    A Behavioural Approach to the Management of
    Stress; A practical guide to techniques.
    Chichester. Wiley.
BENNETT, N. (1976) Teacher Style and Pupil Progress.
    London. Open Books.
BENSON, H. (1977) The Relaxation Response. London.
    Fountain Well Press.
BERNE, E. (1968) Games People Play. The Psychology
    of Human Relationships. Harmonsworth. Penguin
    Books.
BERNE, E. (1972) What do you say after you say
    Hello? The Psychology of Human Destiny. New
    York. Grove Press Inc.
BERNSTEIN, D.A. and BERKOVEC, T.D. (1973) Pro-
    gressive Relaxation Training; a manual for
    helping professions. Champaign, Illinois,
    Research Press.
BERRY, T. (1981) Children and Divorce. Journal

for the Association of Child Psychology and Psychiatry Newsletter, 9, 1-3.

BEST, R. (1980) (ed.) Perspectives in Pastoral Care. London. Heinemann.

BEST, R., JARVIS, C. and RIBBINS, P. (1980) Pastoral Care: Concept and Process. In BEST, R. (ed.) Perspectives in Pastoral Care. London. Heinemann.

BLACKBURN, K. (1975) The Tutor. London. Heinemann.

BOWDLER, D. and GLEISNER, S. (1982) Killer Winks in the Secondary School? A personal and social skills course. Journal of the Association of Educational Psychologists, 5, 10, 64-69.

BOWER, S.A. and BOWER, G.H. (1976) Asserting Yourself. Reading, Massachusets. Addison-Wesley.

BROWN, B. (1974) New Mind, New Body: Biofeedback. New directions for the mind. New York. Harper and Row.

BROWN, B. (1975) (ed.) The Biofeedback Syllabus: A handbook for the psychophysiologic study of biofeedback. Springfield, Illinois, Thomas Press.

BURNS, R.B. (1979) Self Concept. Theory, Measurement, Development and Behaviours. London. Longman.

BUTTON, L. (1974) Developmental Groupwork with Adolescents. Sevenoaks. Hodder & Stoughton.

BUTTON, L. (1980) The Skills of Group Tutoring. In BEST, R. (ed.) Perspectives in Pastoral Care. London. Heinemann.

CANFIELD, J. and WELLS, H.C. (1976) 100 Ways to Enchance Self Concept in the Classroom. Englewood Cliffs, Prentice Hall.

CARROLL, H.C.M. (1977) (ed.) Absenteeism in South Wales: Studies of pupils, their homes and their secondary schools. Swansea: Faculty of Education. University of Swansea.

CARTLEDGE, G. and MILBURN, J.F. (1980) (eds.) Teaching Social Skills to Children: Innovative approaches. New York. Pergamon Press.

CHESLER, M. and FOX, R. (1966) Role-playing Methods in the Classroom. Chicago. Science Research Associates.

CHESTON, M. (1979) It's Your Life: A personal and social course. Exeter. Wheaton.

COHEN, L. (1976) Educational Research in Classrooms and Schools: A manual of materials and methods. London. Harper and Row.

CONGER, D.S. (1973) (ed.) Readings in Life Skills. Training Research and Development Station, Department of Manpower and Immigration.

Saskatchewan, Canada.

CONGER, J. (1977) Adolescence and Youth: Psychological development in a changing world. 2nd edition. New York. Harper and Row.

COOP, R.H. and WHITE, K. (1974) (eds.) Psychological Concepts in the Classroom. New York. Harper and Row.

COOPER, C.L. (1981) (ed.) Improving Interpersonal Relations. Some approaches to social skills training. Aldershot. Gower Publications.

COOPERSMITH, S. (1967) The Antecedents of Self Esteem. San Francisco. W.H. Freeman and Co.

COOPERSMITH, S. and FELDMAN, R. (1974) Fostering a Positive Self-Concept and High Self Esteem in the Classroom. In COOP, R.H. & WHITE (eds.) Psychological Concepts in the Classroom. New York. Harper & Row.

COX, T. (1978) Stress. London. Macmillan Press Ltd.

CURTIS, M.S. (1982) Social Skills Training in the Classroom. British Psychological Society, Division of Educational and Child Psychology, Occasional Papers, 6, 3, 22-31.

DAVID, K. and COWLEY, J. (1979) Counselling and Pastoral Care in Schools. London. Edward Arnold.

DAVIDSON, H.H. and LANG, G. (1960) Childrens' Perceptions of Their Teachers Feelings Towards them Related to Self Perception, School Achievement and Behaviour. Journal of Experimental Education, 29, 2, 107-118.

DeCHARMS, R. (1968) Personal Causation. New York. Academic Press.

DOBSON, C.B. (1982) Stress: The Hidden Adversary. Lancaster. MTP Press.

DOHERTY, K. (1981) A Framework for the Evaluation of Pastoral Care. In HAMBLIN, D. (ed.) Problems and Practice of Pastoral Care. Oxford. Basil Blackwell.

DOUGLAS, J.W.B. (1970) Broken Families and Child Behaviour. Journal, Royal College of Physicians, 4, 203-210.

DOWDING, H. and BOYCE, S. (1979) Getting the Job You Want. London. Ward Lock.

DUNHAM, J. (1977) The Effects of Disruptive Behaviour on Teachers. Education Review, 29, 181-187.

DUVAL, S. and WICKLUND R.A. (1973) Effects of Objective Self-awareness on the Attribution Of Causality. Journal of Experimental Social Psychology, 9, 17-31. Reprinted in ROSENBERG, M

REFERENCES

& KAPLAN, H.B. (1982) Social Psychology of the Self-Concept. Arlington Heights, Illinois, Harlan Davidson Inc.

ELARDO, P. and COOPER, M. (1977) Aware: Activities for Social Development. Reading Massachusetts. Adison Wesley.

ELLIS, J. and BARNES, T. (1979) Life Skills Training Manual. Community Services Volunteers.

ELLIS, R.A.F. and WHITTINGTON, D. (1981) A Guide to Social Skills Training. London. Croom Helm.

FIGG, J. and ROSS, S. (1981) Analysing a School System: A practical exercise. In GILLHAM, W. (ed.) Problem Behaviour in the Secondary School. London. Croom Helm.

FINLAYSON, D.S. and LOUGHRAN, J.L. (1976) Pupils' Perceptions in High and Low Delinquency Schools. Educational Research, 18, 138-144.

FLOWERS, J.V. and BOORAEM, C.D. (1980) Simulation and Role Playing Methods. In KANFER, F.H. and GOLDSTEIN, A.P. (eds.) Helping People Change. Oxford. Pergamon Press.

FROSH, S. (1982) Social Skills Training with Children in Schools. In SPENCE, S. and SHEPHERD, G. (eds.) Developments in Social Skills Training. London. Academic Press.

GALASSI, M.D. and GALASSI, J.P. (1977) Assert Yourself: How to be your own person. New York. Human Sciences Press.

GALL, M.D. (1970) The Use of Questions in Teaching. Review of Educational Research, 40, 709-721.

GALLOWAY, D. (1982a) Persistent Absence From School. Educational Research, 24, 188-196.

GALLOWAY, D. (1982b) A Study of Persistent Absentees from School and their Families. British Journal of Educational Psychology 52, 317-330.

GALLOWAY, D., BALL, T., BLOOMFIELD, D. and SEYD. R. (1982) Schools and Disruptive Pupils. London. Longman.

GOLDFIELD, M.R. and MERAUM, M. (1973) (eds.) Behaviour Change through Self-Control. New York. Holt, Rinehart and Winston.

GOLDIAMOND, I. (1965) Self Control Procedures in Personal Behaviour Problems. Psychological Reports, 17, 851-868.

GREGORY, P. (1980) 'Truancy': A plan for school based action research. Journal of the Association of Educational Psychologists, 5, 3, 30-35.

GRAY, J. (1971) The Psychology of Fear and Stress. London. Weidenfeld and Nicolson.

HAMBLIN, D.H. (1978) The Teacher and Pastoral Care.

Oxford. Basil Blackwell.

HAMBLIN, D.H. (1981) Teaching Study Skills. Oxford. Basil Blackwell.

HAMBLIN D.H. (1981) (ed.) Problems and Practice of Pastoral Care. Oxford. Basil Blackwell.

HARGIE, O.D.W. (1978) The Importance of Teacher Questions in the Classroom. Educational Research, 20, 99-102.

HARGIE, O., SAUNDERS, C. and DICKSON, D. (1981) Social Skills in Interpersonal Communication. London. Croom Helm.

HARGREAVES,D.H.(1975) Interpersonal Relations and Education. London. Routledge and Kegan Paul.

HARGREAVES, D.H. (1978) Deviance: The Interactionist Approach. In GILLHAM, W. (ed.) Reconstructing Educational Psychology. London. Croom Helm.

HAWTON, K., O'GRADY, J., OSBORN, M. and COLE, D. (1982a) Adolescents who take Overdoses: Their characteristics, problems and contact with helping agencies. British Journal of Psychiatry, 140, 118-123.

HAWTON, K., OSBORN, M., O'GRADY, J. and COLE, D. (1982b) Classification of Adolescents who take Overdoses. British Journal of Psychiatry, 140, 124-131.

HAWTON, K., COLE, D., O'GRADY, J. and OSBORN, M. (1982c) Motivational Aspects of Deliberate Self-poisoning in Adolescents. British Journal of Psychiatry, 141, 286-291.

HAYES, B., SLUCKIN, A. and SMITH, A. (1982) Social Skills in a Comprehensive School. Journal of the Association of Educational Psychologists, 5, 8, 42-48.

HERSOV, L. (1976) School Refusal. In RUTTER, M. and HERSOV, L. (eds.) Child Psychiatry: Modern Approaches. Oxford. Blackwell Scientific.

H.M.I. (1977) Truancy and Behavioural Problems in Some Urban Schools. London. HMSO.

HOLDEN, A. (1971) Counselling in Secondary Schools. London. Constable.

HOLMES, T.H. and RAHE, R.H. (1976) The Social Readjustment Rating Scale. Journal of Psychosomatic Research 11, 213-218.

HOPSON, B. and HOUGH, P. (1976) The Need for Personal and Social Education in Secondary Schools and Further Education. British Journal of Guidance and Counselling, 4.1, 16-27.

HOPSON, P. and SCALLY, M. (1979; 1982) Lifeskills Teaching Programmes. Volumes 1 and 2. Leeds. Lifeskills Associates.

HOPSON, B. and SCALLY, M. (1981) Lifeskills

REFERENCES

Teaching, Maidenhead, McGraw Hill.

INSEL, P. and WILSON, G.D. (1971) Measuring Social Attitudes in Children. British Journal of Social and Clinical Psychology, 10, 84-86.

JERSILD, A.T., BROOK, J.S. and BROOK, D.W. (1978) The Psychology of Adolescence. 3rd Edition. New York. Macmillan.

JONES, A. (1979) Counselling Adolescents in Schools. London. Kogan Page.

KAHN, J. and NURSTEN, J. (1968) Unwillingly to School. Oxford. Pergamon Press.

KANFER, F.H. (1980) Self Management Methods. In KANFER, F.H. and GOLDSTEIN, A.P. (eds.) Helping People Change. Oxford. Pergamon Press.

KELLY, G.A. (1955) The Psychology of Personal Constructs. 2 volumes. New York. Norton.

KRUPAR, K.R. (1973) Communication Games: Participant's manual. London. Collier Macmillan.

KUHN, M.H. and McPARTLAND, T.S. (1954) An Empirical Investigation of Self Attitudes. American Sociological Review. 19, 68-76.

LANGRISH, S.V. (1981) Assertiveness Training. In COOPER, C.L. (ed.) Improving Interpersonal Relations. Some approaches to social skills training. Aldershot. Gower Publishing Co.

LAZARUS, R.S. (1966) Psychological Stress and the Coping Process. New York. McGraw Hill.

LEE, R. (1980) Beyond Coping: Some approaches to social education. London. Further Education Curriculum Review and Development Unit.

LEVI, L. (1975) (ed.) Society, Stress and Disease. Volumes 1 & 2. New York. Oxford University Press.

LEVINE, S. and SCOTCH, N.A. (1970) Social Stress. Chicago. Aldine Publishing Co.

LIBERMAN, R.P., DeRISSI, W., KING, L.W. and McCANN.M. (1975) Personal Effectiveness: guiding people to assert themselves and improve their social skills. Champaign Illinois. Research Press.

LORAC, C. and WEISS, M. (1981) Communication and Social Skills. Schools Council Communication and Social Skills Project. Exeter. Wheaton Publications.

LOWENSTEIN, L.F. (1978) The Bullied and Non-bullied Child. British Psychological Society Bulletin, 31, 316-319.

LOWENSTEIN, L.F. (1978) Who is the Bully? British Psychological Society Bulletin, 31, 147-150.

MARLAND, D. (1974) Pastoral Care. London. Heinemann.

MASLOW, A.H. (1968) Towards a Psychology of Being. 2nd edition. New York. Van Nostrand, Rheinhold.

REFERENCES

MASLOW, A.H. (1970) Motivation and Personality. 2nd edition. New York. Harper and Row.

McGRATH, J.E. (1970) (ed.) Social and Psychological Factors in Stress. New York. Holt, Rinehart and Winston.

McGUIRE, J. and PRIESTLEY, P. (1981) Life After School. Oxford. Permanon Press.

MEICHENBAUM, D. (1974) Cognitive Behaviour Modification. New Jersey. General Learning Press.

MILROY, E. (1982) Role-play. A Practical Guide. Aberdeen. Aberdeen University Press.

MONTEMAYOR, R. and EISEN, M. (1977) The Development of Self-conceptions from Childhood to Adolescence. Developmental Psychology, 13, 314-319. Reprinted in ROSENBERG, M. and KAPLAN, H.B. (1982) (eds.) Social Psychology of the Self Concept. Arlington Heights, Illinois. Harlan Davidson Inc.

MUNRO, E.A. and MANTHEI, R.J. (1979) (eds.) Counselling: A skills approach. London. Methuen.

NATIONAL CHILDRENS' BUREAU (1977) Juvenile Delinquency. Highlight 30.

NATIONAL CHILDRENS' BUREAU (1977) Violence, Disruption, and Vandalism in Schools. Highlight 32.

NATIONAL CHILDRENS' BUREAU (1979) Children and Alcohol. Highlight 37.

NATIONAL CHILDRENS' BUREAU (1980) Adolescent Smoking. Highlight 38.

NATIONAL CHILDRENS' BUREAU (1981) Solvent Abuse. Highlight 43. 8 Wakely Street, Islington, London EC1V 7QE.

NICHOLLS, A. and NICHOLLS. H. (1978) Developing a Curriculum: A practical guide. 2nd Edition. London. Unwin Education Books.

O'CONNOR, D. (1984) Glue Sniffing and Volatile Substance Abuse: Case studies of children and young adults. Aldershot. Gower.

OLES, H.J. (1973) Semantic Differential for Third Through Fifth Grade Students. Psychological Reports, 33, 24-26.

OPPENHEIM, A.N. (1966) Questionnaire Design and Attitude Measurement. London. Heinemann.

OSGOOD, C.E., SUCI, G.J. and TANNENBAUM, P.H. (1957) The Measurement of Meaning. Urbana. University of Illinois.

OUSTEN, J. (1981) Differences Between Schools: The implications for school practice. In GILLHAM. W, (ed.) Problem Behaviour in Secondary Schools. London. Croom Helm.

OUSTEN, J., MAUGHAN, B. and MORTIMORE, P. (1980)

271

School Influence on Childrens' Development. In RUTTER, M. (ed.) Scientific Foundation of Child Psychiatry. London. Heinemann.

PHILLIPS, A.S. (1963) Self-concepts in Children. Educational Research, 6, 104-109.

PHILLIPS, B. (1978) School Stress and Anxiety. New York. Human Sciences Press.

PHILLIPS, D. and CALLELY, E. (1981) Pupils Views of Comprehensive Schools or 'What do you think of it so far?'. Links, 7.1, 32-37.

PIK, R. (1981) Confrontation Situations and Teacher Support Systems. In GILLHAM. W, (ed.) Problem Behaviour in the Secondary School. London. Croom Helm.

POITRAS-MARTIN, D. and STONE, G.L. (1977) Psychological Education: A skill-oriented approach. Journal of Counselling Psychology, 24, 153-157.

PRIESTLEY, P., McGUIRE, J., FLEGG, D., HEMSLEY, V. and WELHAM D. (1978) Social Skills and Personal Problem Solving. London Tavistock Pub.

PURKEY, W.W. (1978) Inviting School Success: A self concept approach. Belmont, California. Wadsworth.

RAYMOND, J. (1982a) How Form Tutors Perceive Their Role. Links, 7, 3, 25-30.

RAYMOND, J. (1982b) The Development of a Pastoral Care Curriculum: Bridging the gap between systems work and individual referrals. Journal of The Association of Educational Psychologists, 5, 10, 28-32.

RAYMOND, J. (1985) Intervention in a School with a Class of Disruptive Pupils. Journal of The Association of Educational Psychologists, in press.

RENNIE, J., LUNZER, E.A. and WILLIAMS, W.T. (1974) Social Education: An Experiment in Four Secondary Schools. Schools Council Working Paper 51. London. Evans/Methuen Educational.

REYNOLDS, D., JONES, D. and ST. LEGER, S. (1976) Schools Do Make a Difference. New Society, 29th July. 223-225.

REYNOLDS, D. and SULLIVAN, M. (1981) The effects of School: A radical faith re-stated. In GILLHAM. W, (ed.) Problem Behaviour in the Secondary School. London. Croom Helm.

REYNOLDS. D, and MURGATROYD, S. (1977) The Sociology of Schooling and the Absent Pupil: The school as a factor in the generation of truancy. In CARROLL, H.C.M. (ed.) Absenteeism in South Wales. Swansea. Faculty of

Education. University of Swansea.

RICHARDS, M. and DYSON, M. (1982) Separation, Divorce and the Development of Children: A Review. A report to the D.H.S.S. London. Child Care and Development Group. University of Cambridge. Unpublished.

RICHARDS, M. (1983) Effects of Marital Separation and Divorce in Children. Association of Child Psychology and Psychiatry, Newsletter, 14, 12-15.

ROBINSON, M. (1980) Step-families: A reconstituted family system. Journal of Family Therapy, 2, 45-69.

ROTTER, J.B. (1966) Generalized Expectancies for Internal versus External Control of Reinforcement. Psychological Monographs, 80, 1, 1-28.

RUBIN, K.H. and ROSS, H.S. (1982) (eds.) Peer Relationships and Social Skills in Childhood. New York. Springer-Verlag.

RUSSELL, M.L. and THORESEN, C.E. (1976) Teaching Decision-making Skills to Children. In KRUMBOLTZ, J. and THORESEN, C.E. (eds.) Counselling Methods. New York. Holt, Rinehart and Winston.

RUTTER, M. and GILLER, H. (1983) Juvenile Delinquency: Trends and Perspectives. Harmonsworth. Penguin.

RUTTER, M., MAUGHAN, B., MORTIMORE, P. and OUTSTEN, J. (1979) Fifteen Thousand Hours: Secondary schools and their effects on children. London. Open books.

SEARS, P. and SHERMAN V. (1964) In Pursuit of Self-esteem. California. Wadsworth.

SELIGMAN, M. (1975) Helplessness. San Fransisco. Freeman.

SILCOX, A. (1981) Staff Development and the Problems of Teachers. In HAMBLIN, D.H. (ed.) Problems and Practice of Pastoral Care. Oxford. Blackwell.

SKYNNER, R. and CLEESE, J. (1983) Families and How to Survive Them. London. Methuen.

SOLOMON, D. and OBERLANDER, M.I. (1974) Locus of Control in the Classroom. In COOP, R.H. and WHITE, K. (eds.) Psychological Concepts in the Classroom. New York. Harper and Row.

SPENCE, S. (1980) Social Skills Training with Children and Adolescents: A counsellor's manual. Windsor. NFER.

SPIELBERGER, C.D. and SARASON, I.G. (1975) Stress and Anxiety. Volumes 1 & 2. New York. Halstead

Press.

STANFORD, G. (1977) Developing Effective Classroom Groups: A practical guide for teachers. New York. Hart Publishing Co.

STANTON, G., CLARK, E.P., STRADLING, R. and WATTS, A.G. (1980). Developing Social and Life Skills: Strategies for tutors. London. Further Education Curriculum Review and Development Unit.

SUGARMAN, B. (1973) The School and Moral Development. London. Croom Helm.

TAYLOR, M. (1980) The Language of Pastoral Care. In BEST, R. (ed.) Perspectives in Pastoral Care. London. Heinemann.

TAYLOR, J. and WALFORD, R. (1972) Simulation in the Classroom. Harmonsworth. Penguin.

THOMAS, K.C. (1980) Attitude Assessment. Rediguide 7. TRC Rediguides Ltd. Maidenhead.

THOMPSON, B.L. (1975) Secondary School Pupils' Attitudes to School and Teachers. Educational Research, 18, 1, 62-67.

THORPE, D.P., MEYERS, C.E. and BONSALL, M.R. (1954) What I like to do: An Inventory of Childrens' Interests. Chicago. Science Research Associates.

TROWER, P., BRYANT, B. and ARGYLE, M. (1968) Social Skills and Mental Health. London. Methuen.

TURNER, B. (1974) (ed.) Truancy. London. Ward Lock Educational.

VAN HASSETT, V.B., HERSEN, M., WHITEHILL, M.B. and BELLACK, A.S. (1979) Social Skills Assessment and Training for Children. An evaluative review. Behaviour Research and Therapy, 17, 413-437.

WALCZAK, Y. and BURNS, S. (1984) Divorce: The Child's Point of View. London. Harper and Row.

WALL, W.D. (1968) Adolescents in School and Society. Slough. NFER.

WALL, W.D. (1982) Adolescence: The Search for Identity. British Psychological Society, Division of Education and Child Psychology, Occasional Papers, 6, 3, 3-6.

WALLER, P. and GAA, J. (1974) Motivation in the Classroom. In COOP, R.H. and WHITE, R. (eds.) Psychological Concepts in the Classroom. New York. Harper and Row.

WARR, P.B. and KNAPPER, C. (1968) The Perception of People and Events. New York. Wiley.

WEBB, C. (1978) Talk Yourself Into a Job. Communication Skills Series. London. Macmillan Press.

WILLIAMSON, D. (1980) 'Pastoral Care' or

REFERENCES

'Pastoralization'? In BEST, R. (ed.) Per-
spectives in Pastoral Care. London. Heinemann.
WOODS, P. (1976) Pupils' Views of School. Edu-
cational Research 28, 126-137.
WYLIE, R.C. (1974) The Self-Concept. Volume 1.
Nebraska. University of Nebraska Press.